Sergey's
HTML5
& CSS3
Quick Reference
Third Edition

Includes new
HTML5.1 & CSS4
coverage

By Sergey Mavrody, MFA

2012-2015

Sergey's HTML5 & CSS3

Quick Reference.

HTML5, CSS3 and APIs.

2012-2015

Author Sergey Mavrody, MFA

Editor Nika Mavrody

Find us on the World Wide Web for updates: http://html5.belisso.com
Or contact Sergey directly at belissohtml5@gmail.com

Belisso Corporation

Notice of Rights

Notice of Liability

About the Author

Sergey Mavrody has been working with web technologies since the mid-nineties, focusing on UI design and development, creative direction, information architecture, interactive media, and enterprise applications with rich data visualization and advanced user interface components. Sergey holds two master's degrees. He is also a visual artist and educator with many years experience teaching as professor at the School of the Art Institute of Chicago.

Table of Contents

3. HTML5 Elements......................................31

4. Forms, Attributes & Events 71

In the Chapter 1

I. Intro to HTML5

Overview

About this book

HTML and CSS are the most essential and fundamental web languages: they provide the foundation for the vast majority of web sites and web applications. HTML5 is on track to become the future of the web, offering simple plug-in free Rich Internet Application capabilities, easier development, and enhanced user experience.

Today you can find a wealth of HTML5 information on the web including references, tutorials and tips. There are also a few very good books available which concentrate on certain HTMl5 features. However there is always a need for a relatively concise summary of all that information in one handy reference-style book.

This book is an essential technical dictionary for professional web designers and developers, conveniently summarizing over 3000 pages of (X)HTML5 and CSS3 specifications and covering the most common and fundamental concepts and specs, including tags, attributes, values, objects, properties, methods, events, and APIs. Topics include:

- Introduction to HTML5
- HTML5 and XTML5 syntax rules
- Document semantic structure
- Summary of HTML5 Elements and Attributes
- HTML5 forms
- Global attributes and events
- Summary of CSS3 properties
- HTML5 APIs, including Canvas, SVG, Video, Audio, Web Workers, Web Sockets, Microdata, Geolocation, Web Storage and more.

The author's goal was to create a one-stop reference source which is comprehensive but still concise, simple, easy-to-read, and structured.

The book also offers browser compatibility information.
If the browser logo is present, the element is supported by that browser.
Note, the gray empty circle indicates that the browser is not supported:

IE 6   FF 4

What is HTML?

The well-known acronym 'HTML' stands for HyperText Markup Language. It is the primary markup language for the world wide web, capable of creating web documents by specifying content structure including headings, paragraphs, tables, footers and other elements.

The HTML markup also typically utilizes CSS (Cascading Style Sheets) to describe the visual appearance of content. CSS enables the separation of document HTML content from document visual presentation, such as the layout, colors, and fonts.

HTML allows for the creation of interactive forms as well as the embedding of images, video, audio and other objects. HTML code can embed scripts, such as JavaScript, which contribute to dynamic behavior of web pages.

Major HTML versions

- The first HTML document called "HTML Tags", was published by Berners-Lee in 1991.
- HTML 4.0 was published as a World Wide Web Consortium (W3C) recommendation in 1997, offering three variations: transitional, strict, and frameset.
- XHTML 1.0, a more restrictive subset of HTML markup, was published in 2000-2002. It conforms to XML syntax requirements.
- XHTML 2.0 working drafts were released in 2002-2006. The proposed standard attempted to make a more radical break from the past versions, but sacrificed a backward compatibility. Later the W3C decided to halt any further development of the draft into a standard, in favor of more flexible HTML5 standard.
- HTML5 first public draft was released by the W3C in 2008 and it was completed in 2014.
- HTML 5.1 is currently being developed. This book includes a newly proposed HTML **5.1** and CSS3 building blocks, including an additional: 7 elements, 22 attributes, 18 events, 32 CSS properties and more.
- This is an estimated combined timeline for HTML 5.0, HTML 5.1 and HTML 5.2:

	2013	2014	2015	2016	2017
HTML 5.0	Call for Review	Recommendation			
HTML 5.1	Working Draft		Last Call	Candidate Rec	Recommendation
HTML 5.2			1st Working Draft		Last Call

HTML5

The HTML5 development began in 2004 by an informal group of experts from Apple Computer, the Mozilla Foundation, and Opera Software forming the WHATWG group (Web Hypertext Application Technology Working Group). Ian Hickson of Google, Inc. is the lead author on the HTML5 specification. The WHATWG HTML5 specification was eventually adopted by the World Wide Web Consortium (W3C) in 2007.

- The HTML5 markup is more backward compatible with HTML 4 and XHTML 1.0 vs. XHTML 2.0.

- HTML5 introduces many new elements, including semantic replacements for generic HTML elements. For instance new semantic elements, such as `<header>`, `<footer>`, `<section>`, `<nav>`, `<article>` were created. Many HTML 4 elements were retired (deprecated).

- HTML5 also introduces many additional plugin-free capabilities such as standardized video and audio interface, raster imaging, local database, offline mode, more efficient multi-threaded JavaScript, Cross Document Messaging and more.

XHTML5

XHTML5 is the XML serialization of HTML5. XHTML5 document is served with an XML MIME type, e.g. `application/xhtml+xml`. Also XHTML5 requires stricter well-formed syntax. In XHTML5 document the HTML5 document type declaration is optional and may be omitted. XHTML5 may be utilized to extend HTML5 to some XML-based technologies such as *SVG* and *MathML*.

CSS3

The new version of CSS is introduced and approved in modules which allow for more flexibility to be released. New features of CSS3 are quite extensive:

- Selectors offer a much more specific way of selecting elements, including matching on attributes and attribute values, structural pseudo-classes, target pseudo-class to style only elements that are targeted in the URL, a checked pseudo-class to style any element that is checked such as radio or checkbox elements

- Text Effects and Layout, including hyphenation, 'whitespace', and justification of text

- Paged Media and Generated Content, supporting more options in paged media, such as running headers, footers, page numbering, footnotes and cross-references

- Multi-Column Layout properties allow for multiple column layouts

- Ruby module offers ability to add small annotations on top or next to words, used in Asian scripts

Why use HTML5

HTML5 advantages

- Backward compatibility: HTML5 is wrapping up all previous doctypes

- Simpler Syntax: improved semantics, more productive coding and smaller document size

- New elements and attributes make design and development more flexible

- Plugin-free video and audio and timed media playback

- Smart Web Forms 2.0 functionality (HTML5 supersedes Web Forms 2.0)

- Ability to use in-line *SVG* and *MathML* in with `text/html` MIME type

- Over 20 new plugin-free scripting APIs (application programming interfaces), including: Canvas element 2D graphics, Document editing, Drag-and-drop, Geolocation, Local offline storage, Media capture, Microdata.

- The bottom line: easier development and enhanced user experience

Who this book is for

This diagram below was inspired by Jesse Garrett's diagram The Elements of User Experience. This diagram is centred around typical web application development cycle and various roles involved, most of which would benefit from HTML5 and CSS3 knowledge and/or skills. Anyone who is familiar with HTML and CSS and who is interested in web site/web application development, design and user experience issues would benefit from reading this book.

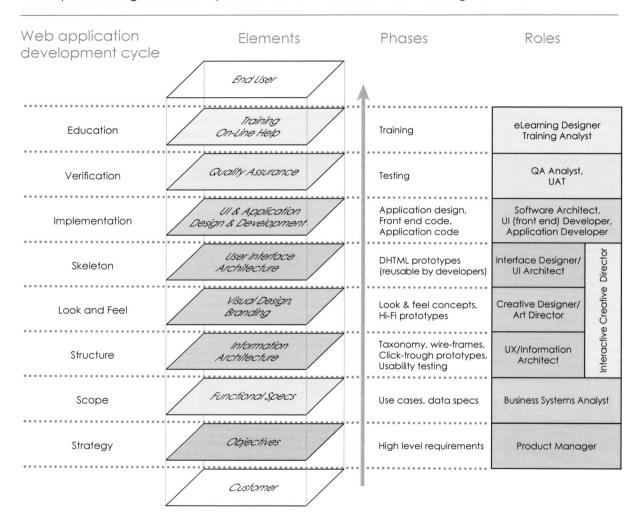

HTML5 Branding

On 18 January 2011, the W3C introduced HTML5 visual branding: the logo and the technology class icons represent aspects of modern Web applications and Web sites. The logo, icons, and website are licensed under *Creative Commons Attribution 3.0 Unported*.

The W3C encourages using this visual branding as a way of showing support for HTML5 if the web site/application is in fact built on HTML5 technologies. The HTML5 visual identity graphics can be downloaded here: http://www.w3.org/html/logo

The logo

The HTML5 logo does not imply the code validity or conformance.

The technology class icons

Semantics

Giving meaning to structure, semantics are front and center with HTML5. A richer set of tags, along with RDFa, microdata, and microformats, are enabling a more useful, data driven web for both programs and your users.

Offline & Storage

Web Apps can start faster and work even if there is no internet connection, thanks to the HTML5 App Cache, as well as the Local Storage, Indexed DB, and the File API specifications.

Device Access

Beginning with the Geolocation API, Web Applications can present rich, device-aware features and experiences, including audio/video input access to microphones and cameras, to local data such as contacts & events, and tilt orientation.

Connectivity

More efficient connectivity means more real-time chats, faster games, and better communication. Web Sockets and Server-Sent Events are pushing (pun intended) data between client and server more efficiently than ever before.

Multimedia

HTML5 introduces built-in media support via the <audio> and <video> elements, without requiring a plug-in or external player, offering the ability to easily embed media into HTML documents.

3D, Graphics & Effects

Between SVG, Canvas, WebGL, and CSS3 3D features, you're sure to amaze your users with stunning visuals natively rendered in the browser.

Performance & Integration

Make your Web Apps and dynamic web content faster with a variety of techniques and technologies such as Web Workers and XMLHttpRequest 2. No user should ever wait on your watch.

CSS3

CSS3 delivers a wide range of stylization and effects, enhancing the web app without sacrificing your semantic structure or performance. Additionally Web Open Font Format provides typographic flexibility and control far beyond anything offered before.

In the Chapter 2

2. HTML Syntax

HTML document

Basics

Generally, HTML document represents a standalone HTML file.

- HTML document is a code assembled of *elements* and text.
- Elements are basic HTML building blocks, represented by HTML tags.
- Elements form a hierarchical nested structure.

Elements and Tags

Each element is denoted by an opening tag, *in this example:* **<title>**, and a corresponding closing tag **</title>**. In some cases a closing tag is not required.

The difference between an element and a tag is that an *element* is a conceptual representation of HTML tag, which can also include its attributes and child tags. See Chapters 3, 4 for detailed element coverage.

```
<!DOCTYPE html>

<html>

<head>
<title>HTML5 Reference</title>

<!-- This is a comment. It does not
render in browser -->

</head>

        <body>

        <h1>Overview</h1>

        <p>The well-known acronym
HTML stands for HyperText Markup
Language.</p>

        </body>

</html>
```

Tag nesting

- Tag is denoted by the less than (<) and greater than (>) inequality signs.
- Nested tag pairs have to be completely within each other, without overlapping with another pair.

```
The <b><em>wrong</b></em> nesting
The <b><em>correct</em></b> nesting
```

Void Elements

Void element has only an opening tag and therefore it can not have any content. A terminating slash may optionally be inserted at the end of the element's tag, immediately before the closing greater-than sign. For a non-void element the terminating slash is illegal.

```
<!--Void elements:-->
<img src=logo.gif><br />
<input type=text>
```

Attributes

An element *in this example:* **input** can have multiple attributes **type, autofocus, name**.

```
<input type=text autofocus
name='first name'>
```

- An attribute is a property of an element.
- Attributes are placed inside the opening tag.
- The tag name and attribute are both separated by white space.
- An attribute is assembled with a name **type** and a value **text**, separated by the equal (=) sign.
- No duplicate attributes allowed within a tag.
- HTML5 attribute value can remain un-quoted if it doesn't contain spaces, quotation marks or inequality signs **type=text**. Otherwise, an attribute value has to be quoted using either single or double quotes **'first name'**.

Boolean attribute

A boolean attribute is a property that represents either a false or true value.

- The absence of a boolean attribute implies a value of "false".

```
<!--boolean value is false:
the field is NOT disabled-->
<input>
```

- The presence of a boolean attribute implies that the value of the attribute is "true".
- Boolean attribute may take the name of the attribute itself as a value **<input disabled=disabled>**.
- In a *polyglot* HTML/XHTML document, a boolean attribute with a true value is coded with a quoted value that matches the attribute name **<input disabled="disabled">**.

```
<!--boolean value is true-->
<input disabled=disabled>
<input disabled="disabled">
<input disabled="">
<input disabled>
```

- In a non-polyglot HTML document the value can be excluded **<input disabled>**.

XHTML5

Polyglot HTML document

A polyglot HTML document is a document that is valid in both *HTML* and *XHTML*.

- A polyglot HTML document obeys both HTML and XHTML syntax rules by using a common subset of both the HTML and XHTML syntax.

- A polyglot document can serve as either HTML or XHTML, depending on browser support and *MIME type*.

- The choice of HTML vs. Polyglot syntax is dependent upon the project objectives, browser support, and other factors.

```
<!--HTML4, HTML5 syntax-->
<input disabled>
<input disabled=disabled>

<!--XHTML 1.0 syntax-->
<input disabled="disabled" />

<!--HTML4, HTML5, XHTML 1.0
conforming Polyglot syntax-->
<input disabled="disabled" />
```

XHTML5 defined

A polyglot HTML5 code essentially becomes an *XHTML5* document if it is served with the XML MIME type [`application/xhtml+xml`]. In a nutshell the HTML5 polyglot document is:

- HTML5 DOCTYPE/namespace. HTML5 no longer needs to refer to a Document Type Definition since HTML5 is no longer formally based on SGML. However, the DOCTYPE is needed for backward compatibility.

- XHTML well-formed syntax

A polyglot document can serve as either HTML or XHTML, depending on browser support and MIME type. A polyglot HTML5 code essentially becomes an XHTML5 document if it is served with the XML MIME type: `application/xhtml+xml` . In a nutshell the XHTML5 document is:

- XML declaration `<?xml version="1.0" encoding="UTF-8"?>` is not required if the default UTF-8 encoding is used.

- HTML DOCTYPE: The `<!DOCTYPE html>` declaration is optional, but it may be used if the document is intended to be a polyglot document that may be served as both HTML or XHTML.

- XHTML well-formed syntax

- XML MIME type: application/xhtml+xml. This MIME declaration is not visible in the source code, but it appears in the HTTP Content-Type header when it's configured on the server. Of course, the XML MIME type is not yet supported by the current version Internet Explorer though IE can render XHTML documents.

- Default XHTML namespace: `<html xmlns="http://www.w3.org/1999/xhtml">`

- Secondary SVG, MathML, Xlink, etc. namespace: To me, this is like a test: if you don't have a need for these namespaces in your document, then using XHTML is overkill. But, essentially, the choice between HTML5 and XHTML5 boils down to the choice of a media type.

Finally, the basic XHTML5 document would look like this:

The XML declaration `<?xml version="1.0" encoding="UTF-8"?>` is not required if the default UTF-8 encoding is used: an XHTML5 validator would not mind if it is omitted.

However, it is strongly recommended to configure the encoding using server HTTP Content-Type header, otherwise this character encoding could be included in the document as part of a meta tag `<meta charset="UTF-8" />`.

This encoding declaration would be needed for a polyglot document so that it's treated as UTF-8 if served as either HTML or XHTML.

The Total Validator Tool - Firefox plugin/desktop app has now the user-selectable option for XHTML5-specific validation.

```
<!DOCTYPE html>

<html xmlns="http://www.
w3.org/1999/xhtml">

<head>

   <title></title>

   <meta charset="UTF-8" />

</head>

<body>

   <svg xmlns="http://www.
w3.org/2000/svg">

     <rect stroke="black" fill="blue"
x="45px" y="45px" width="200px"
height="100px" stroke-width="2"/>

   </svg>

</body>

</html>
```

The main advantage of using XHTML5 would be the ability to extend HTML5 to XML-based technologies such as SVG and MathML. Even though SVG and MathML are supported inline by HTML5 specification, browser support is currently limited. The disadvantage is the lack of Internet Explorer support, more verbose code, and error handling. Unless you need that extensibility, HTML5 is the way to go.

Ultimately, the choice between HTML5 and XHTML5 comes down to the choice of a MIME/content type, that determines what type of document you are using. Unlike XHTML1 vs. HTML4, the XHTML5 vs. HTML5 choice of is exclusively dependent upon the choice of the MIME type, rather than the DOCTYPE.

Document Type and Structure

MIME Type

"MIME" stands for Multipurpose Internet Mail Extensions. MIME type is also called an *Internet Media Type* or *Content Type*. It is similar to file extensions identifying a type of information and it requires at least two components: a type, a subtype, and some optional parameters.

```
<!DOCTYPE html>
  <head>
    <title>HTML5</title>
    <link media=screen type=text/css
    href=styles.css rel=stylesheet>
  </head>
    <body></body>
</html>
```

Common MIME Types

Type	Content Type/Subtype code	Description
Application	application/javascript	JavaScript
	application/xhtml+xml	XHTML
Audio	audio/mpeg	MPEG, MP3 audio
	audio/x-ms-wma	Windows Media Audio
	audio/vnd.rn-realaudio	RealAudio
Image	image/gif	GIF image
	image/jpeg	JPEG image
	image/png	Portable Network Graphics
	image/svg+xml	SVG vector graphics
Message	message/http	Message
Text	text/css	Cascading Style Sheets
	text/csv	Comma-separated values
	text/html	HTML
	text/javascript	JavaScript. This type is obsolete, but allowed in HTML 5. It has cross-browser support, unlike **application/javascript**.
	text/plain	Basic Text
	text/xml	Extensible Markup Language
Video	video/mpeg	MPEG-1 video
	video/mp4	MP4 video
	video/quicktime	QuickTime video
	video/x-ms-wmv	Windows Media Video

The majority of media types could be accessed at the IANA site, the Internet Assigned Numbers Authority: **www.iana.org/assignments/media-types**.

Document Object Model (DOM)

A web browser creates a model of HTML document represented by a tree of objects, such elements, attributes, and text. This model is called *Document Object Model, DOM*. DOM objects could be manipulated by JavaScript. An object instance of a hierarchical DOM tree called a *node*.

```
<div onclick="document.
getElementById('description').
style.display = 'none';">
Hide Description</div>

<div id=description>Overview</div>
```

In this example button action invokes JavaScript,
finding the object ID of the Overview container and hiding the DIV container.

Semantic Elements

(X)HTML5 offers new *block-level* and *inline-level* elements. The new HTML5 *block-level* and elements forming semantic structure of a web page.

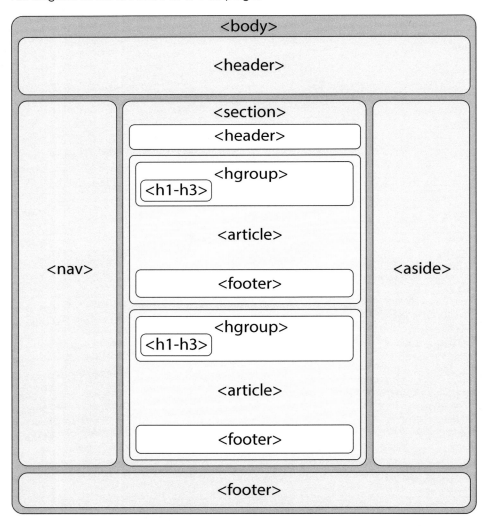

Element	Typical Content	Typical Parent and	Child Elements
`<header>`	Title, logo, banner, Introductory information	Body, Section, Article	Nav, Section
`<hgroup>`	h1-h6 headings	Article, Header	h1, h2, h3, h4, h5, h6
`<nav>`	Primary navigation menu	Body	Section, Nav
`<section>`	Generic page section	Body	Article, Header, Footer, Aside, Nav
`<article>`	Story, subsection, blog post,	Body, Section	Section, Header, Footer
`<address>`		Footer	p, a
`<aside>`	Sidebar content, tip, quotation	Body	Section, Article
`<footer>`	Footer, summary, copyright info, secondary navigation	Body, Section, Article	Nav, Section

The following are the *inline-level* semantic elements: `<del>`, `<s>`, `<ins>`, `<strong>`, `<small>`, `<b>`, `<cite>`, `<i>`, `<q>`, `<em>`, `<code>`, `<mark>`.

Syntax Summary

General Syntax Rules

Rule	HTML5 syntax	XHTML5 syntax
XML declaration	n/a	not required, if the default UTF-8 encoding is used
		`<?xml version="1.0" encoding="UTF-8"?>`
DOCTYPE	required	not required
MIME type	`text/html`	`application/xhtml+xml`
Case sensitive attributes values	not required	required
White space normalization in attribute values	White space characters are not normalized	White space characters are normalized to single space with some exceptions
Low case attributes	not required	required

Rule	HTML5 syntax	XHTML5 syntax
Attribute quotes	not required, except when attribute contains spaces or characters: `"  '  ` = < >`	required
	`<image alt=logo>` `<image alt='company logo'>`	`<image alt="logo" />`
Full boolean attribute	not required, attribute minimization is allowed	required, attribute minimization is illegal

	`<input disabled=disabled>`
	`<input disabled="disabled">`
	`<input disabled="">`
	`<input disabled>`
		`<input disabled="disabled" />`

Terminating slash in void elements	not required	required
	`  or  ;` `<hr> or <hr/>;` `<img> or <img />;` `<input> or <input />`	` ` `<hr />` `<img />` `<input />`
Element names	case insensitive	case sensitive, lower-case
Opening and Closing tags for non-void elements	optional, in some elements, based on certain conditions, see table below	required
Un-escaped Special Characters	Un-escaped ampersands (`&`) and less than signs (`<`) are generally permitted within elements and attribute values. Some exceptions apply.	Un-escaped ampersands (`&`) and 'less than' signs (`<`) are not permitted within elements and attribute values and must be substituted respectively with `&amp;` and `&lt;`

(X)HTML5 void tag syntax

- Void tags has no closing (end) tag: `<input>` ~~`</input>`~~
- HTML5 - terminating slash in void elements is not required: `<input>`
- XHTML5 - terminating slash in void elements is required: `<input />`

List of void tags

area	command	img	meta
base	embed	input	param
br	hr	link	source
col			

HTML5 elements with optional tags

- Optional tags are not applicable for XHTML5 document.
- The Condition column indicates the condition when the tag is optional.
  - Usually, **at least one** condition has to be met to allow an omitted tag
  - Some tags have no condition information available at the time of writing

Element	Start Tag	Condition	End Tag	Condition
`<body>` `</body>`	optional	- *Body* is empty - Not followed by a *space* character - Not followed by a *comment* tag - Except when *script* or *style* element is next	optional	- Not followed by a *comment* tag
`<colgroup>` `</colgroup>`	required	n/a	optional	- Not followed by a *space* character
`<dd></dd>`	required	n/a	optional	- Not followed by a *dt* or *dd* element
`<dt></dd>`	required	n/a	optional	- Not followed by a *dt* or *dd* element - It is the last description term
`<head>` `</head>`	optional	- *Head* is empty, or - Not followed by another element	optional	- Not followed by a *space* character - Not followed by a *comment* element
`<html>` `</html>`	optional	- Not followed by a *comment* element	optional	- Not followed by a *comment* element
`<li></li>`	required	n/a	optional	- Followed by another *li* element - It is the last item within the parent element

Element	Start Tag	Condition	End Tag	Condition
`<optgroup>` `</optgroup>`	required	n/a	optional	■ It is the last *optgroup* element ■ It is the last item within the parent element
`<option>` `</option>`	required	n/a	optional	■ Followed by another *option* element ■ Followed by an *optgroup* element ■ It is the last item within the parent element
`<p></p>`	required	n/a	optional	■ Followed by these tags: *address, article, aside, blockquote, dir, div, dl, fieldset, footer, form, h1, h2, h3, h4, h5, h6, header, hgroup, hr, menu, nav, ol, p, pre, section, table,* or *ul* ■ It is the last item within the parent element
`<tbody>` `</tbody>`	optional	n/a	optional	■ Followed by a *tbody* element ■ Followed by a *tfoot* element ■ It is the last item within the parent element
`<td></td>`	required	n/a	optional	■ Followed by a *td* element ■ Followed by a *th* element ■ It is the last item within the parent element
`<tfoot>` `</tfoot>`	optional	n/a	optional	■ Followed by a *tbody* ■ It is the last item within the parent element
`<th>` `</th>`	required	n/a	optional	■ Followed by a *td* element ■ Followed by a *th* element ■ It is the last item within the parent element
`<thead>` `</thead>`	optional	n/a	optional	■ Followed by a *tbody* ■ Followed by a *tfoot*
`<tr></tr>`	required	n/a	optional	■ Followed by a *tr* element ■ It is the last item within the parent element

The example of a valid HTML5 document omitting optional tags, versus so called *well-formed* XHTML5 document, checked with Total Validator tool:

HTML5

```
<!DOCTYPE html>


    <title>HTML5 document</title>


  <table title=Report>
   <tr>
    <td>1st cell content
    <td>2nd cell content
    <td>3rd cell content

   <tr>
    <td>4th cell content
    <td>5th cell content
    <td>6th cell content

  </table>
```

XHTML5

```
<html xmlns="http://www.
w3.org/1999/xhtml">

<head>
    <title>XHTML5 document</title>
</head>
<body>

  <table title="Report">
   <tr>
    <td>1st cell content</td>
    <td>2nd cell content</td>
    <td>3rd cell content</td>
   </tr>
   <tr>
    <td>4th cell content</td>
    <td>5th cell content</td>
    <td>6th cell content</td>
   </tr>
  </table>
 </body>
</html>
```

Elements by Type

Type	Elements			
Root	■ html			
Metadata	■ head	■ base	■ meta	
	■ title	■ link	■ style	
Scripting	■ script	■ noscript		
Sections	■ body	■ nav	■ h1, h2, h3, h4, h5, h6	■ footer
	■ section element	■ article		■ address
		■ aside	■ header	
Grouping	■ p	■ pre	■ ol	■ dl
	■ hr	■ dialog	■ ul	■ dt
	■ br	■ blockquote	■ li	■ dd

Type	Elements			
Inline Semantics	■ a	■ dfn	■ samp	■ bdo
	■ q	■ abbr	■ kbd	■ ruby
	■ cite	■ time	■ sub	■ rt
	■ em	■ progress	■ sup	■ rp
	■ strong	■ meter	■ span	
	■ small	■ code	■ i	
	■ mark	■ var	■ b	
Edits	■ ins	■ del		
Embedded Content	■ figure	■ embed	■ video	■ canvas
	■ img	■ object	■ audio	■ map
	■ iframe	■ param	■ source	■ area
Tabular Data	■ table	■ col	■ tfoot	■ th
	■ caption	■ tbody	■ tr	
	■ colgroup	■ thead	■ td	
Forms	■ form	■ input	■ datalist	■ textarea
	■ fieldset	■ button	■ optgroup	■ output
	■ label	■ select	■ option	
Interactive Elements	■ details	■ command	■ bb	■ menu
Miscellaneous Elements	■ legend	■ div		

Browser Compatibility Scripting

Due to the fact that HTML5 browser support is inconsistent, JavaScript can be used in order to target specific browser functionality or add missing functionality.

Modernizr

- The most effective HTML5 compatibility detection tool is *Modernizr*, an open source JavaScript library that detects support for HTML5 and CSS3.
- The latest version of *Modernizr* library can be downloaded from modernizr. com web site.

```
<!DOCTYPE html>
<html>
<head><title></title>

   <script src="modernizr.min.js"></script>

</head>
```

HTML5 enabling scripts - Polyfills

- HTML5 Modernizr is a detection tool: it does not add missing HTML5 functionality to older browsers, however Modernizr site has a page "HTML5-Cross-browser-Polyfills", which is a collection of useful links for many various solutions of this kind.

- *Polyfill* is a piece of code or plugin that allows developer to provide a technology browser is missing. Polyfills fill in the gaps to make HTML5 and CSS3 usable today even in older browsers.

New in HTML 5.1

New HTML 5.1 Elements

New	Deprecated
1. details	▪ hgroup (removed in html5)
2. dialog	▪ keygen
3. main	▪ summary (removed in html5)
4. menu	▪ tt (removed in html5)
5. menuitem	
6. picture	
7. summary	

New HTML 5.1 Attributes

New Attribute	Element
▪ allowfullscreen	any element
▪ lang	
▪ itemid	
▪ itemid	
▪ itemprop	
▪ itemref	
▪ itemscope	
▪ itemtype	
▪ translate	
▪ contenteditable	
▪ contextmenu	

New Attribute	Element
■ command ■ default ■ radiogroup ■ title ■ type	menuitem
■ type	menu
■ inputmode	input; textarea
■ menu	button
■ open	details, dialog
■ scoped	style
■ seamless	iframe
■ sortable	table
■ sorted	th

In the Chapter 3

3. HTML5 Elements

General Definitions

Chapter Legend & Conventions

- Attributes listed are specific for each tag, otherwise an element supports all global attributes.
- Global attributes and events listed in Chapter 4.
- Values in { } brackets are variable placeholders for actual values.
- Values in regular text are actual valid values.
- An initial default attribute value is indicated by <u>underline</u>.
- Elements displayed in gray color are deprecated (obsolete).
- The sample code offered is mostly based on HTML5 syntax, not XHTML5.
- If the browser logo is present, the element is supported by that browser. **Note**, the gray empty circle indicates that the browser is not supported:

 IE 6   FF 4

Summary of HTML5 Elements

- This section describes all types of elements that can be used to write an HTML document.
- HTML5 specifications are still in draft mode, and could potentially change.
- The **5** or **5.1** symbols indicates that this is new HTML5 or HTML element or attribute.
- This list includes 7 new HTML**5.1** elements and 22 new HTML**5.1** attributes.

HTML5 Elements

Working Draft → Last Call → Candidate → Recommendation
w3.org/TR/2011/WD-html5-20110525

Tag	Code Example	Description
`<!-- -->`	`<!-- this comment does not render in browser -->`	Comment

`<!DOCTYPE>`	`<!DOCTYPE HTML>`
	
	`<html>`
	`<head>`
	`<title>Title</title>`
	`</head>`
	`<body>World</body>`
	
	`</html>`
		Generally, *Document Type Definition* (DTD) specifies language and version of HTML used for the document.
		
		In HTML 5 the `<!DOCTYPE>` tag is simplified and it does not require a reference to a DTD. The `<!DOCTYPE>` tag is included for backward compatibility.

Tag	Code Example		Description
`<a>`	`<a href=http://html5.belisso.com>Belisso Publishing</a>`		A hyperlink to another page or an *anchor*
	Attribute	**Value**	
	download ❺	{URL}	Target for download
	href	{URL}	Target URL
	hreflang	language_code	Base language of the URL. Use only if the *href* attribute is present
	media	all, aural, braille, handheld, projection, print, screen, tty, tv, {width}, {height}, {device-width}, {device-height}, {orientation}, {grid} {aspect-ratio}, {device-aspect-ratio}, {color}, {color-index}, {monochrome}, {resolution}, {scan}	Defines the device media type of the target URL. This attribute requires the href attribute. Operators and, not and (,) comma could be utilized to combine multiple values. Example: `<a href=media.html media="screen and (aspect-ratio:16/9)">View Video</a>` This attribute is purely advisory.
	type	{MIME type}	It defines the MIME type of the linked resource.
	rel ❺	alternate, author, bookmark help, icon, license, next, nofollow, noreferrer, prefetch, prev, search, stylesheet, tag	Specifies a semantic relationship between the current document and the target URL. ▪ The attribute's value is a set of space-delimited tokens ▪ This attribute has no default value ▪ The *href* attribute is required ▪ Most values supported by browsers
	target	_blank _parent _self _top framename	Specifies target window for the linked document
	charset, coords, name		Deprecated in HTML5

Tip: Use the *download* attribute to specify it on an element to force the referenced resource to be downloaded rather than navigated towards.

Tag	Code Example	Description
`<abbr>`	`<abbr title="United Nations">UN</abbr> is an international organization.`	Abbreviation / acronym. Title attribute may be used to describe the abbreviation.
`<acronym>`		Deprecated in HTML5
`<address>`	`<address>` `Address: 1414 N. Clark ` `Chicago, IL 60610 ` `Ph: 312 285 7867` `</address>`	Address element, renders in italic

`<area>`	`<img src =shapes.gif width=166 height=132 alt=shapes usemap=#map1>`
	
	`<map name=map1>`
	`<area shape=rect coords=0,0,60,90 href=square.htm alt=square>`
	
	`  <area shape=circle coords=50,25,5 href=circle.htm alt=circle>`
	
	`  <area shape=poly coords=152,572,163,611,211, 610,223,574,193,546,152,573 href=pentagon.htm alt=pentagon>`
	`</map>`
		Image map area
		
		Image maps are images with clickable areas (sometimes referred to as "hotspots") that usually link to another page.

Attribute	Value	Description
alt	text	Alternate text for the area. This attribute requires the *href* attribute.
coords	Shape *rect*: left,top,right,bottom Shape *circ*: centerx,centery,radius Shape *poly*: x1,y1,x2,y2 ... xn,yn	Clickable area definition: coordinates
href	{URL}	Target URL of the area
hreflang ❺	{language code}	Base language of the target URL. This attribute requires the *href* attribute

Tag	Code Example	Description
media	all, aural, braille, handheld, projection, print, screen, tty, tv, {width}, {height}, {device-width}, {device-height}, {orientation}, {grid} {aspect-ratio}, {device-aspect-ratio}, {color}, {color-index}, {monochrome}, {resolution}, {scan}	Defines the device media type of the target URL. This attribute requires the href attribute. Operators and, not and (,) comma could be utilized to combine multiple values. Example: `<a href=media.html media="screen and (aspect-ratio:16/9)">View Video</a>` This attribute is purely advisory.
nohref		Not supported in HTML 5.
rel ❺	Alternate, archives, author, bookmark, contact, external, first, help, icon, index, last, license, next, nofollow, noreferrer, pingback, prefetch, prev, search, stylesheet, sidebar, tag, up	Specifies a semantic relationship between the current document and the target URL. ■ The attribute's value is a set of space-delimited tokens ■ This attribute has no default value ■ The *href* attribute is required ■ Most values supported by browsers
shape	rect, rectangle, circ, circle, poly, polygon	Shape of the area
target	_blank, _parent, _self, _top	Where to open the target URL. _*blank*: new window _*self*: same frame _*parent*: parent frameset _*top*: full body of the window
type ❺	{mime type}	Specifies the Multipurpose Internet Mail Extensions type of the target URL. The *href* attribute is required. IE 6 FF SF CH O

Tag	Code Example	Description
`<article>` ❺	```<article>` `Serving as virtual library,` `Wikipedia tackles your` `questions on a wide` `range of subjects.<time` `pubdate datetime=2009-10-` `10T19:15-08:00></time>` `</article>```	External content such as a news article or blog excerpt. The *time* element with *datetime* attribute may be used. IE 9 FF 4 SF 5 CH 7 O 11 iOS 4 An 2.1
`<aside>` ❺	```<article><h1>HTML5</h1>` `<p>HTML5 is the next major` `revision of HTML</p>`  `<aside>` `<p>Generations of HTML:</p>` `<ul>` ` <li>HTML4` ` <li>XHTML1` ` <li>HTML5` `</ul>` `</aside></article>```	Aside content is additional information that can enhance main content, e.g. a tip or a list of facts. *Aside* element should not be used for ads, navigation menu, search boxes, or any other unrelated content. IE 9 FF 4 SF 5 CH 7 O 11
`<audio>` ❺	```<audio src=audiofile.mp3` `controls autoplay></audio>```	Sound content IE 9 FF 4 SF 5 CH 7 O 11

Attribute	Value	Description
autoplay	{boolean}	Audio plays automatically
crossorigin **5.1**	anonymous; use-credentials	Crossorigin handling method
controls	{boolean} controls	Audio controls displayed
loop	{boolean} loop	Audio plays unlimited loop
preload	{boolean} preload	Audio loaded at page load and ready to play
src	{URL}	URL of the audio
mediagroup **5.1**	e.g. audio, video, movie	It can be used to link multiple media elements together by creating a *MediaController*. The value is text; media elements with the same value are automatically linked.
muted	muted	Muted audio state.

Tag	Code Example		Description
`<b>`	The `<b>bold</b>` text		Bold

`<base>`	`<head>`
	`<base href=http://www.domain.`
	`com target=_blank>`
			Default URL and default target for all page links.

	Attribute	**Value**	**Description**
	href	{URL}	Target URL of the area
	target	_blank _parent _self _top	Where to open the target URL. ■ _blank: new window ■ _self: same frame ■ _parent: parent frameset ■ _top: full body of the window
`<basefont>`			Deprecated in HTML5

`<bdi>`	`<ul>`
	`<li>Player <bdi>jim</bdi>: 9pts`
	`<li>Player <bdi>paul</bdi>: 5pts`
	`<li>Player <bdi>إيان</bdi>: 3pts`
	`</ul>`
	
	• **Player john: 9pts**
	• **Player paul: 5pts**
	• **Player إيان : 3pts**
			It represents a span of text that is to be isolated from its surroundings in order to format text bidirectionally.

`<bdo>`	`<bdo dir=rtl>`
	כל המלונות בישראל
	`</bdo>`
	
	`<bdo dir=ltr>`
	All the hotels in Israel
	`</bdo>`
			The bi-directional override tag defines the direction of text display.
			
			כל המלונות בישראל
			
			All the hotels in Israel

	Attribute	**Value**	**Description**
	dir	ltr, rtl	Defines direction. Required.
`<big>`			Deprecated in HTML5
`<blockquote>`			Long quotation
	Attribute	**Value**	**Description**
	cite	{URL}	Target URL of the area

Tag	Code Example		Description

<body>	`<html>`
	`<head>`
	`<title>Title</title>`
	`</head>`
	
	`<body>page content</body>`
	`</html>`
			Browser rendered page content.

	`<p>John Smith ` `(312) 234-5678</p>`		Line break

<button>	`<button type=button name=next`
	`autofocus formnovalidate`
	`form=myForm>Next Page</button>`
			Push button

	Attribute	Value	Description
	autofocus ❺	{boolean}	Sets focus on the button when the page loads. IE 9 FF 4 SF 4 CH 7 O 11
	disabled	{boolean}	Sets button state to disabled.
	form ❺	{text string}	Specifies which form this button belongs to. IE FF 4 SF CH 9 O 11
	formaction ❺	{URL}	Specifies where to submit form data. Overrides the form's *action* attribute. IE FF SF CH O
	formenctype ❺	application/x-www-form-urlencoded multipart/form-data text/plain	Specifies how form-data should be encoded before sending it to a server. Overrides the form's *enctype* attribute. IE FF SF CH O
	formmethod ❺	delete get post put	Specifies how to send form-data. Overrides the form's *action* attribute. IE FF SF CH O

Tag	Code Example		Description
	formnovalidate {boolean}		The form should not be validated when submitted. Overrides the form's *novalidate* attribute. This element is not currently supported by major browsers
	formtarget ⑤	_blank	Where to open the target URL.
		_self	■ *_blank*: new window
		_parent	■ *_self*: same frame
		_top	■ *_parent*: parent frameset
			■ *_top*: full body of the window
	menu **5.1**	{text_string_ID}	It must be specified to give the element's menu.
	name	{text string}	Unique name for the button
	type	button, reset, submit	Button type
	value	{text string}	An initial button value, which can be changed by a script.

`<canvas>` ⑤	`<canvas id=myCanvas height=90 width=90></canvas>`
	
	`<script type=text/javascript> var canvas=document. getElementById('graphics'); var ctx=canvas.getContext('2d'); ctx.fillStyle='#CFEBE2'; ctx.fillRect(0,0,50,80);>`
			HTML rendered graphics.
			
			Basic canvas and text APIs browser support:
			
			IE 9 FF 3 SF 4 CH 7 O 11

	Attribute	**Value**	
	height	{number} pixels, %	Canvas height
	width	pixels	Canvas width

`<caption>`	`<table>`
	`<caption>Revenue</caption>`
	`<tr>`
	`  <th>2009`
	`  <th>2010`
	`<tr>`
	`  <td>$12.6 Billion`
	`  <td>$13.2 Billion`
	`</table>`
			Table caption
			
			Revenue
			2009 $12.6 Billions
			2010 $13.2 Billions

`<cite>`	`<cite>To be or not 2 b?</cite>`		Citation
`<code>`	`<code>return{find(chars. begin())!=chars.end()}</code>`		Programming code text

Tag	Code Example	Description

`<col>`	`<table>`
	
	`<col span=2 style=background-color:Lavender>`
	
	`<col style=background-color:MistyRose>`
	
	`  <tr>`
	`    <td>1st group`
	`    <td>1st group`
	`    <td>2nd group`
	
	`  <tr>`
	`    <td>1st group`
	`    <td>1st group`
	`    <td>2nd group`
	
	`  </table>`
		Applies attributes to a column

	Attribute	Value	Description
	span	{number}	Defines number of columns grouped by the attribute

Tag	Code Example	Description

`<colgroup>`	`<table>`
	
	`<colgroup span=2 style="background-color:#CFEBE2">`
	`<tr>`
	`    <th>Year</th>`
	`    <th>Make</th>`
	`    <th>Model</th>`
	`</tr>`
		Group of table columns. The *colgroup* element can only contain *col* element.
		
		Closing tag **</colgroup>** is not required.

	Attribute	Value	Description
	span	{number}	Defines number of columns grouped by the attribute
	align, char, charoff, valign, width		Deprecated in HTML5

Tag	Code Example	Description
`<data>` ❺	`<p>The first draft is available <data value="2011-02-11">on Monday</data>.</p>`	The data element represents its contents in a machine-readable form.

	Attribute	Value	Description
	value	{text string}	Required. The value is a representation of the element's contents in a machine-readable format.

Tag	Code Example	Description
`<datagrid>`		Currently dropped from HTML5 specs.

Tag	Code Example		Description
`<datalist>` ❺	```Enter phone type: <input type=text list=fone> <datalist id=fone> <option value=Home label=main> <option value=Office> <option value=Mobile> </datalist>```		The *datalist* element provides an auto complete function on input elements, enabling a drop down list of predefined options as the user inputs data. Home main Office Mobile IE FF SF CH O
`<dd>`	```<dl> <dt>CRT <dd>Cathode Ray Tube <dt>LCD <dd>Liquid Crystal Display </dl>```		Definition description In HTML5 the closing tag **</dd>** is not required.
`<del>`	```He shall be <del datetime=2009-10-10T19:15- 08:00>punished</del> <ins>forgiven</ins>```		This element indicates a deleted text. He shall be ~~punished~~ <u>forgiven</u>
	Attribute	**Value**	**Description**
	cite	{URL}	Source of the reason for the change
	datetime	{date and time}	Date and Time of the change
`<details>` ❺.❶	```<details open> <summary><label for=fn>Name & Extension:</label></summary> <p><input type=text id=fn name=fn value="News.pdf"> <p><label><input type=checkbox name=ext checked> Hide extension</ label> </details>```		▪ The *details* element represents a disclosure widget from which the user can obtain additional information or controls. ▪ The first *summary* element child of the element, if any, represents the summary or legend of the details. IE FF SF 6 CH 12 O15
	Attribute	**Value**	**Description**
	open	{boolean}	Indicates expanded detail
`<dfn>`	```<dfn>Definition term</dfn>```		Definition term

Tag	Code Example	Description
<dialog> 5.1	```<dialog>``` ```<h1>Create User</h1>``` ```<main>``` ```<p>Enter Name</p>``` ```<p><input type="text"></p>``` ```</main>``` ```<p><input type=button``` ```onclick="submit()"``` ```value="Submit"></p>``` ```</dialog>```	The *dialog* element represents a part of an application that a user interacts with to perform a task, for example a dialog box, inspector, or window.

	Attribute	Value	Description
	open	{boolean}	It indicates that the dialog is active and that the user can interact with it.

Tag	Code Example	Description
<div>	```<div> <p>Text</p> </div>```	A generic flow container
<dl>	```<dl>``` ```<dt>CRT```	Definition list
<dt>	```<dd>Cathode Ray Tube``` ```<dt>LCD``` ```<dd>Liquid Crystal Display``` ```</dl>```	Definition term
<em>	```The <em>emphasized</em> text```	Emphasized (italicized) text
<embed> 5	```<embed src=AdBanner.swf>```	Embedded media, content or plug-in

IE 6   FF 3   SF 4   CH 7   O 10

	Attribute	Value	Description
	height	{pixels}	Height of the content
	src	{URL}	URL of the content
	type	{type}	Type of the content
	width	{pixels}	Width of the content

Tag	Code Example	Description
<fieldset>	```label{width:120px; float:left;``` ```text-align:right; display:block;``` ```margin-right:0.5em;}``` ```<fieldset name=fSet disabled>``` ```<legend>Address</legend>``` ```<p><label>Street</label><input>``` ```<p><label>City</label><input>``` ```<p><label>Zip Code</label><input>``` ```</fieldset>```	A group of related form elements

Tag	Code Example		Description
	Attribute	Value	Description
	disabled ⑤	{boolean}	Fieldset visibility
	form ⑤	{text string}	Forms associated with fieldset
	name ⑤	{text string}	Fieldset name

`<figcaption>` ⑤ `<figure>` ⑤	`<figure>`
	`  <figcaption>CRT</figcaption>`
	`  <p>Cathode Ray Tube</p>`
	`</figure>`
			Caption for the *figure* element
			
			Figure tag annotates videos, illustrations, photos, etc.
			
			IE 9 FF 4 SF 5 CH 7 O 11

`<font>`			Deprecated in HTML5

`<footer>` ⑤	`<body>`
	`<section>Content</section>`
	`<footer>2010 © Mavrody</footer>`
	`</body>`
			Footer is a layout element
			
			IE 9 FF 4 SF 5 CH 7 O 11

`<form>`	`<form action=action.asp accept-charset=UTF-8 accept-charset=windows-1252>`
	
	`Card Number <input type=text name=number value=123456789>`
	
	`Expiration <input type=text name=date value=01/01/01>`
	
	`<input type=submit value=Submit></form>`
			Form definition
			
			The following form-associated elements could be nested inside the `<form>` tags:
			
			`<input>`, `<textarea>`, `<button>`, `<select>`, `<option>`, `<optgroup>`, `<fieldset>`, `<datalist>`, `<output>`, `<label>`

	Attribute	Value	Description
	accept	{MIME type}	Not supported in HTML 5
	accept-charset	unknown (default), {text string}	A comma delimited list of possible character sets
	action	{URL}	URL where the data is sent
	autocomplete	{boolean}	Form auto-fill
	enctype	application/x-www-form-urlencoded (default), multipart/form-data, text/plain	Indicates how form data should be encoded prior to sending. By default data is encoded so that spaces are converted to (+) symbols, and special characters are converted to the ASCII HEX equivalents.

Tag	Code Example		Description
	method	get (default), post, put, delete	*get* - sends the form data via the URL: {URL} ? name = value & name = value *post* - sends the form data in the body of the request
	name	{text string}	Unique form name
	novalidate ❺	{boolean}	Defines when the form is not validated
	target	_blank, _parent, _self, _top	Where to open the target URL ■ *_blank*: new window ■ *_self*: same frame ■ *_parent*: parent frameset ■ *_top*: full body of the window
`<frame>`, `<frameset>`			Deprecated in HTML5
`<h1>` - `<h6>`	`<h1>Article heading</h1>` `<h2>Article subheading</h2>`		Heading 1 (largest) to Heading 6 (smallest)

`<head>`	`<html>`
	`<head>`
	` <title>Page Title</title>`
	`</head>`
	`<body>Page content.</body>`
	`</html>`
			Head of HTML document
			
			Head can include the following tags:
			
			`<base>`, `<link>`, `<meta>`, `<script>`, `<style>`, `<title>`.

`<header>` ❺	`<header>`
	` <h1>iPhone vs. Android</h1>`
	` <p>Another Comparo</p>`
	`</header>`
	`<article></article>`
			Section / page header
			
			IE 9 FF 4 SF 5 CH 7 O 11

`<hr>`	`<hr>`		Horizontal rule

`<html>`	`<!DOCTYPE HTML>`
	`<html>`
	`<head>`
	` <title>Page Title</title>`
	`</head>`
	`<body>Page content</body>`
	`</html>`
			HTML document definition
			
			All HTML elements are nested inside of html container, except for the **`<!DOCTYPE HTML>`** element which is located before the opening HTML tag.

	Attribute	Value	Description
	manifest ❺	{URL}	Document's cache URL IE 10 FF 4 SF 4 CH 7 O 11
	xmlns	http://www. w3.org/1999/xhtml	XML namespace attribute. required for XHTM serialization.

Tag	Code Example	Description
`<i>`	`British apartment is known as` `<i>flat</i>.`	An alternate content usually rendered in italics. To markup text with stress emphasis use the *em* element.
`<iframe>`	`<iframe src=http://www.` `aeather.com/chicago></iframe>`	In-line frame that embeds another HTML document

Attribute	Value	Description
allowfullscreen **5.1**	{boolean}	It indicates that Document objects in the browsing context are to be allowed to use *requestFullscreen()*
height	{number} pixels, %	*iframe* height
name	{text string}	Unique *iframe* name
sandbox **5**	allow-forms allow-same-origin allow-scripts	*iframe* content restrictions
seamless **5.1**	{boolean}	*iframe* borders and scroll bars will not render ◯ IE 8　◯ FF 4　◯ SF 5　◯ CH 9　◯ O 11
src	{URL}	The URL of the document to show in the *iframe*
srcdoc **5**	{HTML code}	The HTML of the document showing in the *iframe* ◯ IE　● FF　✦ SF　◉ CH　O O 10
width	{number} px, %	*iframe* width

Tag	Code Example	Description
`<img>`	`<img src=map.gif alt="Map of` `the North America" width=200>`	External image

Attribute	Value	Description
alt	{text string}	Short description of the image, text alternative for assistive technologies

Tag	Code Example		Description
	crossorigin	anonymous use-credentials	It permits images from third-party sites that allow cross-origin access to be used with *canvas*.
	height width	{number} pixels, %	Height/width of an image
	ismap	{URL}	Server-side image map
	sizes **5.1**	a valid source size list: `<source-size-list>` `=` `[<source-size>#,]?` `<source-size-value>` `<source-size> =` `<media-condition>` `<source-size-value>` `<source-size-` `value> = <length>`	If the *srcset* attribute has any *image candidate strings* using a width descriptor, the *sizes* attribute must also be present, and the value must be a *valid source size list*.
	src	{URL}	Reference to the image location
	srcset **5.1**	One or more *image candidate strings*, each separated by comma	Images to use in different situations (e.g. high-resolution displays, small monitors, etc)
	usemap	{URL}	URL of an image map
<input>	`<input name=ssn required autocomplete=on>`		User-editable data control

	Attribute	Value	Description
	accept	audio/* video/* image/* {a MIME type with no parameters}	A comma-delimited list of MIME types Valid only with `type=file`
	alt	{text string}	Short description of the image. Valid only with `type=image`

Tag	Code Example	Description
Tip: the `autocomplete =off` value could be useful to protect sensitive data.	autocomplete <u>on</u> off	If "on", browser will store form's input values and it will predict the value for the field when the user starts to type in that field again. IE 9 FF 4 SF 5 CH 7 O 11
	autofocus ⑤ {boolean}	Atomatic focus on the input field. This attribute is invalid with `type=hidden` IE 9 FF 4 SF 5 CH 7 O 11
	checked {boolean}	Indicates that the input element should be checked when it first loads. Valid with `type=checkbox` and `type=radio`
	dirname	Removed from HTML 5.1 specifications
	disabled {boolean}	Disables the input element so that the user can not write text in it, or select it. Cannot be used with `type=hidden`.
	form ⑤ {text string}	Associates control with one or more form IDs when an input field located outside the form IE 8 FF SF CH O 11
	formaction ⑤ {URL}	Specifies where to submit form data. Overrides the form's *action* attribute. IE FF SF CH O 10
	formenctype ⑤ application/x-www-form-urlencoded multipart/form-data text/plain	Specifies how form-data should be encoded before sending it to a server. Overrides the form's *enctype* attribute. IE FF SF CH O 10

Tag	Code Example		Description
	formmethod ⑤	delete get post put	Specifies how to send form-data. Overrides the form's *action* attribute. IE 10 FF 4 SF 5.1 CH 9 O 11
	formnovalidate ⑤	true false	Overrides the form's *novalidate* attribute
	formtarget ⑤	_blank _self _parent _top	Overrides the form's target attribute, where to open the target URL. ■ *_blank*: new window ■ *_self*: same frame ■ *_parent*: parent frameset ■ *_top*: full body of the window
	height ⑤	{number} pixels, %	Height of an input field
	inputmode 5.1	verbatim, latin, latin-name, latin-prose, full-width-latin, kana, kana-name, katakana, numeric, tel, email, url,	It specifies what more helpful input mechanism for users entering content into the form control.
	list ⑤	{datalist_id}	Reference to a drop down data list with predefined options.
	max ⑤	{number}	Field's maximum legal value
	maxlength minlength	{number}	Input field's maximum/minimum number of characters allowed
	min ⑤	{number}	Field's minimum legal value
	multiple ⑤	{boolean}	Multiple values allowed
	name	{text string}	Field's unique name
	pattern ⑤	{text string: JavaScript pattern}	Specifies a regular expression against which the control's value is to be checked.
	placeholder ⑤	{text string}	Short hint such as a sample value
	readonly	{boolean}	Value of the field is not editable

Tag	Code Example		Description
	required ❺	{boolean}	Required input field. This attribute cannot be used with the types: hidden, image, button, submit, reset. `[required] {` `border-color: #88a;` `-webkit-box-shadow: 0 0 3px rgba(0, 0, 255, .5);}` `<input required>`
	size	{number}	Length of the field measured by number of visible characters
	src	{URL}	URL of the image when input `type=image`
	step ❺	{number} any	Specifies the required granularity of the value, by limiting the allowed values. This attribute is legal when `type=date`, `datetime`, `datetime-local`, `month`, `week`, `time`, `number`, or `range`.
	type	button, checkbox, *color*, *date*, *datetime*, *datetime-local*, *email*, file, hidden, image, *month*, number, password, radio, *range*, reset, *search*, submit, *tel*, text, *time*, *url*, *week*	Element type. HTML5 *input* element introduced several new values for the *type* attribute, highlighted on the left and described in the next chapter.
	value	{text string}	▪ Initial control value ▪ Illegal with `type=file` ▪ Required for *checkbox*, *radio button*
	width ❺	{number} pixels, %	Width of the input field
`<ins>`	`<ins>Date</ins>` of the insertion		Inserted text
	Attribute	Value	Description
	cite	{URL}	A URL to an additional info
	datetime	{yyyy/mm/dd}	Date and time of the insertion
`<kbd>`	Type `<kbd>www.ebay.com</kbd>` into browser address bar.		Keyboard text entered by user

Tip: see the next chapter for detailed coverege of the new ❺ *type* attribute values

Tag	Code Example	Description
<keygen> ❺	```<form action=processkey.cgi method=post enctype=multipart/ form-data> <p><keygen name=mykey> <p><input type=submit value="Submit this key"></form>```	The *keygen* element represents a control for generating a public-private key pair and for submitting the public key from that pair.

Attribute	Value	Description
autofocus	{boolean}	Sets focus on the button when the page loads.
challenge	{boolean}	If present, the value of the *keygen* is set to be challenged when submitted.
disabled	{boolean}	Disables the input element when it first loads so that the user cannot write text in it, or select it.
form	{text string}	Unique form name the input field belongs to.
keytype	{rsa}	Key type definition. RSA is a signature algorithm for public key encryption.
name	{text string}	Unique element name.

Tag	Code Example	Description
<label>	```label { width:120px; float:left; text-align:right; display:block; margin-right:0.5em;}``` `<p><label for=str>Street</label> <input id=str>` `<p><label for=city>City</label> <input id=city>` `<p><label for=zip>Zip Code</label> <input id=zip>`	The *label* element uses unique id to associate label with input for usability and accessibility applications. You can also assign CSS properties to it.

Attribute	Value	Description
for	{id}	Defines label/input association. If this attribute is not present, the label is associated with its contents.
form	{text string}	Unique form name. Defines label/ forms association.

Tag	Code Example	Description

`<legend>`	`<fieldset>`
	`<legend>Address</legend>`
	`   <p>Street <input type=text>`
	`   <p>City <input type=text>`
	`   <p>Zip Code <input`
	`type=text>`
	`</fieldset>`
		The *legend* element provides title for the *fieldset*, *figure*, and the *details* elements.
		
		Address
		Street

Tag	Code Example	Description

`<li>`	`<ol>`
	`   <li>New York`
	`   <li>Los Angeles`
	`   <li>Chicago`
	`</ol>`
		List item. Closing tag `</li>` is not required in HTML5.

Attribute	Value	Description
value	{number}	Value of the first list item within the *ol* element.

Tag	Code Example	Description

`<link>` ❺	`<head>`
	`    <link rel=stylesheet`
	`type=text/css href=style.css>`
	`</head>`
		Link to external resource. It must appear in the head of the document and it is usually used to point to a style sheets file.

Attribute	Value	Description
href	{URL}	The URL of the resource
crossorigin	anonymous use-credentials	It is intended for use with external resource links.
hreflang	{language code}	Language definition
media	screen, tty, tv, projection, handheld, print, braille, aural, <u>all</u>	Type of device the document designed for. ■ *screen* - Computer screens ■ *tty* - Teletypes and terminals ■ *tv* - Televisions ■ *projection* - Projectors ■ *handheld* - Handhelds ■ *print* - For on-screen viewing, print preview, and printed output ■ *braille* - Braille devices ■ *aural* - Speech synthesizers ■ *all* - All devices

Tag	Code Example		Description
	rel	alternate, archives, author, first, help, icon, index, last, license, next, pingback, prefetch, prev, search, stylesheet, sidebar, tag, up	■ Relationship between the document and the destination URL ■ The *href* attribute must be present ■ Accepts multiple values, separated by a space
	sizes	{number}	Sizes of the linked resource when `rel=icon`.
	type	{mime type}	Specifies the Multipurpose Internet Mail Extensions type of the target URL. This attribute requires the *href* attribute

<main> 5.1	`<main>`
	`<h1>Heading</h1>`
	`<article>Article 1</article>`
	`<article>Article 2</article>`
	`</main>`
			The *main* semantic element represents the main content of the body of a document or application.

<map>	`<img src =shapes.gif width=166 height=132 alt=shapes usemap=#shapemap>`
	
	`<map name=shapemap>`
	`<area shape=rect coords=0,0,60,90 href=square.htm alt=square>`
	`</map>`
			■ Client-side image-map with clickable areas.
			■ The *name* attribute is required in the map element.

	Attribute	Value	Description
	name	{text string}	Unique name

Tag	Code Example	Description
<mark> 5	`<p>The <mark>name</mark> attribute is required.</p>`	Marked / highlighted text IE 9 FF 4 SF CH7 O11.1 The name attribute is required.
<marquee>	`<marquee behavior="slide" direction="right">Animated text </marquee>`	A nonstandard element. It animates text across the page. IE 6 FF SF CH 2 O 10

Tag	Code Example		Description
`<menu>` **5.1**	```<menu label=stars> <li> <button type=menu value="Edit" menu="editemenu"> <menu id="edit" type="popup"> <menuitem onclick="fcopy()" label="Copy"> <menuitem onclick="fpaste()" label="Paste"></menu> </li> </menu>```		The *menu* element represents a list of commands.

Attribute	Value	Description
label	{text string}	Defines a visible label for the menu
type	context, toolbar, popup	Menu type

Tag	Code Example	Description
`<menuitem>` **5.1**	```<menu type=popup id=formmenu> <input type=submit id=submitB> <menuitem command=submitB default label=Submit> </menu>```	The *menuitem* element represents a command that the user can invoke from a popup menu (either a context menu or the menu of a menu button)

Attribute	Value	
checked	{boolean}	Whether the control is checked
command **5.1**	{text string}	It defines the attribute's value as being the ID of another element that defines a command.
default **5.1**	{boolean}	Mark the command as being a default command
disabled	{boolean}	Whether the form control is disabled
icon **5.1**	{URL}	URL to the icon for the command
label	{text string}	User-visible label
radiogroup **5.1**	{text string}	Name of group of commands to treat as a radio button group
title **5.1**	{text string}	Hint describing the command
type **5.1**	commnd, checkbox, radio	Type of command

Tag	Code Example	Description

<meta>	`<!DOCTYPE HTML>`
	`<html><head>`
	`<title>Title</title>`
	
	`<meta name=keywords`
	`content="HTML5, CSS3, RDF">`
	
	`</head><body></body></html>`
		Meta information about page: refresh rates, character encoding, author, descriptions, keywords for search engines.

Attribute	Value	
charset	{character encoding}	Character encoding declaration
content	{text string}	Meta information associated with *http-equiv* or *name*
http-equiv	{content-language}, {content-type}, {default-style}, {expires}, {refresh}, {set-cookie}	HTTP message header attribute
name	author, description, keywords, generator, revised, others	Property name

Tag	Code Example	Description
<meter> ❺	`<meter min=0 max=100 value=50>` `</meter>`	Predefined measurement range, but not a single number

IE 9   FF 4   SF 6   CH 8   O

Shipment Status

Attribute	Value	Description
high low	{number}	High/low range limit
max	{number}	Maximum value. Default is **1**
min	{number}	Minimum value. Default is **0**
optimum	{number}	■ Measurement's value is the best value. Higher then the "high" value indicates that the higher value is better ■ Lower than the "low" value: the lower value is better ■ The in between value: neither high nor low values are good

Tag	Code Example		Description
	value	{number}	Measured value

`<nav>` ❺	`<nav>`
	`<a href=index.htm>Home</a>`
	`<a href=prod.htm>Products</a>`
	`<a href=cont.htm>Contacts</a>`
	`</nav>`
			Block-level semantic layout element which defines navigational section
			
			IE 9 FF 4 SF 5 CH 7 O 11

`<noframes>`			Deprecated in HTML5

`<noscript>`	`<script src=script.js type="text/javascript">`
	`</script>`
	`<noscript>This browser does not support JavaScript</noscript>`
			noscript section. It defines alternate content for browsers that recognizes the *script* element, but does not support the script in it.

`<object>`	`<object type=video/quicktime data=wedding.mov width=380 height=320></object>`		Embedded object such as image, audio, video, Java applet, ActiveX, Flash or PDF.

	Attribute	Value	Description
	data	{URL}	URL to the object's data
	form	{text string}	Form this button related to
	height, width	{number} pixels	Height, width of the object
	name	{text string}	Unique object name
	typemustmatch	{boolean}	It indicates that the resource specified by the *data* attribute is only to be used if the value of the *type* attribute and the *Content-Type* of the aforementioned resource match. The attribute must not be specified unless both the *data* attribute and the *type* attribute are present.
	type	{MIME_type}	Multipurpose Internet Mail Extensions type of the target URL. This attribute requires the *href* attribute
	usemap	{URL}	URL of the image map

Tag	Code Example		Description

`<ol>`	`<ol start=3>`
	`  <li>Mars`
	`  <li>Jupiter`
	`  <li>Saturn`
	`</ol>`
			Ordered list
			
			3. Mars
			4. Jupiter
			5. Saturn

	Attribute	Value	Description
	reversed ❺	{boolean}	Descending list order
	type	{1, A, a, I, i}	The numeral marker type definition ■ 1 - Decimal numbers. Default. ■ a - Lowercase alphabetical list ■ A - Uppercase alphabetical list ■ i - Roman lowercase numbers ■ I - Roman uppercase numbers
	start	{number}	Initial list number

Tag	Code Example		Description

`<optgroup>`	`<select>`
	`<optgroup label=fruits>`
	`  <option>Apple`
	`  <option>Peach`
	`<optgroup label=veggies>`
	`  <option>Tomato`
	`  <option>Onion`
	`</select>`
			Group of related options in a select list. Closing tag `</optgroup>` is not always required in HTML5.
			
			Peach
			fruits
			 Apple
			 Peach
			veggies
			 Tomato
			 Onion

	Attribute	Value	Description
	label	{text string}	Option group label
	disabled	{boolean}	Disables option group options

Tag	Code Example		Description

`<option>`
 	
Tip: the closing tag `</option>` is not always required in HTML5
	`<select>`
	`  <option>Apple`
	`  <option>Peach`
	`  <option>Cherry`
	`</select>`
			Drop-down list option

	Attribute	Value	Description
	disabled	{boolean}	Disabled option
	label	{text string}	Alternative label to the option item
	selected	{boolean}	Initially selected option
	value	{text string}	Initial value of the option item

Tag	Code Example		Description
`<output>` 5	`<form action=myAction.asp>` `  <output name=total></output>`		Output element definition. Could be used for data calculations. IE FF 4 SF 5.1 CH 7 O 11
	Attribute	**Value**	**Description**
	for	id of another element	Element association
	form	{text string}	Forms association
	name	{text string}	Unique object name for the form
`<p>`	`<p>Paragraph text</p>`		Paragraph

`<param>`	`<object type=application.edo>`
	`   <param name=ac_1 value=abc>`
	`This page requires the use`
	`of plug-in`
	
	`</object>`
			Object parameter

	Attribute	**Value**	**Description**
	name	{text string}	Defines a unique name for the parameter. Required attribute.
	value	{text string}	Specifies the value of the parameter. Required attribute.

`<picture>` 5.1	`<picture>`
	
	`<source`
	`media="(min-width: 45em)"`
	`srcset="large.jpg">`
	
	`<source`
	`media="(min-width: 32em)"`
	`srcset="med.jpg">`
	
	`<img src="small.jpg" alt="The`
	`president giving an award.">`
	
	`</picture>`
			The *picture* element itself does not display anything; it merely provides a container which provides multiple sources to its contained *img* element to allow a specific image resource, based on the screen pixel density, viewport size, image format, and other factors. It accepts *global* attributes.
			
			The *picture* element is somewhat different from the similar *video* and *audio* elements: the source element's *src* attribute has no meaning when the element is nested within a *picture* element, and the resource selection algorithm is different.

`<pre>`	`<pre>This text should    be`
	`     displayed    preserving`
	`spacing  and  ignoring   word`
	`     wrap</pre>`
			Pre-formatted text. Text is displayed in a fixed-width font such as Courier, preserving spacing and ignoring word wrap.

Tag	Code Example		Description

<progress> ⑤	Downloading now. please wait...
	
	`<progress value=30 max=100>`
	`   <span id=downl>30</span>%`
	`</progress>`
			Animated task in-progress indication
			
			IE 10 FF 4 SF 6 CH 8 O11
			
			Downloading now. please wait...

	Attribute	Value	Description
	max	{number}	Task completion measurement
	value	{number}	Overall task measurement

| <q> | `<p>The phrase <q cite=http://`
`en.wikipedia.org>to be, or not`
`to be</q> comes from William`
`Shakespeare's Hamlet.</p>` | | Quotation

The phrase to "be, or not to be" comes from William Shakespeare's Hamlet. |

	Attribute	Value	Description
	cite	{URL}	Quotation source

<ruby> ⑤		<ruby> tag defines ruby container. ■ Ruby annotations are used in East Asian typography to display an explanation/pronunciation. ■ <ruby> tag normally used together with the <rt> and the <rp> tags. IE 9 FF SF 5.5 CH 8 O15
	`<ruby>` 　蘋果	
<rb> ⑤	`  <rt>`	The *rb* element marks the base text component of a ruby annotation.
<rtc> ⑤	`    <rp>(</rp>apple<rp>)</rp>`	The *rtc* element marks a ruby text container in a ruby annotation.
<rp> ⑤	`  </rt>` `</ruby>`	<rp> tag defines a non-supporting browser content. Example: 蘋果(apple)
<rt> ⑤		<rt> tag defines explanation/ pronunciation annotation. Example: **apple** 蘋果

Tag	Code Example	Description
`<s>`		Deprecated in HTML5
`<samp>`	`<samp>return{find(chars.` `begin())!=chars.end()}</samp>`	Sample programming code. Most browsers display the **`<samp>`** tag in a so called 'monospace' font - usually 'Courier New'.

`<script>`	`<script type=text/javascript`
	`defer src=common.js>`
	
	`  function goMain()  {`
	`  window.location="main.jsp";}`
	
	`</script>`
		Client-side script definition

Attribute	Value	
async **5**	{boolean}	Asynchronous script execution
crossorigin **5.1**	anonymous; use-credentials	Crossorigin handling method
type	text/ecmascript text/javascript application/ecmascript application/javascript text/vbscript	Script MIME type
charset	charset	Script character encoding
defer	{boolean}	Script execution time options: - Immediately (default) - After the page has rendered
src	{URL}	Target URL to an external JavaScript file

Tag	Code Example	Description

`<section>` **5**	`<article>`
	`  <header>`
	`    <h1>ABC Interactive</h1>`
	`  </header>`
	
	`  <section>`
	`    <h2>Services</h2><p></p>`
	`  </section>`
	
	`  <section>`
	`    <h2>Location</h2><p></p>`
	`  </section>`
	`</article>`
		Layout semantic section definition
		
		IE 9 FF 4 SF 5 CH 7 O 11

Tag	Code Example		Description

`<select>`	`<select>`
	
	  `<option>Visa`
	  `<option>Master Card`
	  `<option>American Express`
	
	`</select>`
			Selectable drop down list

Attribute	Value	Description
autofocus ❺	{boolean}	Places focus on the input field
autocomplete **5.1**	{the value meaning} {the expected input}	It can be used to turn this feature on
disabled	{boolean}	Disables the list
form ❺	{text string}	Form association
multiple	{boolean}	Multiple items can be selected
name	{text string}	Unique list name
size	{number}	Visible number of the list items

Tag	Code Example	Description

`<small>`	`<footer>`
	`<small>2010 © Mavrody</small>`
	`</footer>`
		Small element usually utilized for a fine print and legal disclaimers.

Tag	Code Example	Description

`<source>` ❺	`<video controls autoplay>`
	
	  `<source src=mymovie.mp4`
	  `type='video/mp4;`
	  `codecs="theora, vorbis"'>`
	
	  `<source src=mymovie.ogv`
	  `type='video/ogg;`
	  `codecs="avc1.42E, mp4a.40"'>`
	
	`</video>`
		Multiple media source for *video* and *audio* elements. If the media attribute is omitted, it is the default: the media resource is for all media.
		
		The *codecs* parameter may need to be assigned to specify the resource encoding.
		
		IE 9 FF 4 SF 5 CH 10 O11

Attribute	Value	Description
media	screen, tty, tv, projection, handheld, print, braille, aural, <u>all</u>	Type of media resource, for browsers to decide if it shall download it or not
src	{URL}	The URL of the media
type	{mime type}	Multipurpose Internet Mail Extensions type of the embedded content

Tag	Code Example	Description

`<span>`	```<div>```
	
	```The <span style=color:blue> span tag</span> is utilized to apply styles, classes and <span class=index>JavaScript </span> events to a text string or to a group of elements.```
	
	```</div>```
		span is a generic container/section which does not carry any semantic information.
		
		■ Span is utilized to apply styles, classes and JavaScript events to a text string or to a group of elements.
		
		■ 'span' is an *inline*-level section unlike the 'div' element, which is a *block*-level section.

`<strike>`		Deprecated in HTML5
`<strong>`	```This is a matter of a great <strong>importance</strong>, while <strong>this matter even <strong>more important </strong></strong>```	*Strong* is importance indicator. This element could be nested to emphasize stronger importance.

`<style>`	```<!DOCTYPE html>```
	```<html><head><title></title>```
	
	``` <style type=text/css>```
	``` p {color:blue;}```
	``` </style>```
	
	```</head>```
	```<body>```
	
	``` <p>Blue paragraph</p>```
	
	``` <div>```
	``` <style type=text/css```
	``` media=screen scoped>```
	``` p {color:green;}```
	``` </style>```
	
	``` <p>Green paragraph</p>```
	``` </div>```
		Defines page-level *Cascading Style Sheets* classes, as opposed to an external CSS file.
		
		■ Style element usually appear inside the *head* element
		
		■ The *scoped* attribute is required if the *style* element placed within the *body* element

Attribute	Value	Description
type	text/css	Content-type

Tag	Code Example		Description
	media	screen tty tv projection handheld print braille aural all	Type of device the document designed for ■ *screen* - Computer screens ■ *tty* - Teletypes and terminals ■ *tv* - Televisions ■ *projection* - Projectors ■ *handheld* - Handhelds ■ *print* - For on-screen viewing, print preview, and printed output ■ *braille* - Braille devices ■ *aural* - Speech synthesizers ■ *all* - All devices
	scoped **5.1**	{boolean}	The HTML5 *scoped* attribute applies styles to a parent element. If this attribute is not present, styles will be applied to the whole document. IE ◯ FF 21 ● SF ◯ CH ◯ O ◯
<sub>	Water is a substance with chemical formula H<sub>2</sub>O		Defines subscripted text which could be used in mathematical expressions and in some languages. Water is a substance with chemical formula H_2O
<summary> **5.1**	<details> <summary>Design</summary> This article is about the general concept of design. </details>		'Summary' is a header for the *detail* element IE ◯ FF ◯ SF 6 CH 12 O 15
<sup>	The amount of energy is directly proportional to the mass of body: E = mc<sup>2</sup>		*sup* defines superscripted text which could be used for mathematical expressions, and in some languages. The amount of energy is directly proportional to the mass of body: $E = mc^2$

Tag	Code Example	Description

`<table>`	`<table summary=contribution>`
	
	`<tr>`
	`<th>1st column header cell`
	`<th>2nd column header cell`
	
	`<tr>`
	`<td>1st row, 1st cell`
	`<td>1st row, 2nd cell`
	
	`</table>`
		Table element typically represents 2-dimensional data, in the form of grid of cells.
		
		■ Tables should not be used to control page layout
		■ Initially there has been a debate about possible removal of the *summary* attribute

Attribute	Value	Description
border	{numeric}	It is a border indicator.
sortable **5.1**	{boolean}	It indicates that the user agent is to allow the user to sort the table.
frame, cellpadding, cellspacing, rules, width		Deprecated in HTML5

Tag	Code Example	Description

`<thead>`	`<table summary=payments>`
	
	`<thead class=hd>`
	`<tr>`
	`<th>Name`
	`<th>Amount`
	`</thead>`
		t-header, *t-body* and *t-footer* elements utilized to group table cells for a CSS control over a group.
		
		■ If you use one of these 3 elements, you should use all of them
		■ The following apply to each of the 3 elements:
		  - Must have a **`<tr>`** tag inside
		  - Closing tags are optional
		  - Global attributes supported
		  - Element-specific attributes are deprecated: align, char, charoff, valign
		■ The **`<td>`** tag is illegal inside of the *t-header* element

`<tbody>`
 	
Tip: use *tbody* to show/hide groups of rows
	`<tbody class=bd>`
	`<tr>`
	`<td>John`
	`<td>$100`
	`<tr>`
	`<td>Ann`
	`<td>$50`
	`</tbody>`	

`<tfoot>`	`<tfoot class=ft>`
	`<tr>`
	`<td>Total`
	`<td>$150`
	`</tfoot>`
	
	`</table>`	

Name	Amount
John	$100
Ann	$50
Total	**$150**

Tag	Code Example	Description

`<td>`	`<table>`
	
	`<tr>`
	`<th` *colspan*`=3 id=cont>Contact`
	
	`<tr>`
	`<th id=fn>First Name`
	`<th id=ln>Last Name`
	`<th id=ph>Phone`
	
	`<tr>`
	`<td` *headers*`='cont fn'>John`
	`<td` *headers*`='cont ln'>Smith`
	`<td` *headers*`='cont ph'>312235`
	
	`</table>`
		Table cell
		
		■ Closing `</td>` tag is not required
		■ The code example illustrates use of attributes *colspan* and *headers*.

Contact		
First Name	**Last Name**	**Phone**
John	Smith	312-235-5678
Ann	Jackson	202-123-4567

Attribute	Value	Description
headers	{text string}	Accessibility attribute - text string consisting of an unordered set of unique space-separated header IDs
colspan	{number}	Number of columns this cell spans
rowspan	{number}	Number of rows this cell spans
abbr, align, axis, char, charoff, height, nowrap, scope, valign		Deprecated in HTML5

Tag	Code Example	Description
`<textarea>`	`<textarea rows=5 cols=10>` `To be or not to be</textarea>`	Multi-line text area

Attribute	Value	Description
autofocus ❺	{boolean}	Places focus on the input field. Invalid with `type="hidden"`.
cols	{number}	Number of characters visible in a single row of the text-area
dirname	{text string}	It enables the submission of the directionality of the element, and gives the name of the field that contains this value during form submission.
disabled	{boolean}	Disables the input element when it first loads so that the user can not write text in it, or select it. Cannot be used with `type=hidden`

Tag	Code Example		Description
	form ⑤	{text string}	Associates control with form ID(s)
	inputmode **5.1**	verbatim, latin, latin-name, latin-prose, full-width-latin, kana, kana-name, katakana, numeric, tel, email, url,	It specifies what more helpful input mechanism for users entering content into the form control.
	maxlength ⑤ minlength	{number}	Maximum/minumum number of characters allowed
	name	{text string}	Field's unique name
	placeholder ⑤	{text string}	Short hint such as a sample value or a brief description of the expected format.
	readonly	{boolean}	Value of the field is not editable
	required ⑤	{boolean}	Defines a required input field's. This attribute cannot be used with the following types: hidden, image, button, submit, reset
	rows	{number}	Number of rows in the text-area
	wrap ⑤	hard, soft	Content wrapping type ■ The *hard* type takes advantage of the *cols* attribute to set line breaks ■ The *soft* type adds no line breaks

Tag	Code Example		Description
`<th>`	`<tr><th>Header</th></tr>`		Table header cell

	Attribute	Value	Description
	abbr		
	colspan, rowspan	{number}	Indicates the number of columns/rows this cell should span
	headers		
	scope	col, colgroup, row, rowgroup	Header cells that will use this header's information
	sorted **5.1**		
	abbr, align, axis, char, charoff, height, nowrap, valign, width		Deprecated in HTML5

Tag	Code Example	Description
`<time>`	The Apollo 11 landed the first humans on the Moon on `<time datetime="1969-07-20T17:40">` July 20, 1969 at 20:17:40`</time>`	Inline semantic element.

Attribute	Value	
datetime	{datetime}	Specifies the date or time that the element represents in any one of the following formats: ■ Date: **1995-12-30** ■ Time: **23:59:12.30** ■ Date and time. 'Z' is a time zone designator. Date and time separated by 'T': **1995-12-30T23:59** **1995-12-30T23:59:58Z** **1995-12-30T23:59:58-08:00**

Tag	Code Example	Description

`<title>`	`<head>`
	`<title>Google</title>`
	`</head>`
		HTML document title, appears in the browser's tab/title bar

`<tr>`	`<table>`
	  `<tr>`
	  `<td>Cell 1</td>`
	  `<td>Cell 2</td>`
	  `<td>Cell 3</td>`
	  `</tr>`
	`</table>`
		Table row
		
		Attributes deprecated in HTML5: align, char, charoff, valign

Tag	Code Example	Description

`<track>`	`<video width="720" height="480">`
	
	`<source src="jaws.mp4" type="video/mp4">`
	
	`<source src="jaws.ogg" type="video/ogg">`
	
	`<track src="subtitles_en.vtt" kind="subtitles" srclang="en" label="English">`
	
	`<track src="subtitles_no.vtt" kind="subtitles" srclang="no" label="Russian">`
	
	`</video>`
		It specifies explicit external timed text tracks for media elements.

Attribute	Value	
default	default	The track is enabled if the user's preferences do not indicate that another track is more appropriate
kind	captions, chapters, descriptions, metadata, subtitles	The type of the text track
label	{text}	The title of the text track
src	{url}	Required: the URL of the track file
srclang	{language_code}	the language of the track text data

Tag	Code Example	Description
`<u>` ❺	`<p>The <u>see</u> is full of fish.</p>`	This element (underline) was deprecated in HTML 4. The `<u>` tag is redefined in HTML5, to indicate a stylistically different text, e.g. misspelled words or proper names.

`<ul>`	`<ul>`
	`  <li>Mars`
	`  <li>Jupiter`
	`  <li>Saturn`
	`</ul>`
		Unordered (or un-numbered) list which is typically rendered as a series of bulleted items.

`<var>`	`I expect at least <var>n</var> number of guests to arrive.`	Variable

Tag	Code Example	Description
`<video>` 5	`<video src=mymovie.vid controls autoplay loop preload>This video is not supported by your browser </video>`	Video IE 9 FF 4 SF 4 CH8 O11

Attribute	Value	Description
autoplay	{boolean}	Video plays automatically
crossorigin 5.1	anonymous; use-credentials	Crossorigin handling method
controls	{boolean} controls	Video controls displayed
height width	{number} pixels	Height/width of the video player
loop	{boolean} loop	Video plays unlimited loop
poster	{URL}	Specifies an image to be displayed while the video is loading.
preload	{boolean} preload	Video loaded at page load and ready to play
src	{URL}	URL of the video
mediagroup 5.1	e.g. audio, video, movie	It can be used to link multiple media elements together by creating a *MediaController*. The value is text; media elements with the same value are automatically linked.
muted	muted	Muted audio state.

Tag	Code Example	Description
`<wbr>`	`<p>To be<wbr>or<wbr>not to be</p>`	Word breaking opportunity: preventing breaking lines at the wrong place.

HTML5 Browser Compatibility

	Desktop					Mobile		
	IE	FireFox	Safari	Chrome	Opera	iOS	Opera	Android
Audio Element	9	3.5	4	6	10.5	4	✕	2.3
Border Radius	9	3	3.2	6	10.5	3.2	✕	2.1*
Box-Shadow	9	3.5	3.2	6	10.5	3.2	✕	2.1
Canvas (basic)	9	3	3.2	6	10.5	3.2	10	2.1
Details & Summary	✕	✕	7	36	27	7.1	✕	4.1
Multi-column Layout	11	38*	7*	36*	11.1*	3.2*	8	37*
Media Queries	9	3.5	4	6	10.5	3.2	10	2.1
Progress and Meter	11*	31	7	36	27	8*	✕	4.4
Rubi	9*	4*	6*	6*	27	✕	✕	✕
Semantic Elements	9	4	5	6	11.1	4	10*	2.1
Selectors (advanced)	9	3.5	3.2	6	10.5	3.2	10	2.1
Text Overflow	6*	31*	7	36	27	7.1	8*	37
Video	9	3.5	4	6	10.5	4	✕	2.3
Overall compliance	**92%**	**92%**	**99%**	**99%**	**99%**	**92%**	**46%**	**92%**

* indicates partial support

? indicates unknown support

✕ indicates no support

In the Chapter 4

4. Forms, Attributes & Events

HTML5 Forms aka Web Forms 2.0

Web Forms 2.0 draft specification was superseded by HTML5 Forms specification. Form elements and attributes in HTML5 provide a higher degree of semantics vs. HTML4 while also offering a simplified markup and user interface styling.

A wide range of web forms functionality is now available without the use of JavaScript, Ajax libraries or plug in-based technologies, utilizing the updated HTML markup.

This section provides an overview of new input element types and attributes and the next chapter offers a more complete summary.

Input and Output elements

HTML5 <input> types and attributes

Type	Description	Example
date ❺	ISO 8601 encoded year, month, and day. Format: yyyy-mm-dd The screenshot example is rendered by *Opera* for Windows. `<input type=date>`	
datetime ❺ datetime-local ❺	*Datetime* type allows for user selection of a date and time: ISO 8601 encoded year, month, day, hour, minute, second, fractions of a second, and expressed in UTC, the Coordinated Universal Time. Format: yyyy-mm-dd HH:MMZ The *datetime-local* type displays no timezone. Format: yyyy-mm-dd HH:MM `<input type=datetime>`	

Type	Description	Example
month ❺	ISO 8601 encoded year, and a month. Format: yyyy-mm `<input type=month>`	
week ❺	ISO 8601 encoded year, and a week. Format: yyyy-mmW `<input type=week>`	
color ❺	Color picker control. ■ **placeholder** ❺ attribute represents a hint text intended to aid the user with data entry `<input type=color placeholder=black>`	
tel ❺	Telephone number. ■ **placeholder** ❺ attribute represents a hint text intended to aid the user with data entry ■ **pattern** ❺ attribute defines a regular expression against which the control's value is to be validated ■ **autocomplete** ❺ attribute, if "on", browser will store the input values and it will predict the value for the field when the user starts to type in that field again. The "off" value prevents the browser from using "autocomplete" which could be useful to protect sensitive data.	`<input type=tel` *placeholder*=" (000)000-0000" *pattern*="^\(?\d{3}\)?[-\s]\d{3}[-\s]\d{4}.*?$" *autocomplete*>` (000)000-0000
time ❺	Hour, minute, seconds, fractional seconds. `<input type=time>`	10:21

Type	Description	Example
range 5	'Range' slider widget contains a value from a range of numbers. ■ **min** and **max** 5 attributes indicate the defined range of values for the element	`<input type=range min=5 max=10>`
search 5	'Search' input. ■ **placeholder** 5 attribute as a hint ■ **autofocus** 5 attribute gives field instant focus ■ **results** attribute gives a drop down with the number of results requested. It is not an HTML5 attribute: it is *Webkit* browser specific only.	`<input type=search results=5 autofocus placeholder=Search...>` Search... html5 ×
number 5	Accepts numerical value only. ■ **step** 5 attribute specifies the increment input can be updated ■ **min** and **max** 5 attributes indicate the defined range of values ■ **value** attribute sets the initial value	`<input type=number value=20 step=1 min=5 max=50>` Hours: 20

email 5	Accepts email value only.
	
	■ **required** 5 attribute could simplify input validation code and error styling
	
	■ **oninvalid** 5 event can be used for validations
		`input[required] { background: yellow;}`
		
		`input: invalid { background-color:orange; border: 2px red solid;}`
		
		`input: valid { border: 1px solid green;}`
		
		`<input type=email required>`
		
		Email myemail@domain

Type	Description	Example

url ➎	Accepts URL value only
	
	■ **list** ➎ attribute can retrieve predefined values
	
	■ New *datalist* ➎ element can store values for the **list** attribute
		`<input type=url`
		list`=link_set name=link>`
		
		`<datalist id=link_set>`
		
		`<option label=Orbitz`
		`  value=http://www.orbitz.com>`
		
		`  <option label=Kayak`
		`  value=http://www.kayak.com>`
		
		`</datalist>`
		
		http://www.orbitz.com — Orbitz
		http://www.kayak.com — Kayak
		http://www.expedia.com — Expedia

HTML5 <output> element

Element	Description	Example

output ➎	**<output>** is HTML5 tag to representing the results of data calculations
	
	■ **onforminput** ia a new form event
		`<input type=number value=20>`
		
		`<output name=rate`
		onforminput=`"..." >0</output>`
		`<output name=total`
		onforminput=`"..." >0</output>`
		
		Hours: 20
		Rate: $ 30
		Total: $ 600

Input Type/Attribute Matrix (partial list)

	Text, Search, URL, Tel	Email	Password	Datetime, Date, Week, Month, Time	Number, Datetime-local	Range	Color	Checkbox, Radio	File	Button	Image
accept									✓		
alt											✓
autocomplete	✓	✓	✓	✓	✓	✓	✓				
checked								✓			
files									✓		
formaction										✓	✓
formenctype										✓	✓
formmethod										✓	✓
formnovalidate										✓	✓
formtarget										✓	✓
height, width											✓
list	✓	✓		✓	✓	✓	✓				
max, min				✓	✓	✓					
maxlength	✓	✓	✓								
multiple		✓							✓		
pattern	✓	✓	✓								
placeholder	✓	✓	✓								
readonly	✓	✓	✓	✓	✓						
required	✓	✓	✓	✓	✓			✓	✓		
size	✓	✓	✓								
src											✓
step				✓	✓	✓					
value	✓	✓	✓	✓	✓	✓	✓	✓	✓	✓	✓

Attributes

This list includes 22 new HTML **5.1** attributes.

Attribute	Value	Element	Description
abbr	Text*	th	Alternative label to use for the header cell when referencing the cell in other contexts
accept	Set of comma-separated tokens* consisting of valid MIME types with no parameters	input	Hint for expected file type in file upload controls
accept-charset	Ordered set of unique space-separated tokens, ASCII case-insensitive, consisting of labels of ASCII-compatible character encoding	form	Character encoding to use for form submission
accesskey	Ordered set of unique space-separated tokens, case-sensitive, consisting of one Unicode code point in length	**Global attribute: all elements**	Keyboard shortcut to activate or focus element
action	Valid non-empty URL potentially surrounded by spaces	form	URL to use for form submission
allowfullscreen **5.1**	Boolean attribute	iframe	Whether to allow the iframe's contents to *userequestFullscreen()*
alt	Text*	area; img; input	Replacement text for use when images are not available
async	Boolean attribute	script	Execute script asynchronously
autocomplete	"on"; "off"	form	Default setting for autofill feature for controls in the form
autocomplete	Autofill field name and related tokens*	input; select; textarea	Hint for form autofill feature

Attribute	Value	Element	Description
autofocus	Boolean attribute	button; input; keygen; select; textarea	Automatically focus the form control when the page is loaded
autoplay	Boolean attribute	audio; video	Hint that the media resource can be started automatically when the page is loaded
border	The empty string, or "1"	table	Explicit indication that the table element is not being used for layout purposes
challenge	Text	keygen	String to package with the generated and signed public key
charset	Encoding label*	meta	Character encoding declaration
charset	Encoding label*	script	Character encoding of the external script resource
checked	Boolean attribute	menuitem; input	Whether the command or control is checked
cite	Valid URL potentially surrounded by spaces	blockquote; del; ins; q	Link to the source of the quotation or more information about the edit
class	Set of space-separated tokens	**Global attribute: all elements**	Classes to which the element belongs
cols	Valid non-negative integer greater than zero	textarea	Maximum number of characters per line
colspan	Valid non-negative integer greater than zero	td; th	Number of columns that the cell is to span
command 5.1	ID*	menuitem	Command definition
content	Text*	meta	Value of the element
contenteditable	"true"; "false"	**Global attribute: all elements**	Whether the element is editable
contextmenu	ID*	**Global attribute: all elements**	The element's context menu
controls	Boolean attribute	audio; video	Show user agent controls

Attribute	Value	Element	Description
`coords`	Valid list of integers*	area	Coordinates for the shape to be created in an image map
`crossorigin`	"anonymous"; "use-credentials"	audio; img; link; script; video	How the element handles cross-origin requests
`data`	Valid non-empty URL potentially surrounded by spaces	object	Address of the resource
`datetime`	Valid date string with optional time	del; ins	Date and (optionally) time of the change
`datetime`	Valid strings: month, date, year-less date, time, floating date and time,time-zone offset, global date and time, week, non-negative integer, duration	time	Machine-readable value
`default` 5.1	Boolean attribute	menuitem	Mark the command as being a default command
`default`	Boolean attribute	track	Enable the track if no other text track is more suitable
`defer`	Boolean attribute	script	Defer script execution
`dir`	"ltr"; "rtl"; "auto"	**Global attribute: all elements**	The text directionality of the element
`dir`	"ltr"; "rtl"	bdo	The text directionality of the element
`dirname`	Text*	input; textarea	Name of form field to use for sending the element's directionality in form submission
`disabled`	Boolean attribute	button; menuitem; fieldset; input; keygen; optgroup; option; select; textarea	Whether the form control is disabled
`download`	Text	a; area	Whether to download the resource instead of navigating to it, and its file name if so
`draggable` 5.1	"true"; "false"	**Global attribute: all elements**	Whether the element is 'draggable'

Attribute	Value	Element	Description
dropzone 5.1	Unordered set of unique space-separated tokens, ASCII case-insensitive, consisting of accepted types and drag feedback*	**Global attribute: all elements**	Accepted item types for drag-and-drop
enctype	"application/x-www-form-urlencoded"; "multipart/form-data"; "text/plain"	form	Form data set encoding type to use for form submission
for	ID*	label	Associate the label with form control
for	Unordered set of unique space-separated tokens, case-sensitive, consisting of IDs*	output	Specifies controls from which the output was calculated
form	ID*	button; fieldset; input; keygen; label; object; output; select; textarea	Associates the control with a form element
formaction	Valid non-empty URL potentially surrounded by spaces	button; input	URL to use for form submission
formenctype	"application/x-www-form-urlencoded"; "multipart/form-data"; "text/plain"	button; input	Form data set encoding type to use for form submission
formmethod	"GET"; "POST"	button; input	HTTP method to use for form submission
formnovalidate	Boolean attribute	button; input	Bypass form control validation for form submission
formtarget	Valid browsing context name or keyword	button; input	Browsing context for form submission
headers	Unordered set of unique space-separated tokens, case-sensitive, consisting of IDs*	td; th	The header cells for this cell

Attribute	Value	Element	Description
`height`	Valid non-negative integer	canvas; embed; iframe; img; input; object; video	Vertical dimension
`hidden`	Boolean attribute	**Global attribute: all elements**	Whether the element is relevant
`high`	Valid floating-point number*	meter	Low limit of high range
`href`	Valid URL potentially surrounded by spaces	a; area	Address of the hyperlink
`href`	Valid non-empty URL potentially surrounded by spaces	link	Address of the hyperlink
`href`	Valid URL potentially surrounded by spaces	base	Document base URL
`hreflang`	Valid BCP 47 language tag	a; area; link	Language of the linked resource
`http-equiv`	Text*	meta	Pragma directive
`icon` 5.1	Valid non-empty URL potentially surrounded by spaces	menuitem	Icon for the command
`id`	Text*	**Global attribute: all elements**	The element's ID
`inputmode` 5.1	"verbatim"; "latin"; "latin-name"; "latin-prose"; "full-width-latin"; "kana"; "kana-name"; "katakana"; "numeric"; "tel"; "email"; "url"	input; textarea	Hint for selecting an input modality
`ismap`	Boolean attribute	img	Whether the image is a server-side image map
`itemid` 5.1	Valid URL potentially surrounded by spaces	**Global attribute: all elements**	Global identifier for a *microdata* item
`itemprop` 5.1	Unordered set of unique space-separated tokens, case-sensitive, consisting of valid absolute URLs, defined property names, or text*	**Global attribute: all elements**	Property names of a *microdata* item

Attribute	Value	Element	Description
itemref 5.1	Unordered set of unique space-separated tokens, case-sensitive, consisting of IDs*	**Global attribute: all elements**	Referenced elements
itemscope 5.1	Boolean attribute	**Global attribute: all elements**	Introduces a *microdata* item
itemtype 5.1	Unordered set of unique space-separated tokens, case-sensitive, consisting of valid absolute URL*	**Global attribute: all elements**	Item types of a *microdata* item
keytype	Text*	keygen	The type of cryptographic key to generate
kind	"subtitles"; "captions"; "descriptions"; "chapters"; "metadata"	track	The type of text track
label	Text	menuitem; menu; optgroup; option; track	User-visible label
lang	Valid BCP 47 language tag or the empty string	**Global attribute: all elements**	Language of the element
list	ID*	input	List of auto complete options
loop	Boolean attribute	audio; video	Whether to loop the media resource
low	Valid floating-point number*	meter	High limit of low range
manifest	Valid non-empty URL potentially surrounded by spaces	html	Application cache manifest
max	Varies*	input	Maximum value
max	Valid floating-point number*	meter; progress	Upper bound of range
maxlength	Valid non-negative integer	input; textarea	Maximum length of value
media	Valid media query	link; style	Applicable media

Attribute	Value	Element	Description
`mediagroup`	Text	audio; video	Groups media elements together with an *implicitMediaController*
`menu`	ID*	button	Specifies the element's designated pop-up menu
`method`	"GET"; "POST"; "dialog"	form	HTTP method to use for form submission
`min`	Varies*	input	Minimum value
`min`	Valid floating-point number*	meter	Lower bound of range
`minlength`	Valid non-negative integer	input; textarea	Minimum length of value
`multiple`	Boolean attribute	input; select	Whether to allow multiple values
`muted`	Boolean attribute	audio; video	Whether to mute the media resource by default
`name`	Text*	button; fieldset; input; keygen; output; select; textarea	Name of form control to use for form submission and in the *form.elements* API
`name`	Text*	form	Name of form to use in *thedocument.forms* API
`name`	Valid browsing context name or keyword	iframe; object	Name of nested browsing context
`name`	Text*	map	Name of image map to reference from the *usemap* attribute
`name`	Text*	meta	*Metadata* name
`name`	Text	param	Name of parameter
`novalidate`	Boolean attribute	form	Bypass form control validation for form submission
`open` 5.1	Boolean attribute	details	Whether the details are visible
`open` 5.1	Boolean attribute	dialog	Whether the dialog box is showing
`optimum`	Valid floating-point number*	meter	Optimum value in gauge

Attribute	Value	Element	Description
`pattern`	Regular expression matching the JavaScript Pattern production	input	Pattern to be matched by the form control's value
`placeholder`	Text*	input; textarea	User-visible label to be placed within the form control
`poster`	Valid non-empty URL potentially surrounded by spaces	video	Poster frame to show prior to video playback
`preload`	"none"; "metadata"; "auto"	audio; video	Hints how much buffering the media resource will likely need
`radiogroup` 5.1	Text	menuitem	Name of group of commands to treat as a radio button group
`readonly`	Boolean attribute	input; textarea	Whether to allow the value to be edited by the user
`rel`	Set of space-separated tokens*	a; area; link	Relationship between the document containing the hyperlink and the destination resource
`required`	Boolean attribute	input; select; textarea	Whether the control is required for form submission
`reversed`	Boolean attribute	ol	Number the list backwards
`rows`	Valid non-negative integer greater than zero	textarea	Number of lines to show
`rowspan`	Valid non-negative integer	td; th	Number of rows that the cell is to span
`sandbox`	Unordered set of unique space-separated tokens, ASCII case-insensitive, consisting of "allow-forms", "allow-pointer-lock", "allow-popups", "allow-same-origin", "allow-scripts and "allow-top-navigation"	iframe	Security rules for nested content
`spellcheck`	"true"; "false"	**Global attribute: all elements**	Whether the element is to have its spelling and grammar checked

Attribute	Value	Element	Description
scope	"row"; "col"; "rowgroup"; "colgroup"	th	Specifies which cells the header cell applies to
scoped 5.1	Boolean attribute	style	Whether the styles apply to the entire document or just the parent sub-tree
seamless 5.1	Boolean attribute	iframe	Whether to apply the document's styles to the nested content
selected	Boolean attribute	option	Whether the option is selected by default
shape	"circle"; "default"; "poly"; "rect"	area	The kind of shape to be created in an image map
size	Valid non-negative integer greater than zero	input; select	Size of the control
sizes	Unordered set of unique space-separated tokens, ASCII case-insensitive, consisting of sizes*	link	Sizes of the icons (forrel="icon")
sortable 5.1	Boolean attribute	table	Enables a sorting interface for the table
sorted 5.1	Set of space-separated tokens, ASCII case-insensitive, consisting of neither, one, or both of "reversed" and a valid non-negative integer greater than zero	th	Column sort direction
span	Valid non-negative integer greater than zero	col; colgroup	Number of columns spanned by the element
src	Valid non-empty URL potentially surrounded by spaces	audio; embed; iframe; img; input; script; source; track; video	Address of the resource
srcdoc	The source of an iframe srcdoc document*	iframe	A document to render in the *iframe*

Attribute	Value	Element	Description
`srclang`	Valid BCP 47 language tag	track	Language of the text track
`srcset` 5.1	Comma-separated list of image candidate strings	img	Images to use in different situations (e.g. high-resolution displays, small monitors, etc)
`start`	Valid integer	ol	Ordinal value of the first item
`step`	Valid floating-point number greater than zero, or "any"	input	Granularity to be matched by the form control's value
`style`	CSS declarations*	**Global attribute: all elements**	Presentational and formatting instructions
`tabindex`	Valid integer	**Global attribute: all elements**	Whether the element is focusable, and the relative order of the element for the purposes of sequential focus navigation
`target`	Valid browsing context name or keyword	a; area	Browsing context for hyperlink navigation
`target`	Valid browsing context name or keyword	base	Default browsing context for hyperlink navigation and form submission
`target`	Valid browsing context name or keyword	form	Browsing context for form submission
`title`	Text	**Global attribute: all elements**	Advisory information for the element
`title`	Text	abbr; dfn	Full term or expansion of abbreviation
`title`	Text	input	Description of pattern (when used with *pattern* attribute)
`title` 5.1	Text	menuitem	Hint describing the command
`title`	Text	link	Title of the link
`title`	Text	link; style	Alternative style sheet set name
`translate`	"yes"; "no"	**Global attribute: all elements**	Whether the element is to be translated when the page is localized

Attribute	Value	Element	Description
`type`	Valid MIME type	a; area; link	Hint for the type of the referenced resource
`type`	"submit"; "reset"; "button"; "menu"	button	Type of button
`type`	Valid MIME type	embed; object; script; source; style	Type of embedded resource
`type`	input type keyword	input	Type of form control
`type`	"popup"; "toolbar"	menu	Type of menu
`type` 5.1	"command"; "checkbox"; "radio"	menuitem	Type of command
`type`	"1"; "a"; "A"; "i"; "I"	ol	Kind of list marker
`typemustmatch`	Boolean attribute	object	Whether the type attribute and the Content-Type value need to match for the resource to be used
`usemap`	Valid hash-name reference*	img; object	Name of image map to use
`value`	Text	button; option	Value to be used for form submission
`value`	Text*	data	Machine-readable value
`value`	Varies*	input	Value of the form control
`value`	Valid integer	li	Ordinal value of the list item
`value`	Valid floating-point number	meter; progress	Current value of the element
`value`	Text	param	Value of parameter
`width`	Valid non-negative integer	canvas; embed; iframe; img; input; object; video	Horizontal dimension
`wrap`	"soft"; "hard"	textarea	How the value of the form control is to be wrapped for form submission

An asterisk (*) indicates that the actual rules are more complicated than indicated in the table above.

Events

HTML Event Handler Attributes

Most HTML tags can be interacted with by events. There are many of different ways an event can occur, including:

- User interaction using keyboard key press or mouse click
- Automatic page processing, such as page loading
- At set time-intervals or after a delay
- JavaScript can be attached to an event using JavaScript *event handler*, which could trigger an action.
- Event Handlers correspond to HTML tag attributes.
- JavaScript defines the five types of events:
  - form
  - keyboard
  - mouse
  - media
  - window
- This list includes 18 HTML **5.1** events.

```
<input type=button value=Confirm
onclick="alert('Are you sure?')">
```

List of Events

Event	Interface	Targets	Description
abort	Event	Window	Fired at the Window when the download was aborted by the user
autocomplete **5.1**	Event	form elements	Fired at a form element when it is auto-filled
autocompleteerror **5.1**	Event	form elements	Fired at a form element when a bulk auto-fill fails
DOMContentLoaded **5.1**	Event	Document	Fired at the Document once the parser has finished
afterprint	Event	Window	Fired at the Window after printing
afterscriptexecute **5.1**	Event	script elements	Fired at script elements after the script runs (just before the corresponding load event)

Event	Interface	Targets	Description
beforeprint	Event	Window	Fired at the Window before printing
beforescriptexecute 5.1	Event	script elements	Fired at script elements just before the script runs; canceling the event cancels the running of the script
beforeunload	BeforeUnloadEvent	Window	Fired at the Window when the page is about to be unloaded, in case the page would like to show a warning prompt
blur	Event	Window, elements	Fired at nodes losing focus
cancel 5.1	Event	dialog elements	Fired at dialog elements when they are canceled by the user (e.g. by pressing the Escape key)
change	Event	Form controls	Fired at controls when the user commits a value change (see also the change event of input elements)
click	MouseEvent	Elements	Normally a mouse event; also synthetically fired at an element before its activation behavior is run, when an element is activated from a non-pointer input device (e.g. a keyboard)
close 5.1	Event	dialog elements, WebSocket	Fired at dialog elements when they are closed, and at *WebSocket* elements when the connection is terminated
connect 5.1	MessageEvent	SharedWorkerGlobalScope	Fired at a shared worker's global scope when a new client connects
contextmenu 5.1	Event	Elements	Fired at elements when the user requests their context menu

Event	Interface	Targets	Description
error	Event	Global scope objects, Workerobjects, elements, networking-related objects	Fired when unexpected errors occur (e.g. networking errors, script errors, decoding errors)
focus	Event	Window, elements	Fired at nodes gaining focus
hashchange	HashChangeEvent	Window	Fired at the Window when the fragment identifier part of the document's address changes
input	Event	Form controls	Fired at controls when the user changes the value (see also the change event of input elements)
invalid	Event	Form controls	Fired at controls during form validation if they do not satisfy their constraints
languagechange 5.1	Event	Global scope objects	Fired at the global scope object when the user's preferred languages change
load	Event	Window, elements	Fired at the Window when the document has finished loading; fired at an element containing a resource (e.g. img, embed) when its resource has finished loading
loadend 5.1	Event orProgressEvent	img elements	Fired at img elements after a successful load (see also media element events)
loadstart 5.1	ProgressEvent	img elements	Fired at img elements when a load begins (see also media element events)

Event	Interface	Targets	Description
message	MessageEvent	Window, EventSource, WebSocket, MessagePort, BroadcastChannel, Dedicated-Worker-Global-Scope, Worker	Fired at an object when it receives a message
offline	Event	Global scope objects	Fired at the global scope object when the network connections fails
online	Event	Global scope objects	Fired at the global scope object when the network connections returns
open 5.1	Event	EventSource, WebSocket	Fired at networking-related objects when a connection is established
pagehide	PageTransitionEvent	Window	Fired at the Window when the page's entry in the session history stops being the current entry
pageshow	PageTransitionEvent	Window	Fired at the Window when the page's entry in the session history becomes the current entry
popstate	PopStateEvent	Window	Fired at the Window when the user navigates the session history
progress	ProgressEvent	img elements	Fired at *img* elements during a CORS-same-origin image load (see also media element events)
readystatechange	Event	Document	Fired at the Document when it finishes parsing and again when all its sub resources have finished loading
reset	Event	form elements	Fired at a form element when it is reset
select 5.1	Event	Form controls	Fired at form controls when their text selection is adjusted (whether by an API or by the user)

Event	Interface	Targets	Description
show **5.1**	RelatedEvent	menu elements	Fired at a menu element when it is shown as a context menu
sort	Event	table elements	Fired at table elements before it is sorted; canceling the event cancels the sorting of the table
storage	StorageEvent	Window	Fired at Window event when the corresponding *localStorage* or *sessionStorage* storage areas change
submit	Event	form elements	Fired at a form element when it is submitted
toggle	Event	details element	Fired at details elements when they open or close
unload	Event	Window	Fired at the Window object when the page is going away

In the Chapter 5

5. CSS3

CSS Overview

'CSS' stands for *Cascading Style Sheets*. Cascading Style Sheets are similar to style sheets found in word processing and page layout application programs. CSS is not part of HTML but rather a standalone standard language, designed to enable the separation of document content (typically coded in HTML) from document presentation, represented by layout, typography and visual elements.

CSS Levels

The CSS specifications are maintained by the World Wide Web Consortium. CSS has 3 main levels. Levels are similar to versions or generations, and include levels CSS1, CSS2, CSS3. Each generation of CSS builds upon the last, adding new features. CSS4 is currently in the early draft stage. Each CSS specification maintained as individual document. This chapter is organized using these individual specifications. Each specification is on a different level of completion which is reflected in the chart below.

CSS3

Taxonomy & Status (October 2014)

- W3C Recommendation
- Candidate Recommendation
- Last Call
- Working Draft
- Obsolete or inactive
- Related non-W3C Technologies

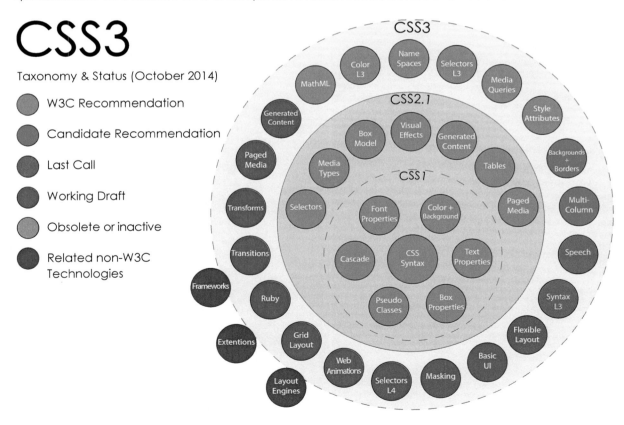

CSS3 Basics

- CSS attributes and values can be manipulated by JavaScript.

- Some browsers offer browser specific properties.

- CSS comments are used to add notes to the code. A CSS comment is denoted by (/*) and (*/) signs. Comments placed between these signs are not rendered by browsers.

- CSS can be applied as a predefined universal *rule* or as *inline* HTML attribute specific to a single HTML element.

- A style, applied to HTML element via HTML 'style' property also called an *inline style*. Inline style can control one HTML element at a time.

- A rule can be reusable: it can control multiple HTML elements.

Anatomy of a CSS Rule

A CSS rule includes HTML selector and CSS declaration.

	HTML tag, Class, or ID	CSS Declaration
Syntax concept	selector	{ property: attribute; }
This book's syntax Syntax	div	height = <u>auto</u> | <length> | inherit
Code example: - CSS - JavaScript	div	`{height: 100px;}` `object.style.height="100px"`

CSS Properties

- Multiple property values should be delimited by space.

- *Shorthand* property combines values of multiple properties in one simplified declaration. Shorthand property can be used to minimize syntax by combining several related property values into a single "super-property".

- If property is not specified, the initial default property value applies.

Typical CSS property locations

- In most cases the external CSS is preferred, because one set of rules can control multiple HTML elements and multiple HTML documents.

- HTML comment tags (`<!--    -->`) may be used to hide CSS from incompatible browsers.

Location	Method of CSS Rule Declaration	Example

External CSS file	Embedded rule definition via the <link> HTML tag	`<head>`
		
		`  <link href=styles.css rel=stylesheet type=text/css>`
		
		`</head>`

External CSS file	Embedded rule definition via the **@import** CSS declaration into:
	
	- **<head>** of the document
	- another CSS file. This allows for nesting of multiple CSS files
		`<head>`
		`<style type=text/css>`
		`<!--`
		`  @import url(styles.css);`
		`-->`
		`</style>`
		`</head>`

<head> of the HTML document	Embedded rule definition via the **<style>** tag	`<head>`
		`<style type=text/css media=all>`
		`<!--`
		`  .style1 {color:#eeeeee;}`
		`-->`
		`</style>`
		`</head>`

HTML element	Inline HTML 'style' attribute within the **<body>** of HTML document
	
	Tip: the style attribute needs no quotes as long as the values are space delimited
		`<body>`
		`  <p style=height:100%;color:blue>`
		`</body>`

CSS Cascading Priority

■ CSS can 'cascade': it applies properties/values in order of priority.

■ A higher priority style overwrite a lower priority style.

low	Priority Type	Comment	Example

1	Browser default	Browser default value is determined by W3C initial value specifications. It has the lowest priority and can be overwritten.	`<p style=font-weight:bold>`
			`Sample text</p>`
			`<!-- The 'bold' value overwrites default browser value 'normal'-->`

2	CSS property definition in HTML document	CSS rule or CSS inline style overwrites a default browser value.	`.myclass`
			`{font-weight: bold;}`
			
			`<p class=myclass>text</p>`

3	Parent inheritance	If a property is not specified, it will be inherited from a parent element.	`<div style=color: blue>`
			`    <p>Text</p>`
			`</div>`

4	Rule order	Last rule declaration has a higher priority	`div {width: auto;}` `div {width: 90%;}`
5	Selector specificity	A specific contextual selector (#heading p) overwrites generic definition	`#heading p {color: blue;}` `p {color: black;}`
6	Importance	The '!important' value overwrites the previous priority types.	`.myclass {` `font-size:12px !important;}`

7	Media Type	A property definition applies to all media types, unless a property had a media-specific CSS defined.	`<style type="text/css"`
			`media="print">`
			
			`.mystyle {color: blue;}`

8	Inline	A style applied to an HTML element via HTML 'style' property overwrites all the previous priority types.	`<p style=font-weight: bold>` `Sample text</p>`
9	User defined	Most browsers have the accessibility feature: a capability to load a user defined CSS.	
high			

CSS Properties

Section definitions & conventions

- CSS3 specifications are still in draft mode and could potentially change.

- In this chapter of the book, shorthand properties are formatted in bold.

- The description section has CSS properties and values delimited by single quotes.

- In this chapter of the book, a set of property values represented by a conceptual syntax 'Syntax', which describes rules these values can be assigned.

- Syntax Syntax section describes several types of values, using distinctive display conventions:

  - Variable data values denoted by the less than (<) and greater than (>) brackets (e.g., `<image>`, `<length>`, `<color>`, etc.). These are placeholders for actual values.

  - Variable data values, that have the same set of values wile sharing the same name as a property, appear in single quotes (e.g., `<'column-width'>`, `<'text-emphasis-style'>`, `<'background-color'>`, etc.)

  - Constant keyword values must appear literally, without any delimiting characters (e.g., normal, hidden, blue, auto, etc.). The slash (/) and the comma (,) must also appear literally.

- Pipe character (|) is a substitution for "or", meaning that values delimited by pipe character (|) generally can not be used together within a single property.

- A plus symbol (+) separates options that could be used together in any order, within one property.

- An ampersand (&) separates values which must all occur, in any order.

- An asterisk symbol (*) indicates that the preceding value may occur zero or more times. This Syntax example `[<URL> + [,* ]]` represents a list of multiple comma-delimited URLs. Two optional numbers in curly brackets `{X,Y}` indicate that the preceding group occurs **X** to **Y** times.

- The 'inherit' value defines whether the value is inherited from its parent. It applies to every CSS property, though it is omitted from the Syntax row in order to simplify the content. For instance, the 'float' property Syntax would be: `left | right | none | inherit`.
  On the other hand, note that not every property has the 'inherited' quality, defining whether a property value is inherited from a parent element by default.

- In this section of the book an initial default property value is indicated by <u>underline</u>.

- In case an initial value indicator is omitted, it means initial value is not defined by standards and it is implementation dependent.

- The characters <, >, [,], |, &, +, * , and underlining are not used in CSS syntax that way, but they rather a convention of the Syntax row of this book.

- The ➋, ➌ symbols indicate the CSS version.

- The color text of this kind (visible:) indicates a property value.

- Legend for the browser compatibility indicator:

  - [*]Partial support,

  - [m,w] Browser-specific syntax required, e.g. *-ms-* , *-webkit-* , *-moz-* , *-o-*

  - **Note**, the gray empty circle indicates that the browser is not supported

IE 9[m]   SF 5[w]   CH 10[*]

CSS Box Syntax

It is essential to understand the CSS *box-object Syntax*. This Syntax defines the key CSS layout properties and element relationship to other page elements. The box Syntax properties are: *margin, background, border, padding, width* and *height*. Think of each web page element as being an invisible rectangle with an invisible border and an invisible outer space.

- Margin: a transparent space immediately outside of the invisible box, separating an element from other elements

- Padding: a transparent space inside the invisible box but before the content, separating an element from its border and content (e.g. text)

- Border: between the padding and the margin. The border could be virtual (invisible)

- Background: combined padding and content space

- Width and Height: define content area dimensions only

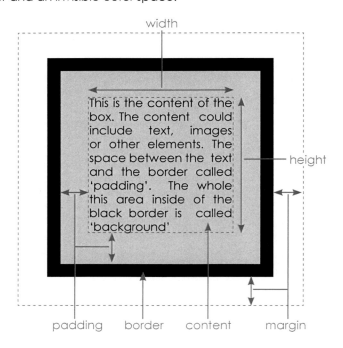

Background & Borders L3

Draft → Last Call → Candidate → Recommendation
http://www.w3.org/TR/css3-background/

Property	Values	
background	Syntax	[<bg-layer>] + [,*]
	Description	Shorthand property. Comma-separated items define the number of background layers. Each layer may include: <bg-image> + <bg-position> [/ <bg-size>] + <repeat-style> + <attachment> + <box> + <'background-color'>
	Example	`section {background:50% url('img.gif') / 8em scroll repeat-x border-box blue;}` //single layer
background-attachment	Syntax	<attachment: [<u>scroll</u>	fixed	local]> + [,*]
	Description	Defines scrolling method for multiple comma separated background images with regard to the viewport: ■ scroll: fixed to the element, scrolls with the document ■ fixed: fixed with regard to the viewport ■ local: inherits element's content position, scrolls with content
	Example	`div {background: url(stripe.png) fixed, url(logo.png) scroll;}`

Property	Values	
background-clip ❸	Syntax	<box:[<u>border-box</u>	content-box	padding-box]> + [,*]
	Description	Defines an extension of a background into a border:

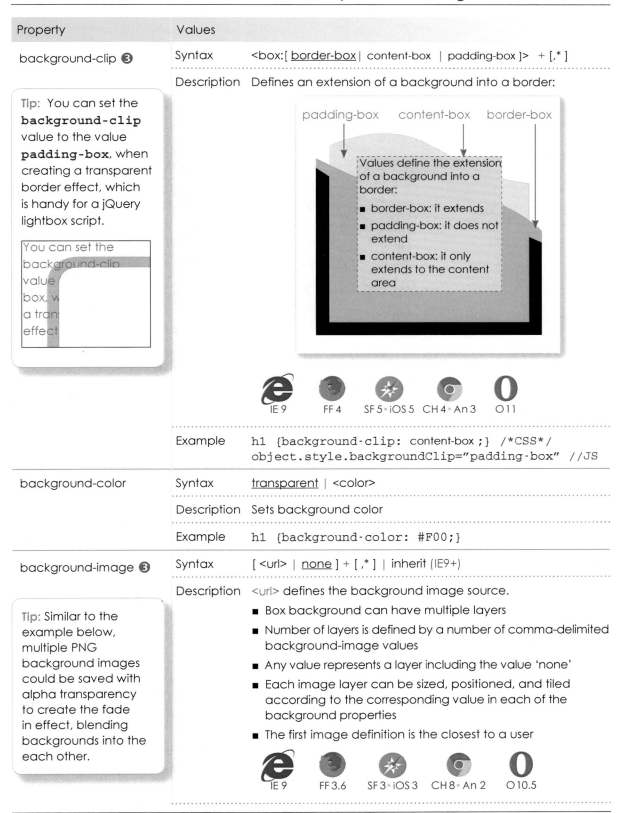

Tip: You can set the **background-clip** value to the value **padding-box**, when creating a transparent border effect, which is handy for a jQuery lightbox script.

padding-box   content-box   border-box

Values define the extension of a background into a border:

- border-box: it extends
- padding-box: it does not extend
- content-box: it only extends to the content area

IE 9   FF 4   SF 5 · iOS 5   CH 4 · An 3   O 11

	Example	h1 {background-clip: content-box ;} /*CSS*/ object.style.backgroundClip="padding-box" //JS
background-color	Syntax	<u>transparent</u>	<color>
	Description	Sets background color
	Example	h1 {background-color: #F00;}
background-image ❸	Syntax	[<url>	<u>none</u>] + [,*]	inherit (IE9+)
	Description	<url> defines the background image source.

Tip: Similar to the example below, multiple PNG background images could be saved with alpha transparency to create the fade in effect, blending backgrounds into the each other.

- Box background can have multiple layers
- Number of layers is defined by a number of comma-delimited background-image values
- Any value represents a layer including the value 'none'
- Each image layer can be sized, positioned, and tiled according to the corresponding value in each of the background properties
- The first image definition is the closest to a user

IE 9   FF 3.6   SF 3 · iOS 3   CH 8 · An 2   O 10.5

Property	Values

Example	`{background:url(sky.png) top left no-repeat,`
	`url(water.png) bottom left no-repeat,`
	`url(portrait.png) top  left no-repeat;}`
	`object.style.backgroundImage="url(sky.png)"`

background-origin ❸	Syntax	<box: [border-box | content-box | padding-box]> + [,*]
	Description	Defines when background position is relative to a box. See the **background-clip** property for the illustration.
Tip: not applicable if the **background-attachment** value is **fixed**.		 IE 9　FF 4　SF 5 • iOS 5　CH 4 • An 3　O 10.6

	Example	`.class2 {background: url('img.jpg');`
		`background-origin: content-box;}`
		`object.style.backgroundOrigin="border-box"`

background-position	Syntax	[[top | bottom] | [<length%> | <lengthPixels> | left | center | right] [<length%> | <lengthPixels> | top | center | bottom] | [center | [left | right] [<length%> | <lengthPixels>] + [center | [top | bottom] [<length%> | <lengthPixels>]
	Description	■ If only one keyword, the second value will be "center" ■ The initial value is top left corner: 0 0. It could be set either by percentage or by keyword values "top left" ■ The percentages and positions could be mixed ■ Percentages refer to size of background positioning area, minus the size of background image

Property	Values	

	Example	`.class1, .class2`
		`{background-image:url(img.jpg)}`
		
		`.class1 {background-position: left top;}`
		`/* 0px 0px */`
		
		`.class2 {background-position:`
		`left 15px top 20px;}  /* 15px 20px */`
		
		`.class3 {background:url(img.jpg)top center}`
		`/* shorthand: 50%, 0% */`
		
		`object.style.backgroundOrigin="content-box"`
		`//JavaScript`

background-size	Syntax	`<bg-size: [<width > + <height>]	cover	contain]> + [,*]`
	Description	Preserving original aspect ratio to fit inside the background positioning area could be achieved by values: ■ contain: scale the image to the largest size. ■ cover: scale the image to the smallest size. The original aspect ratio could be modified by manipulating the width and height values. ■ The first value is the width, the second is the height. ■ Possible 'width' and 'height' values: [auto	pixels	%] ■ If the second value is absent, it is implied to be 'auto'.
	Example	■ This image is stretched to fit horizontally 4 times. The aspect ratio is fixed:
		`.class1 {background-size: 25% auto;}` `object.style.backgroundSize="50px 100px"`

Property	Values	
background-repeat	Syntax	<repeat-style: [repeat-x | repeat-y | [repeat] | space | round | no-repeat]> + [,*]
	Description	Background repeat behavior: ■ repeat: Vertically and horizontally ■ repeat-x: Horizontally only ■ repeat-y: Vertically only ■ no-repeat: Displayed only once ■ round: Repeated as much as needed to fit within the background area. If it doesn't fit a whole number of times, it will be scaled to fit. ■ space: Repeated as often as will fit within the background positioning area to avoid clipping, and then the images will be spaced out to fill the area. First and last images touch the edges of the area:
	Example	`body {background-repeat: space;` `background-image: url(sculpture.png) white;}`
border	Syntax	<border-width> + <border-style> + <color>
	Description	Shorthand property
	Example	`.class1 {border: 2px red solid;}` `object.style.border="2px red solid"`
border-color	Syntax	<color>
	Description	Defines one common color for all 4 borders
	Example	`.class1 {border-color:#003333;}`
border-top-color border-right-color border-bottom-color border-left-color	Syntax	<color>
	Description	Defines individual color for each of 4 optional borders
	Example	`.class1 {border-top-color:#003333;` `            border-right-color: blue;}`

Property	Values	
border-style	Syntax	<u>none</u> | hidden | dotted | dashed | solid | double | groove | ridge | inset | outset
	Description	Defines one common style for all 4 borders
	Example	`.class1 {border-style: dashed solid;}` `object.style.borderStyle="dashed solid"`
border-top-style border-right-style border-bottom-style border-left-style	Syntax	<u>none</u> | hidden | dotted | dashed | solid | double | groove | ridge | inset | outset
	Description	Defines individual style for each of 4 optional borders
	Example	`.class1 {border-top-style: dashed;` `              border-left-style: solid;}`
border-width	Syntax	\<numeric\> | thin | <u>medium</u> | thick
	Description	Defines one common width for all 4 borders. Numeric can be in pixels, points or em.
	Example	`.class1 {border-width: 1.6em;}`
border-top-width border-right-width border-bottom-width border-left-width	Syntax	\<numeric_fixed\> | thin | <u>medium</u> | thick
	Description	Defines individual width for each of 4 optional borders. Numeric can be in pixels, points or em.
	Example	`.class1 {border-top-width: thin;` `              border-left-width: 2px;}`
border-radius ❸	Syntax	[\<radius_fixed\> | \<radius_%\>] + [* 1,4]
	Description	Shorthand. Defines one common radius for all 4 corners. Fixed value can be in pixels, points or em: 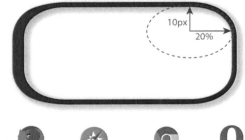

	Example	`.class1 {border: solid black 6px;`
		`              border-left-width: 14px;`
		`              border-radius: 20%/40px;}`
		
		`object.style.borderRadius="8px"`

IE 9   FF 4   SF 5ᵂ • iOS 3ᵂ   CH 10 • An 2ᵂ   O 10.6

> **Tip:** You can create an image with rounded corners: DIV container with rounded corners and background image. An optional transparent GIF could be placed inside.

Property	Values	
border-top-left-radius ❸	Syntax	[<radius_fixed> | <radius_%>] [< radius_fixed> | <radius_%>]
border-top-right-radius	Description	Defines individual radius for each of 4 corners. Fixed value can be in pixels, points or em.
border-bottom-right-radius	Example	.class1{ border-top-left-radius: 10px 20% 1em; border-top-right-radius: 10px 20%;}
border-bottom-left-radius		
border-top	Syntax	<border-width> + <border-style> + <color>
border-right	Description	Shorthand properties
border-bottom	Example	.class1 {border-top: 2px solid red; border-right: 2px dashed blue; border-bottom: solid red; border-left: 2px dashed blue;}
border-left		
border-collapse	Syntax	<u>separate</u> | collapse
	Description	Two adjacent table cell types:
		■ separated: each have their own borders
		■ collapsed: share borders
	Example	table {border-collapse: collapse;}
border-image ❸	Syntax	<'border-image-source'> + <'border-image-slice'> [/<'border-image-width'>? [/<'border-image-outset'>]?] ? + <'border-image-repeat'>
	Description	Shorthand property. Defines an image to overwrite border styles specified by the 'border-style' properties and it creates an additional background layer. all browser support
	Example	border: solid 50px; border-image:url(images/flower.png) 35 repeat stretch; -webkit-border-image:url(images/flower.png) 35 repeat stretch; -moz-border-image:url(images/flower.png) 35 repeat stretch;

Property	Values	
border-image-slice ❸	Syntax	[[<number_pixels> | <number %>] + [*1,4]] + fill
	Description	Initial value: **100%**. Four values represent inward offsets from the top, right, bottom, and left edges of the image, dividing it into nine regions: four corners, four edges and a middle. The middle image part is discarded (treated as transparent) unless the 'fill' keyword is present. ■ <number_%>: relative to the size of the image. ■ <number_pixels>: pixels in a bitmap image or vector coordinates in a vector image. ■ Optional 'fill' keyword preserves the middle part of the border-image. all browser support 25% 20% 30% 15%
	Example	`border-image-slice: 25% 30% 15% 20% fill;`
border-image-source ❸	Syntax	none | <image>
	Description	Defines an image overwriting the *border-style* properties creating an additional background layer.
border-image-width ❸	Syntax	[<width_pixels> | <width %> | <integer> | auto]
	Description	Initial value: '**1**'. Definition of the border image is drawn inside an area called the border image area. The four values of *border-image-width* specify offsets dividing the border image area into nine parts: distances from the top, right, bottom, and left sides of the area. ■ <width_%>: the size of the border image area: the width for horizontal offsets, the height for vertical offsets. ■ <integer>: multiples of the corresponding *border-width*. ■ auto: border image width is the original width or height of the corresponding image slice.
	Example	`.class1 {border-image-width: 2;}`
border-image-outset ❸	Syntax	[<length_pixels> | <number_integer>]
	Description	■ <length_pixels>: initial value: '**0**'. Top, right, bottom, left value of the border image area beyond the border box. ■ <integer>: multiples of the corresponding *border-width*. all browser support
	Example	`.class1 {border-image-outset: 0 1em;}`

Property	Values	
border-image-repeat ❸	Syntax	stretch	repeat	round	space
	Description	Border image scaling methods: ■ stretch: stretched to fill the area. ■ repeat: tiled (repeated) to fill the area. ■ round: tiled to fill the area. If it does not fit the area with a whole number of tiles, the image is re-scaled. ■ space: tiled to fill the area. If it does not fit with a whole number of tiles, a space is added between the tiles.
	Example	.class1 {border-image-repeat: round stretch space repeat;}
box-decoration-break ❸	Syntax	slice	clone
	Description	Border and padding method at the column/line break: ■ clone: independent border and padding for each box ■ slice: one common border and padding for both boxes IE FF 4 SF CH
	Example	.class {box-decoration-break: slice;}
box-shadow ❸	Syntax	none	[inset & [<offset-x> <offset-y> <blur-radius> <spread-radius> <color>]]
	Description	■ inset: optional keyword which defines an inner shadow ■ <offset-x>: horizontal shadow offset ■ <offset-y>: vertical shadow offset ■ <blur-radius>: shadow edge softness. 0 is sharp ■ The -webkit prefix: Safari and Chrome compatibility ■ The -moz prefix: Firefox compatibility Box Shadow

Property	Values	

	Example 1	`.class1 {border:1px solid blue;`
		`background-color: #FFFF00;`
		`width: 120px; height: 120px;`
		`box-shadow: 10px 10px 20px 0px gray;`
		`-webkit-box-shadow: 10px 10px 20px 0px gray;`
		`-moz-box-shadow: 10px 10px 20px 0px gray;}`

	Example 2	`/* since box-shadow property is incompatible`
		`with most of Internet Explorer versions, this`
		`IE-specific alternative could be used*/`
		
		`.class1 { filter:`
		`progid:DXImageTransform.Microsoft.Shadow`
		`(color=#C6CDD5,direction=90,strength=4)`
		`progid:DXImageTransform.Microsoft.Shadow`
		`(color=#C6CDD5,direction=180,strength=4)}`

Box Syntax

Draft → Last Call →Proposal → Recommendation
http://www.w3.org/TR/css3-box/

Property	Values	
clear	Syntax	none	left	right	both
	Description	Element side where other floating elements are not allowed.
	Example	`.class1 {clear: left;}`
display	Syntax	<u>inline</u>	block	inline-block	list-item	run-in	compact	table	inline-table	table-row-group	table-header-group	table-footer-group	table-row	table-column-group	none	table-column	table-cell	table-caption	ruby	ruby-base	ruby-text	ruby-base-group	ruby-text-group	<template>
	Description	Element display method. Element is displayed as: ■ block: block / paragraph. Allows no elements next to it. Exception: a float property assigned to another element. ■ inline: on the line of the current block ■ list-item: block box and a list-item in-line box ■ none: block is not created ■ run-in: either block or in-line boxes, depending on context ■ table, inline-table, table-row-group, table-column, table-column-group, table-header-group, table-footer-group, table-row, table-cell, and table-caption: these values define table-style element behavior

	Example	`.class1 {display: inline;}`
		
		`object.style.display="inline"`

Property	Values	
float	Syntax	left | right | <u>none</u> | <page-floats>
	Description	Defines box floating method/direction. The property does not apply to elements that are absolutely positioned.
	Example	`.class1 {float: right;}`
height width	Syntax	<u>auto</u> | <length_fixed> | <length_%>
	Description	Defines height and width of an element
	Example	`.class1 {width: 12px; height: 50%;}`
max-height max-width min-height min-width	Syntax	<u>auto</u> | <length_fixed> | <length_%>
	Description	Defines maximum or minimum height / width of an element.
	Example	`.class1 {max-height: 120px;}` `object.style.minWidth="20px"`

margin
 	
Tip: Centering a DIV container:
`div {`
`margin:0 auto;`
`width:100px; }`
	Syntax	[<length_fixed> | <length_%> | auto]{1,4}

	Description	Shorthand property. Margin defines transparent space around elements, outside of the border: from 1 to 4 values.

	Example	`.class1 {margin: inherit 0 10%;}`
		`/* top:inherit;left & right:0, bottom:10%*/`
		
		`.class2 {margin: auto;}`
		`/* top, left, bottom, right: auto */`
		
		`.class3 {margin: 15px 10px;}`
		`/* top & bottom:15px; left & right:10px */`
		
		`object.style.margin="10px"`

margin-bottom margin-left margin-right margin-top	Syntax	<length_fixed> | <length_%> | auto
	Description	■ Initial value: 0 ■ Acceptable 'width_numeric' units: [px | pt | % | em]
	Example	`.class1 {margin-top: 8%;}` `object.style.margin-left="10px"`
padding	Syntax	[<length_fixed> | <length_%> | auto]{1,4}
	Description	Shorthand property. Padding defines the space around content, inside of the element border. It can have 1-4 values.

	Example	`.class1 {padding: inherit 0 10%;}`
		`/* top:inherit; left & right:0, bottom:10% */`
		
		`.class2 {padding: 15px;}`
		`/* top, left, bottom, right: 15px */`
		
		`.class3 {padding: 15px 10px;}`
		`/* top & bottom:15px; left & right:10px */`

Property	Values	
padding-bottom	Syntax	<length_fixed> | <length_%>
padding-left	Description	■ Initial value: **0** ■ Acceptable <width_numeric> units: [px | pt | % | em]
padding-right		
padding-top	Example	`.class1 {padding-top: 8%;}` `object.style.paddingTop="8%"`
overflow	Syntax	[visible | hidden | scroll | auto | no-display | no-content] {1,2}
	Description	■ Shorthand for *overflow-x* and *overflow-y* properties. ■ The second property value is optional. If it has one value, it defines both *overflow-x* and *overflow-y*.
	Example	`.class1 {overflow: scroll auto;}  /*equal to` `{overflow-x:scroll; overflow-y:auto}*/`
overflow-style ❸	Syntax	<u>auto</u> | [scrollbar | panner | move | marquee] [, [scrollbar | panner | move | marquee]]*
	Description	Inherited. Defines the *overflow* property method: a list of scrolling methods in order of preference/browser support. ■ auto: browser chooses the scrolling method and displays a scroll bar when it detects the clipped content. ■ move - the content is draggable by a mouse pointer. ■ scrollbar - regular scroll bar. ■ marquee - the content moving autonomously of user events. ■ panner - two nested rectangles: the smaller rectangle represents a visible content view that can be moved (panned) by the user within the larger rectangle. ◯ no browser support Lorem ipsum dolor sit amet, consectetur adipisicing elit, sed do eiusmod tempor incididunt ut labore et dolore magna aliqua. Ut enim ad minim veniam, quis nostrud exercitation ullamco laboris nisi ut aliquip ex ea commodo consequat. Duis aute panner method
	Example	`.class1 {overflow-style: marquee-block;}`

Property	Values	
overflow-x ❸ overflow-y ❸	Syntax	<u>visible</u> | hidden | scroll | auto | no-display | no-content
	Description	Horizontal *x* or vertical *y* content overflow method: ■ visible: the content is not clipped, but partially hidden. ■ hidden: the content is clipped and no scrolling is available. ■ scroll: the content is clipped and the scrolling is always on. ■ auto: browser chooses the scrolling method and displays a scroll bar when it detects the clipped content. ■ no-display: if the content doesn't fit in the box, the box is not displayed, as if **display:none** is set. ■ no-content: if the content doesn't fit in the box, the content is hidden, as if **visibility:hidden** is set. IE 6 FF 1.5 SF 3 • iOS 3 CH 2 • An 2 O9.5
	Example	`.class1 {overflow-x: scroll;}` `object.style.overflowY="hidden"`
rotation ❸	Syntax	<angle>
	Description	■ Box rotation angle. ■ Initial value: **0**. no browser support
	Example	`.class1 {rotation: 45deg;}` `object.style.rotation="90deg"`
rotation-point ❸	Syntax	<bg-position>
	Description	■ Rotation center (pivot) point. ■ Initial value: **50% 50%**. no browser support
	Example	`.class1 {rotation-point: top left;}`
text-overflow ❸	Syntax	<u>clip</u> | ellipsis | <string> | initial
	Description	Unofficial. Text overflow method can be used to give a visual indication where text has been clipped. ■ <string>: renders the specified string (the clipped text) ■ ellipsis: renders an ellipsis [...] to indicate clipped text ■ clip: clips the text all browsers support
	Example	`.class1 {text-overflow: ellipsis;}` `object.style.textOverflow="clip" //JavaScript`

Property	Values	
visibility	Syntax	<u>visible</u>	hidden	collapse
	Description	Inherited. This property specifies whether the boxes generated by an element are rendered. Invisible boxes still affect layout unless the **display** is **none**.
		■ visible: the box is visible.
		■ hidden: the box is hidden, but still it affects layout by taking up the same space.
		■ collapse: it applies for internal table objects: rows, row groups, columns, and column groups (similar to **hidden**).
	Examples	`.class1 {visibility: hidden;}`

Color L3

Draft → Last Call → Candidate → Recommendation
http://www.w3.org/TR/css3-color/

Property	Values	
color ❸	Syntax	\<color>	attr(X,color)
	Description	Inherited
		■ \<color>: a keyword or a numerical RGB value. See Appendix for the list of keyword values.
		■ attr(X,color): the function returns color as value of attribute X
	Example	`h1 {color: rgb(240,6,10);}`
opacity ❸	Syntax	\<alphavalue>
Tip: RGBA declaration allows you to set opacity via the Alpha channel, as part of the color value **rgba (255,0,0,0.5)**	Description	Values range between **0.0** (transparent) to initial value **1.0** (opaque)
		IE 9 · FF 4 · SF 5 · iOS 3 · CH 11 · An 2 · O 11
	Example	`.class1 {opacity: 0.7;}`
		`.class2 {background-color: rgba(255,0,0,0.7);}`
		`object.style.opacity=0.7`

111

Flexible Box Layout L1

Draft ➔ Last Call ➔ Candidate ➔ Recommendation
http://www.w3.org/TR/css-flexbox-1/

Property	Values	
flex-direction	Syntax	<u>row</u> | row-reverse | column | column-reverse
	Description	Defines how flexbox items are placed in the container: ■ row: the flex container's *main axis* has the same orientation as the inline axis of the current writing mode. The *main-start* and *main-end* directions are equivalent to the *inline-start* and *inline-end* directions, respectively, of the current writing mode. ■ row-reverse: same as *row*, except the *main-start* and *main-end* directions are swapped. ■ column: the flex container's main axis has the same orientation as the *block axis* of the current writing mode. The *main-start* and *main-end* directions are equivalent to the *block-start* and *block-end* directions, respectively, of the current writing mode. ■ column-reverse: same as *column*, except the *main-start* and *main-end* directions are swapped.
	Example	`div { display: flex; flex-direction: column;}` The red box The long green box The blue blue blue blue box
flex-wrap	Syntax	nowrap | wrap | wrap-reverse
	Description	The property controls whether the flex container is single-line or multi-line, and the direction of the cross-axis, which determines the direction new lines are stacked in. ■ nowrap: the flex container is single-line. The cross-start direction is equivalent to either the inline-start or block-start direction of the current writing mode, whichever is in the cross axis, and the cross-end direction is the opposite direction of cross-start. ■ row-reverse: the flex container is multi-line. The cross-start direction is equivalent to either the inline-start or block-start direction of the current writing mode, whichever is in the cross axis, and the cross-end direction is the opposite direction of cross-start. ■ column: same as wrap, except the cross-start and cross-end directions are swapped.

Property	Values	
| | Example | ```
.class1 {
    display:-webkit-flex; -webkit-flex-wrap:wrap;
    display:flex; flex-wrap:wrap;}
``` |
flex-flow	Syntax	<flex-direction> || <flex-wrap>
	Description	The flex-flow property is a shorthand for setting the *flex-direction* and *flex-wrap* properties, which together define the flex container's main and cross axes.
	Example	`.class1 {flex-flow: row-reverse wrap-reverse;}`
order	Syntax	<integer>
	Description	Initial value: **0**. Defines order of elements within a flexible box.
	Example	`.class1 {order: 2;}`
flex	Syntax	none | [<'flex-grow'> <'flex-shrink'>? + <'flex-basis'>]
	Description	*Flex* is a shorthand property. It specifies the flex *grow factor* and flex *shrink factor*, and the flex *basis*. When a box is a flex item, flex is consulted instead of the main size property to determine the main size of the box. If a box is not a *flex item*, flex has no effect. ■ flex-grow: this value sets *flex-grow longhand* and specifies the *flex grow factor*, which determines how much the *flex item* will grow relative to the rest of the flex items in the flex container when positive free space is distributed. When omitted, it is set to *1*. ■ flex-shrink: this value sets *flex-shrink longhand* and specifies the flex *shrink factor*, which determines how much the *flex item* will shrink relative to the rest of the flex items in the flex container when negative free space is distributed. When omitted, it is set to *1*.
```

Property	Values	

		■ flex-basis: This value sets the *flex-basis longhand* and specifies the *flex basis*: the initial *main size* of the flex item, before free space is distributed according to the flex factors. It takes the same values as the width property (except *auto* is treated differently) and an additional content keyword. When omitted from the flex shorthand, its specified value is *0%*. If the specified flex-basis is *auto*, the used flex basis is the computed value of the flex item's main size property. If that value is itself *auto*, then the used flex basis is automatically-determined based on its content (i.e. sized as for content).
		
		■ Most common *flex* values. **initial** is the initial value:
		  - **flex:initial**. Equivalent to **flex:0 1 auto**
		  - **flex:auto**. Equivalent to **flex:1 1 auto**
		  - **flex:none**. Equivalent to **flex:0 0 auto**
		  - **flex:\<integer>**. Equivalent to **flex:\<integer> 1 0%**
		
		all browsers support

	Example	`.class1 { flex:3 1 0%; }`
flex-grow flex-shrink	Syntax	\<number>
	Description	It sets the flex grow/shrink factor to the provided \<number>. Initial value: *Flex-grow*: **0**. *Flex-shrink:* **1**.
	Example	`.class1 {flex-grow: 2;}`
flex-basis	Syntax	<u>auto</u> | content | \<width>
	Description	It sets the the initial length of a flexible item. ■ auto: when specified on a flex item, the auto keyword retrieves the value of the main size property as the used flex-basis. If that value is also auto, then the used value is content. ■ content: indicates automatic sizing, based on the flex item's content. ■ \<width>: For all other values, percentage values of *flex-basis* are resolved against the flex item's containing block, i.e. its flex container, and if that containing block's size is indefinite, the result is the same as a main size of auto.
	Example	`.class1 {flex-basis: 100px;}`

Property	Values	
justify-content	Syntax	<u>flex-start</u> | flex-end | center | space-between | space-around
	Description	It aligns flex items along the main axis of the current line of the flex container. Typically it helps distribute extra free space leftover when either all the flex items on a line are inflexible, or are flexible but have reached their maximum size. ■ flex-start: flex items are packed toward the start of the line. ■ flex-end: flex items are packed toward the end of the line. ■ center: flex items are packed toward the center of the line. ■ space-between: flex items are evenly distributed in the line. ■ space-around: flex items are evenly distributed in the line, with half-size spaces on either end **flex-start** **flex-end** **center** **space-between** **space-around**
	Example	`.class1 { justify-content: flex-end;}`
align-items align-self	Syntax	<u>auto</u> | flex-start | flex-end | center | baseline | stretch
	Description	*Flex items* can be aligned in the cross axis of the current line of the flex container, similar to justify-content but in the perpendicular direction. *align-items* sets the default alignment for all of the flex container's items, including anonymous flex items. *align-self* allows this default alignment to be overridden for individual flex items. ■ flex-start: the *cross-start* margin edge of the flex item is placed flush with the *cross-start* edge of the line. ■ flex-end: the *cross-end* margin edge of the flex item is placed flush with the *cross-end* edge of the line. ■ center: the flex item's margin box is centered in the *cross axis* within the line. ■ baseline: if the flex item's inline axis is the same as the *cross axis*, this value is identical to *flex-start*. ■ stretch: if the *cross size* property of the flex item computes to **auto**, and neither of the cross-axis margins are **auto**, the flex item is stretched.

Property	Values		
	Illustration	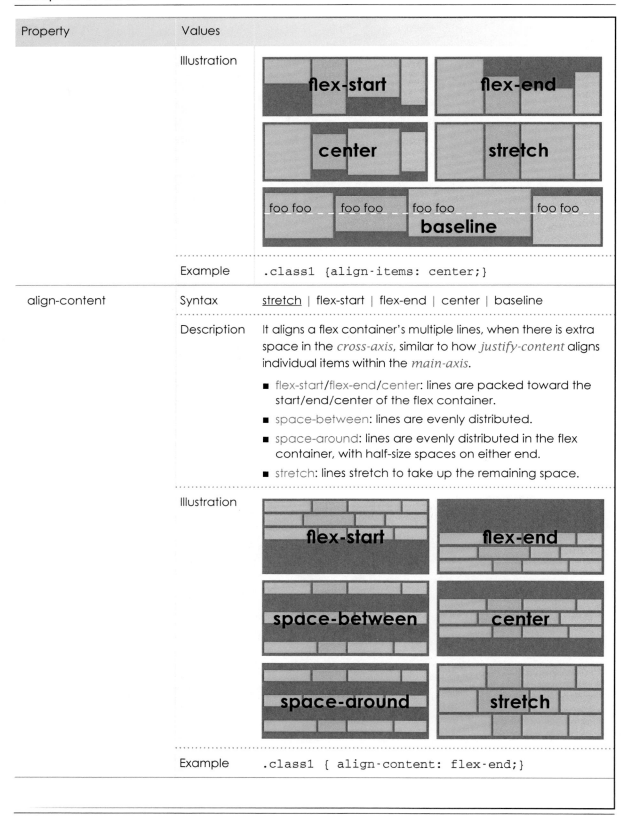	
	Example	`.class1 {align-items: center;}`	
align-content	Syntax	stretch | flex-start | flex-end | center | baseline	
	Description	It aligns a flex container's multiple lines, when there is extra space in the *cross-axis*, similar to how *justify-content* aligns individual items within the *main-axis*. ■ flex-start/flex-end/center: lines are packed toward the start/end/center of the flex container. ■ space-between: lines are evenly distributed. ■ space-around: lines are evenly distributed in the flex container, with half-size spaces on either end. ■ stretch: lines stretch to take up the remaining space.	
	Illustration		
	Example	`.class1 { align-content: flex-end;}`	

Fonts Module Level 3

Draft → Last Call → Candidate → Recommendation
http://www.w3.org/TR/css-fonts-3/

Property	Values	
font	Syntax	[[<'font-style'> + <'font-variant'> + <'font-weight'>] <'font-size'> [/ <'line-height'>] <'font-family'>]	caption	icon	menu	message-box	small-caption	status-bar	<appearance>
	Description	Inherited. Shorthand property for setting *font-style*, *font-variant*, *font-weight*, *font-size*, *line-height* and *font-family* properties, and to control system font values: ■ caption: captioned controls: buttons, drop-downs, etc. ■ icon: labeling icons ■ menu: drop down menus and menu lists ■ message-box: dialog boxes. ■ small-caption: small control labels ■ status-bar: window status bars ■ <appearance> ❸: text styling values for system controls: icon, window, desktop, workspace, document, tooltip, status-bar, dialog, message-box, button, caption, range, small-caption, push-button, hyperlink, radio-button, checkbox, menu-item, tab, menu, menubar, pull-down-menu, pop-up-menu, list-menu, radio-group, checkbox-group, outline-tree, field, combo-box, signature, password

	Example	`.class {font: x-large/1.5em "Palatino", serif;}`
		
		 `button p {font: menu;}`

font-family	Syntax	[<family-name>	<generic-family>] + [, *]
	Example	`p {font-family: Arial, Gill, sans-serif;}`
font-feature-settings	Syntax	normal	<string> [<integer>	on	off]?
	Description	These descriptor define initial settings that apply when the font defined by an *@font-face* rule is rendered. They do not affect font selection.
	Example	`p {font-feature-settings: normal ;}`

Property	Values	
font-kerning	Syntax	auto	normal	none
	Description	Kerning is the contextual adjustment of inter-glyph spacing. This property controls metric kerning, kerning that utilizes adjustment data contained in the font. ■ auto: Specifies that kerning is applied at the discretion of the user agent ■ normal: Specifies that kerning is applied ■ none: Specifies that kerning is not applied
	Example	`.class {font-kerning: none;}`
font-language-override	Syntax	normal	<string>
	Description	Authors can control the use of language-specific glyph substitutions and positioning by setting the content language of an element. ■ normal: specifies that when rendering with OpenType fonts, the content language of the element is used to infer the OpenType language system ■ <string>: single three-letter case-sensitive OpenType language system tag, specifies the OpenType language system to be used instead of the language system implied by the language of the element

	Example	A font may lack support for a specific language. In this situation authors may need to use the typographic conventions of a related language that are supported by that font:
		
		`<body lang="mk">`
		`    <!-- Macedonian lang code -->`
		
		`body { font-language-override: "SRB"; }`
		`    <!-- Serbian language tag -->`
		
		`<h4>Член 9</h4>`
		`<p>Никој човек нема да биде подложен </p>`
		
		The Macedonian text here will be rendered using Serbian typographic conventions, with the assumption that the font specified supports Serbian.

Property	Values	
font-size	Syntax	none	<length>	<percentage>	[larger	smaller]	[xx-small	x-small	small	<u>medium</u>	large	x-large	xx-large]
	Description	It indicates the desired height of glyphs from the font. For scalable fonts, the font-size is a scale factor applied to the EM unit of the font. For non-scalable fonts, the font-size is converted into absolute units and matched against the declared font-size of the font, using the same absolute coordinate space for both of the matched values.
	Example	.class1 {font-size: 12px;}
font-size-adjust	Syntax	<u>none</u>	<number>
	Description	Inherited. Preserving the readability by maintaining the 'aspect value' of lowercase letters vs. their uppercase counterparts and adjusting the *font-size* so that the *x-height* is the fixed regardless of the font used. 'Aspect value' = font x-height / font size.
	Example	.class1 {font-size-adjust: 0.5;}
font-stretch	Syntax	<u>normal</u>	ultra-condensed	condensed	extra-condensed	semi-condensed	semi-expanded	expanded	extra-expanded	ultra-expanded
	Description	Inherited
	Example	.class1 {font-style: extra-expanded;}
font-style	Syntax	<u>normal</u>	italic	oblique
	Description	Inherited
	Example	.class1 {font-style: italic;}
font-variant	Syntax	<u>normal</u>	none	[<common-lig-values> + <discretionary-lig-values> + <historical-lig-values> + <contextual-alt-values> + stylistic(<feature-value-name>) + historical-forms + styleset(<feature-value-name> #) + character-variant(<feature-value-name> #) + swash(<feature-value-name>) + ornaments(<feature-value-name>) + annotation(<feature-value-name>) + [small-caps	all-small-caps	petite-caps	all-petite-caps	unicase	titling-caps] + <numeric-figure-values> + <numeric-spacing-values> + <numeric-fraction-values> + ordinal + slashed-zero + <east-asian-variant-values> + <east-asian-width-values> + ruby]
	Description	These descriptor defines initial settings that apply when the font defined by an *@font-face* rule is rendered.
	Example	.class1 {font-variant: none;}

Property	Values	
font-variant-alternates	Syntax	normal | [stylistic(<feature-value-name>) + historical-forms + styleset(<feature-value-name> #) + character-variant(<feature-value-name> #) + swash(<feature-value-name>) + ornaments(<feature-value-name>) + annotation(<feature-value-name>)]
	Description	This property can provide a control over the variety of alternate glyphs in addition to the default glyphs. ■ historical-forms: Enables display of historical forms Jesuits ► Jeſuits ■ stylistic(<feature-value-name>): Enables stylistic alternates *quick* ► *quick* ■ styleset(<feature-value-name> #): Enables stylistic sets **incroyable** ► **incroyable** ■ character-variant(<feature-value-name> #): Enables display of specific character variants ■ ornaments(<feature-value-name>): Enables replacement of default glyphs with ornaments, if provided in the font. • ► ❦ ❧ ❁ ■ annotation(<feature-value-name>): Enables display of alternate annotation forms. 519 ► ⑤①⑨ ■ swash(<feature-value-name>): Enables swash glyphs *Quick* ► *Quick*
	Example	In the case of the swash Q in the example shown above, the swash could be specified using these style rules: ```css @font-feature-values Jupiter Sans { @swash { delicate: 1; flowing: 2; } } h2 { font-family: Jupiter Sans, sans-serif; } /* show the 2nd swash variant in h2 headings */ h2:first-letter { font-variant-alternates: swash(flowing); } <h2>Quick</h2> ``` When Jupiter Sans is present, the 2nd alternate swash alternate will be displayed. When not present, no swash character will be shown, since the specific named value "flowing" (chosen by the author) is only defined for the Jupiter Sans family.

Property	Values	
font-variant-caps	Syntax	<u>normal</u> | small-caps | all-small-caps | petite-caps | all-petite-caps | unicase | titling-caps
	Description	It allows the selection of small capitals glifs.
		These glyphs are specifically designed to blend well with the surrounding normal glyphs, to maintain the weight and readability which suffers when text is simply re-sized to fit this purpose.
		■ normal: None of the features listed below are enabled.
		■ small-caps: Enables display of small capitals. Small-caps glyphs typically use the form of uppercase letters but are reduced to the size of lowercase letters.
		qed ▶ QED
		■ all-small-caps: Enables display of small capitals for both upper and lowercase letters.
		■ petite-caps: Enables display of petite capitals.
		■ all-petite-caps: Enables display of petite capitals for both upper and lowercase letters.
		■ unicase: Enables display of mixture of small capitals for uppercase letters with normal lowercase letters.
		■ titling-caps: Enables display of titling capitals. Uppercase letter glyphs are often designed for use with lowercase letters, so they don't look to strong. When used in all uppercase titling sequences they can appear too strong.
	Example	Using small caps to improve readability in acronym-laden text.
		Quotes rendered italicized; small-caps on the first line:
| | | ```
blockquote
{ font-style: italic; }
``` |
| | | ```
blockquote:first-line
{ font-variant: small-caps; }
``` |
| | | ```
<blockquote>
I'll be honor-bound to slap them like a
haddock.
</blockquote>
``` |
```

Property	Values	
font-variant-east-asian	Syntax	normal | [[full-width | proportional-width] + ruby] + [jis78 | jis83 | jis90 | jis04 | simplified | traditional]]
	Description	Allows control of glyph substitution and sizing in East Asian text.

- normal: None of the features listed below are enabled.
- jis78: Enables rendering of JIS78 forms.

麹町 ▶ 麴町

- jis83: Enables rendering of JIS83 forms.
- jis90: Enables rendering of JIS90 forms.
- jis04: Enables rendering of JIS2004 forms. Fonts generally include glyphs defined by the Japanese national standard but it's sometimes necessary to use older variants.
- simplified: Enables rendering of simplified forms.

- traditional: Enables rendering of traditional forms, which still used in some contexts.

大学 ▶ 大學

- full-width: Enables rendering of full-width variants.
- proportional-width: Enables rendering of proportionally-spaced variants.

欧文フォント ▶ 欧文フォント

- ruby: Enables display of ruby variant glyphs. Since ruby text is generally smaller than the associated body text, font designers can design special glyphs for use with ruby that are more readable than scaled down versions of the default glyphs.

Only glyph selection is affected, there is no associated font scaling or other change that affects line layout. The red ruby text below is shown with default glyphs (left) and with ruby variant glyphs (right). Note the slight difference in stroke thickness.

しんかんせん　　しんかんせん
新幹線　新幹線

	Example	`flowing: 2;`

Property	Values	
font-variant-ligatures	Syntax	normal	[[common-ligatures	no-common-ligatures] + [discretionary-ligatures	no-discretionary-ligatures] + [historical-ligatures	no-historical-ligatures] + [contextual	no-contextual]]	none
	Description	Ligatures and contextual forms are ways of combining glyphs to produce more harmonized forms. ■ normal: it specifies that common default features are enabled. For OpenType fonts, common ligatures and contextual forms are on by default, discretionary and historical ligatures are not. ■ common-ligatures: Enables common ligatures. For OpenType fonts, common ligatures are enabled by default. fi ► fi ■ no-common-ligatures: Disables common ligatures. ■ discretionary-ligatures: Enables display of discretionary ligatures. Which ligatures are discretionary or optional is decided by the type designer. WORDS ► WORDS ■ no-discretionary-ligatures: Disables discretionary ligatures. ■ historical-ligatures: Enables display of historical ligatures. tz ► ß ■ no-historical-ligatures: Disables historical ligatures. ■ contextual: Enables display of contextual alternates. Although not strictly a ligature feature, this feature is commonly used to harmonize the shapes of glyphs with the surrounding context. *labor of love* ► *labor of love* ■ no-contextual: Disables display of contextual alternates. ■ none: Specifies that all types of ligatures are disabled.
	Example	.class1 {font-variant-ligatures: contextual;}

Property	Values	
font-variant-numeric	Syntax	normal | [[lining-nums | oldstyle-nums] + [diagonal-fractions | stacked-fractions] + [proportional-nums | tabular-nums] + ordinal + slashed-zero]
	Description	Specifies control over numerical forms. The example below shows how proportional numbers are used while tabular numbers are used so that columns of numbers line up properly:

	Lining	Old-Style
Proportional	409,280	409,280
	367,112	367,112
	155,068	155,068
	171,792	171,792
Tabular	409,280	409,280
	367,112	367,112
	155,068	155,068
	171,792	171,792

- normal: None of the features listed below are enabled.
- lining-nums: Enables display of lining numerals.
- oldstyle-nums: Enables display of old-style numerals.
- proportional-nums: Enables proportional numerals.
- tabular-nums: Enables display of tabular numerals.
- diagonal-fractions: Enables lining diagonal fractions.

$$2 \ 1/3 \quad \blacktriangleright \quad 2\tfrac{1}{3}$$

- stacked-fractions: Enables lining stacked fractions.

$$2 \ 1/3 \quad \blacktriangleright \quad 2\frac{1}{3}$$

- ordinal: Enables display of letter forms used with ordinal.

$$\text{1st} \quad \text{17th} \quad \text{2a} \quad \blacktriangleright \quad \text{1}^{\text{st}} \quad \text{17}^{\text{th}} \quad \text{2}^{\text{a}}$$

- slashed-zero: Enables display of slashed zeros.

$$4000 \quad \blacktriangleright \quad 4000$$

| | Example | In the case of 'ordinal', although ordinal forms are often the same as superscript forms, they are marked up differently. For superscripts, the variant property is only applied to the sub-element containing the superscript: |

```
sup { font-variant-position: super; }
```

x²

For ordinals, the variant property is applied to the entire ordinal number rather than just to the suffix:

```
.ordinal { font-variant-numeric: ordinal; }
```

<span class="ordinal">17th</span>

In this case only the "th" will appear in ordinal form, the digits will remain unchanged. Depending upon the typographic traditions used in a given language, ordinal forms may differ from superscript forms.

Property	Values	
font-variant-position	Syntax	<u>normal</u> | sub | super
	Description	This property is used to enable typographic subscript and superscript glyphs.
		These are alternate glyphs designed within the same em-box as default glyphs and are intended to be laid out on the same baseline as the default glyphs, with no re-sizing or repositioning of the baseline.
		They are explicitly designed to match the surrounding text and to be more readable without affecting the line height (top) vs. typical synthesized subscripts (bottom):
		$$C_{10}H_{16}N_5O_{13}P_3$$ $$C_{10}H_{16}N_5O_{13}P_3$$
		■ normal: None of the features listed below are enabled.
		■ sub: Enables display of subscript variants.
		■ super: Enables display of superscript variants
	Example	A typical user agent default style for the sub element:
| | | ```
sub { vertical-align: sub;
      font-size: smaller;
      line-height: normal; }
``` |
| | | Using font-variant-position to specify typographic subscripts in a way that will still show subscripts in older user agents: |
| | | @supports (font-variant-position: sub) { |
| | | ```
sub { vertical-align: baseline;
      font-size: 100%;
      line-height: inherit;
      font-variant-position: sub; } }
``` |
		Browsers that support the 'font-variant-position' property will select a subscript variant glyph and render this without adjusting the baseline or font-size.
		Older user agents will ignore it and use the standard defaults for subscripts.
font-weight	Syntax	<u>normal</u> | bold | bolder | lighter | 100 | 200 | 300 | 400 | 500 | 600 | 700 | 800 | 900
	Example	`.class1 {font-weight: bold;}`

Generated Content: Paged Media

Draft → Candidate → Proposal → Recommendation
http://www.w3.org/TR/css-gcpm-3/

IE 8   FF 4   SF 3 • iOS 3 CH 4 • An 3   O 11

CSS3 paged media is defined as a continuous media describing page specific behavior and elements:

- Page size, orientation, breaks, margins, border, and padding.
- Headers, footers and page numbering. Widows and orphans.
- In the page Syntax, the document appears in a CSS 'page box'. It consists of border , margin, padding and other properties. The properties of a page box are determined by the *@page* rule set
- Page box size specified by the 'size' property.

Property	Values	
string-set ❸	Syntax	[[<custom-ident> <content-list>] [, <custom-ident> <content-list>]*] | none
	Description	■ Copies the text content of an element into a named string, which functions as a variable.
		■ The text content of this named string can be retrieved using the string() function. Since these variables may change on a given page, an optional second value for the string() function allows to choose which value is used.
	Example	`h1 { string-set: header content(before) ':' content(text); }`
running ❸	Syntax	<custom-ident>
	Description	■ Copies the text content of an element into a named string, which functions as a variable (running header).
		■ The text content of this named string can be retrieved using the string() function. Since these variables may change on a given page, an optional second value for the string() function allows to choose which value is used.
	Example	`h2 { running: chapter;font-size: 18pt;}`
		`@page {@top-center{content:element(chapter);}}`
footnote-display ❸	Syntax	<u>block</u> | inline | compact
	Description	■ auto: automatic, may place the footnote body on a later page than the footnote reference.
		■ line: due to lack of space, the user agent introduces a forced page break at the start of the line containing the footnote reference, so that both fall on the next page.
		■ block: as with line, except a forced page break is introduced before the footnote paragraph.
	Example	`.myfootnote {footnote-display: inline;}`

Property	Values	
footnote-policy ❸	Syntax	<u>auto</u> | line | block
	Description	A footnote is display method: block or inline element
	Example	`.myfootnote {footnote-policy: line;}`
bookmark-label ❸	Syntax	<content-list> | <u>none</u>
	Description	Defines a bookmark label.
	Example	`.class1 {bookmark-label: "review";}`
bookmark-level ❸	Syntax	<u>none</u> | <integer>
	Description	Defines a bookmark level.
	Example	`.class1 {bookmark-level: 1;}`
bookmark-state ❸	Syntax	<u>open</u> | closed
	Description	Defines the initial state of a bookmark link
	Example	`.class1 {bookmark-state: closed;}`

CSS Grid Layout Level 1

Draft ➜ Last Call ➜ Candidate ➜ Recommendation
http://www.w3.org/TR/css-grid-1/

Property	Values	
grid	Syntax	<'grid-template'> | [<'grid-auto-flow'> [<'grid-auto-columns'> [/ <'grid-auto-rows'>]?]?]
	Description	The grid property is a shorthand that sets all of the explicit grid properties (grid-template-rows, grid-template-columns, and grid-template-areas) as well as all the implicit grid properties (grid-auto-rows, grid-auto-columns, and grid-auto-flow) in a single declaration.
		If <'grid-auto-rows'> value is omitted, it is set to the value specified for grid-auto-columns. Other omitted values are set to their initial values.
		IE 10ᵐ FF SF CH

Property	Values	
Tip: Use grid system to design layout similar to the grids traditionally used in magazines and newspapers. Grid systems bring visual structure and balance to design. Grids can enhance the user experience by creating predictable cognitive patterns.	Example 1	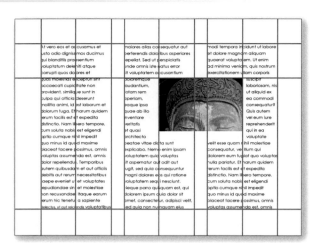

	Example 1	In addition to accepting the grid-template shorthand syntax for setting up the explicit grid, the grid shorthand can also easily set up parameters for an auto-formatted grid.
		For example, grid: row 1fr; is equivalent to
		`grid-template: none;`
		`grid-auto-columns: 1fr;`
		`grid-auto-rows: 1fr;`
		`grid-auto-flow: row;`
	Example 2	Similarly, grid: column 1fr / auto is equivalent to
		`grid-template: none;`
		`grid-auto-columns: 1fr;`
		`grid-auto-rows: auto;`
		`grid-auto-flow: column;`

grid-template-columns	Syntax	none	<track-list>	subgrid <line-name-list>?
grid-template-rows	Description	These properties specify, as a space-separated *track list*, the line names and track sizing functions of the grid.
		Each *track sizing function* can be specified as a length, a percentage of the grid container's size, a measurement of the contents occupying the column or row, or a fraction of the free space in the grid. It can also be specified as a range using the *minmax()* notation.

Property	Values	

	Track List Syntax	■ <track-list> = [<line-names>? [<track-size> | <repeat()>]] + <line-names>?
		   - <track-size> = minmax(<track-breadth> , <track-breadth>) | <track-breadth>
		   - <track-breadth> = <length> | <percentage> | <flex> | min-content | max-content | auto
		   - <line-names> = (<custom-ident>*)
		 ■ <line-name-list> = [<line-names> | repeat([<positive-integer> | auto], <line-names>+)]+

	Values	■ <length>: A non-negative length. ■ <percentage>: A non-negative percentage values, which are relative to the inline size of the grid container in column grid tracks, and the block size of the grid container in row grid tracks. ■ <flex>: A non-negative dimension with the unit *fr* specifying the track's flex factor. Each <flex>-sized track takes a share of the remaining space in proportion to its flex factor. ■ max-content: Represents the largest max-content contribution of the grid items occupying the grid track. ■ min-content: Represents the largest min-content contribution of the grid items occupying the grid track. ■ minmax(min, max): Defines a size range greater than or equal to *min* and less than or equal to *max*. ■ auto: As a maximum, identical to *max-content*. As a minimum, represents the largest minimum size (as specified by *min-width*/*min-height*) of the grid items occupying the grid track.
	Example 1	Given the following grid-template-columns declaration: `grid-template-columns: 100px 1fr max-content minmax(min-content, 1fr);` Five grid lines are created: ■ At the start edge of the grid container. ■ 100px from the start edge of the grid container. ■ A distance from the previous line equal to half the free space (the width of the grid container, minus the width of the non-flexible grid tracks). ■ A distance from the previous line equal to the maximum size of any grid items belonging to the column between these two lines. ■ A distance from the previous line at least as large as the largest minimum size of any grid items belonging to the column between these two lines, but no larger than the other half of the free space.

Property	Values	

	Example 2	Additional examples of valid grid track definitions:
		
		`grid-template-rows:`
		`1fr minmax(min-content, 1fr);`
		
		`grid-template-rows:`
		`10px repeat(2, 1fr auto minmax(30%, 1fr));`
		
		`grid-template-rows:`
		`calc(4em - 5px)`

grid-template-areas	Syntax	none | <string>+
	Description	The syntax of the grid-template-areas property also provides a visualization of the structure of the grid, making the overall layout of the grid container easier to understand. ■ none: The grid doesn't define any named grid areas. ■ <string>+: A row is created for every separate string listed for the grid-template-areas property, and a column is created for each cell in the string.
	Example	In this example, the *grid-template-areas* property is used to create a page layout where areas are defined for header content (head), navigational content (nav), footer content (foot), and main content (main). The template creates 3 rows and 2 columns, with 4 named grid areas. The head area spans both columns and the first row of the grid.

```
<style type="text/css">

  #grid {    display: grid;
             grid-template-areas: "head head"
             "nav  main"
             "foot .   " }

        #grid > header { grid-area: head; }
        #grid > nav    { grid-area: nav; }
        #grid > main   { grid-area: main; }
        #grid > footer { grid-area: foot; }

</style>
```

Property	Values	
grid-template	Syntax	none | subgrid | <'grid-template-columns'> / <'grid-template-rows'> | [<track-list> /]? [<line-names>? <string> <track-size>? <line-names>?]+
	Description	The grid-template property is a **shorthand** for setting grid-template-columns, grid-template-rows, and grid-template-areas in a single declaration. It has several distinct syntax forms: ■ none: Sets all three properties to their initial values (none). ■ subgrid: Sets *grid-template-rows* and *grid-template-columns* to **subgrid**, and grid-template-areas to its initial value. ■ <'grid-template-columns'> / <'grid-template-rows'>: Sets *grid-template-columns* and *grid-template-rows* to the specified values, respectively, and sets grid-template-areas to **none**.

	Example	`grid-template: auto 1fr auto / auto 1fr;`
		
		The shorthand above is equivalent to:
		
		`grid-template-columns: auto 1fr auto;`
		`grid-template-rows: auto 1fr;`
		`grid-template-areas: none;`

grid-auto-columns, grid-auto-rows	Syntax	<u>auto</u> | <track-size>
	<track-size> syntax	■ <track-size> = minmax(<track-breadth> , <track-breadth>) | <track-breadth> ■ <track-breadth> = <length> | <percentage> | <flex> | min-content | max-content | auto
	Description	If a grid item is positioned into a row or column that is not explicitly sized by *grid-template-rows* or *grid-template-columns*, implicit grid tracks are created to hold it. This can happen either by explicitly positioning into a row or column that is out of range, or by the auto-placement algorithm creating additional rows or columns. The *grid-auto-columns* and *grid-auto-rows* properties specify the size of such implicitly-created tracks.

Property	Values	
	Description	■ <length>: A non-negative length. ■ <percentage>: A non-negative percentage values, which are relative to the inline size of the grid container in column grid tracks, and the block size of the grid container in row grid tracks. ■ <flex>: A non-negative dimension with the unit *fr* specifying the track's flex factor. Each <flex>-sized track takes a share of the remaining space in proportion to its flex factor. ■ max-content: Represents the largest max-content contribution of the grid items occupying the grid track. ■ min-content: Represents the largest min-content contribution of the grid items occupying the grid track. ■ minmax(min, max): Defines a size range greater than or equal to *min* and less than or equal to *max*. ■ auto: As a maximum, identical to *max-content*. As a minimum, represents the largest minimum size (as specified by *min-width*/*min-height*) of the grid items occupying the grid track.
	Example	This example illustrates A Grid with an implicit row and four implicit columns, two of which are zero-sized.

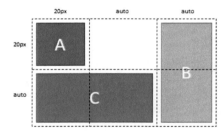

```
<style type="text/css">

#grid { display: grid;
        grid-template-columns: 20px;
        grid-template-rows: 20px }
#A { grid-column: 1; grid-row: 1; }
#B { grid-column: 5; grid-row: 1 / span 2; }
#C { grid-column: 1 / span 2; grid-row: 2; }

</style>

<div id="grid">
        <div id="A">A</div>
        <div id="B">B</div>
        <div id="C">C</div>
</div>
```

Property	Values	
grid-auto-flow	Syntax	[row | column] + dense
	Description	Grid items that aren't explicitly placed are automatically placed into an unoccupied space in the grid container by the auto-placement algorithm. ■ row: The auto-placement algorithm places items by filling each row in turn, adding new rows as necessary. If neither row nor column is provided, row is assumed. ■ column: The auto-placement algorithm places items by filling each column in turn, adding new columns as necessary. ■ dense: If specified, the auto-placement algorithm uses a "dense" packing algorithm, which attempts to fill in holes earlier in the grid if smaller items come up later.
	Example	A form arranged using automatic placement: 3 columns, each auto-sized to their contents. No rows are explicitly defined. The *grid-auto-flow* property is row which instructs the grid to search across its three columns starting with the first row, adding rows as needed until sufficient space is located to accommodate the position of any auto-placed grid item.

```
<style type="text/css">
form { display: grid; grid-auto-flow: row;
grid-template-columns: (labels) auto (controls)
auto (oversized) auto;}
form > label {
grid-column: labels; grid-row: auto;}
form > input, form > select {
grid-column: controls; grid-row: auto; }
#department {
grid-column: oversized; grid-row: span 3;}
</style>
```

Property	Values	
grid-row-start	Syntax	<grid-line>
grid-column-start	<grid-line> syntax	<u>auto</u> | <custom-ident> | [<integer> && <custom-ident>?] | [span && [<integer> + <custom-ident>]]
grid-row-end grid-column-end	Description	The *grid-row-start*, *grid-column-start*, *grid-row-end*, and *grid-column-end* properties determine a grid item's size and location within the grid by contributing a line, a span, or nothing (automatic) to its grid placement, thereby specifying the inline-start, block-start, inline-end, and block-end edges of its grid area. ■ <custom-ident>: First attempt to match the grid area's edge to a named grid area: if there is a named line with the name "**<custom-ident>-start (for grid-*-start) / <custom-ident>-end**" (for grid-*-end), contributes the first such line to the grid item's placement. ■ <integer> && <custom-ident>?: Contributes the Nth grid line to the grid item's placement. If a negative integer is given, it instead counts in reverse, starting from the end edge of the explicit grid. If a name is given as a **<custom-ident>**, only lines with that name are counted. If not enough lines with that name exist, all lines in the implicit grid are assumed to have that name for the purpose of finding this position. A **<integer>** value of zero makes the declaration invalid. ■ span && [<integer> || <custom-ident>]: Contributes a grid span to the grid item's placement such that the corresponding edge of the grid item's grid area is N lines from its opposite edge. If a name is given as a **<custom-ident>**, only lines with that name are counted. If not enough lines with that name exist, all lines in the implicit grid are assumed to have that name for the purpose of counting this span. If the **<integer>** is omitted, it defaults to **1**. Negative integers or zero are invalid. ■ auto: indicating auto-placement
	Example	The grid item is placed between the lines indicated by index: ```grid-column-start: 4; grid-column-end: auto; /* Line 4 to line 5 */```

Property	Values	
grid-row, **grid-column**	Syntax	\<grid-line\> [/ \<grid-line\>]?
	Description	■ The *grid-row* and *grid-column* are shorthands for *grid-row-start*/*grid-row-end* and *grid-column-start*/*grid-column-end*, respectively.
		■ If two **\<grid-line\>** values are specified, the *grid-row-start*/*grid-column-start* longhand is set to the value before the slash, and the *grid-row-end*/*grid-column-end* longhand is set to the value after the slash.
		■ When the second value is omitted, if the first value is a **\<custom-ident\>**, the *grid-row-end*/*grid-column-end* longhand is also set to that **\<custom-ident\>**; otherwise, it is set to **auto**.
		See the *grid-row-start* property for the syntax and values.
grid-area	Syntax	\<grid-line\> [/ \<grid-line\>]{0,3}
	Description	■ If four **\<grid-line\>** values are specified, *grid-row-start* is set to the first value, *grid-column-start* is set to the second value, *grid-row-end* is set to the third value, and *grid-column-end* is set to the fourth value.
		■ When *grid-column-end* is omitted, if *grid-column-start* is a **\<custom-ident\>**, *grid-column-end* is set to that **\<custom-ident\>**; otherwise, it is set to **auto**.
		■ When *grid-row-end* is omitted, if *grid-row-start* is a **\<custom-ident\>**, *grid-row-end* is set to that **\<custom-ident\>**; otherwise, it is set to **auto**.
		■ When *grid-column-start* is omitted, if grid-row-start is a **\<custom-ident\>**, all four longhands are set to that value. Otherwise, it is set to **auto**.
		See the *grid-row-start* property for the syntax and values.

Image Values & Replaced Content

Draft → Last Call → Candidate → Recommendation
http://www.w3.org/TR/css3-images/

IE   FF   SF   CH   O11

CSS can be used to insert and move content around a document, in order to create footnotes, counters, running headers and footers, section numbering, and lists.

CSS can also define replaced images while scaling and cropping them.

Property	Values	
image-orientation ❸	Syntax	<u>auto</u> | <angle>
	Description	Initial: **0deg**. Applies to: images. Defines the image angle.
	Example	`.class1 {image-orientation: 90deg;}`
image-resolution ❸	Syntax	[from-image + <resolution>] snap?
	Description	Initial: **1dppx**. Defines the image resolution. ■ from-image: the image must be rendered at the image's native / specified / default resolution (**1dppx**). ■ <resolution>: defines image rendering resolution. ■ snap: The "snap" keyword combined with specified resolution is rounded to the nearest value that would map one image pixel to an integer number of device pixels.
	Example	`.class1 {image-resolution: 2dppx snap;}`
object-fit	Syntax	<u>fill</u> | contain | cover | none | scale-down
	Description	Defines scaling method for the contents of a replaced element as: intrinsic size ■ fill: exactly fill the replaced element, potentially changing the aspect ratio. ■ contain: completely fit the replaced element while retaining the aspect ratio. ■ cover: completely fill the replaced element while being cropped and retaining the aspect ratio. ■ none: retain the original size and aspect ratio while potentially being cropped. ■ scale-down: similar to 'none' or 'contain' values, whichever would result in a smaller size.
	Example	`.class1 {object-fit: cover;}`
object-position	Syntax	<position>
	Description	Initial value: **50% 50%**. Applies to: replaced elements. Defines the alignment of the replaced element inside its box. The <position> value is defined as syntax of *background-position*.
	Example	`.class1 {object-position: top left;}`

Line

Draft → Last Call → Candidate → Recommendation
w3.org/TR/2002/WD-css3-linebox-20020515

This module specifies the properties of line within block elements, baseline alignment and the placement of drop cap initial letters. Most of the properties are new to CSS3.

Property	Values	
alignment-adjust ❸	Syntax	<u>auto</u> | baseline | before-edge | text-before-edge | middle | central | after-edge | text-after-edge | ideographic | alphabetic | hanging | mathematical | <length_%> | <length_fixed>
	Description	Inline elements. Defines precise alignment of elements lacking the desired baseline that is on the start-edge: ■ <length_%>: value multiplied by calculated 'line-height' ■ <length_fixed>: offset lengths of the start-edge ■ auto: browser defined
		Alignment of elements that is at the intersection of: ■ baseline: start-edge / dominant-baseline ■ before-edge: start-edge / before-edge ■ text-before-edge: start-edge / 'text-before-edge' ■ central: start-edge / 'central' baseline ■ middle: start-edge / 'middle' baseline ■ after-edge: start-edge / after-edge ■ text-after-edge: start-edge / 'text-after-edge' baseline ■ ideographic: start-edge / 'ideographic' baseline ■ alphabetic: start-edge / 'alphabetic' baseline ■ hanging: start-edge / 'hanging' baseline ■ mathematical: start-edge / 'mathematical' baseline.
	Example	`.class1 {alignment-adjust: text-after-edge;}`
alignment-baseline ❸	Syntax	<u>baseline</u> | use-script | before-edge | text-before-edge | after-edge | text-after-edge | central | middle | ideographic | alphabetic | hanging | mathematical
	Description	Inline element. Defines alignment to the baseline of its parent.
	Example	`.class1 {alignment-baseline: hanging;}`

Property	Values	
baseline-shift ❸	Syntax	baseline	sub	super	<percentage>	<length>
	Description	Inline element alignment relative to a dominant baseline. ■ baseline: no baseline shift ■ sub	super: subscript	superscript ■ <length_%>	<length_fixed>: shift based on specific value
	Example	`.class1 {baseline-shift: 5px;}`
dominant-baseline ❸	Syntax	auto	use-script	no-change	reset-size	alphabetic	hanging	ideographic	mathematical	central	middle	text-after-edge	text-before-edge
	Description	Inline elements. Definition of a scaled-baseline-table value based on three components: - baseline-identifier for the dominant baseline - script-related definition for additional baseline-identifiers - baseline-table font-size
	Example	`.class1 {dominant-baseline: ideographic;}`
drop-initial-after-adjust ❸	Syntax	central	middle	after-edge	text-after-edge	mathematical	ideographic	alphabetic	hanging	<percentage>	<length>
	Description	Applies to: `::first-letter` pseudo element Drop cap alignment for the primary connection point
	Example	`.d::first-letter {drop-initial-after-adjust:5%}`
drop-initial-after-align ❸	Syntax	<'alignment-baseline'>
	Description	Applies to: `::first-letter` pseudo element. Defines alignment line within the multiple line box. The line number being defined by the 'drop-initial-value' property.
	Example	`.dropcap::first-letter {drop-initial-after-baseline: central;}`
drop-initial-before-adjust ❸	Syntax	before-edge	text-before-edge	middle	central	after-edge	text-after-edge	ideographic	hanging	mathematical	<percentage>	<length>
	Description	Applies to: `::first-letter` pseudo element
	Example	`.dropcap::first-letter {drop-initial-before-adjust: hanging;}`

Property	Values	
drop-initial-before-align ❸	Syntax	<u>caps-height</u> | <'alignment-baseline'>
	Description	Applies to: `::first-letter` pseudo element. Defines the alignment line at the secondary connection point
	Example	`.d::first-letter {drop-initial-before-align: before-edge;}`
drop-initial-value ❸	Syntax	<u>initial</u> | <integer>
	Description	Applies to: `::first-letter` pseudo element. Number of lines occupied by a drop cap. no browser support To be, or not to be: that is the question: whether 'tis nobler in the mind to suffer the slings and arrows of
	Example	`.dropcap::first-letter {drop-initial-value: 3;}`
drop-initial-size ❸ **Tip:** due to the lack of browser support, use this workaround: `.d::first-letter {float:left; margin:0 2px 0; font-size:3em; padding:2px;}`	Syntax	<u>auto</u> | <line> | <length> | <percentage>
	Description	Applies to: `::first-letter` pseudo element Defines the partial dropping of the initial letter. Values other than 'auto' remove the secondary connection line constraint. The drop initial letter is sized using: ■ auto: typographic font attributes ■ <line_number>: number of lines (e.g. integer) ■ <length>: absolute length value (e.g. pixels) ■ <percentage>: relative length value (e.g. %)
	Example	`.dropcap::first-letter {drop-initial-size: 4;}`
inline-box-align ❸	Syntax	initial | last | <integer>
	Description	Inline-block-level elements. Identifies which line of a multi-line text block aligns with the previous and next element. ■ initial: the initial line ■ last: the last line ■ <integer>: specifies the line number
	Example	`.class1 {inline-box-align: last;}`
line-height ❸	Syntax	<u>normal</u> | number | <length> <percentage> | none
	Description	Inherited. All elements. Specifies a distance between two text baselines. AKA 'leading' in traditional typography.
	Example	`.class1 {line-height: 2em;}`

Property	Values	
line-stacking ❸	Syntax	<'line-stacking-strategy'> + <'line-stacking-ruby'> + <'line-stacking-shift'>
	Description	Inherited. Applies to: block elements. Shorthand property. Definition for the line box spacing rules.
	Example	`p {line-stacking: include-ruby max-height;}`
line-stacking-ruby ❸	Syntax	exclude-ruby	include-ruby
	Description	Inherited. Block elements. Line stacking method for elements containing elements with `display:ruby-text` or `display:ruby-text-container`. The ruby annotation elements are: ■ exclude-ruby: ignored for line stacking. ■ include-ruby: considered for line stacking.
	Example	`.class1 {line-stacking-ruby: include-ruby;}`
line-stacking-shift ❸	Syntax	consider-shifts	disregard-shifts
	Description	Inherited. Block elements. Line stacking method for elements with `baseline-shift` attribute. The *stack-height* definition: ■ consider-shifts: considers top-edge and bottom-edge of characters with a `baseline-shift` property. ■ disregard-shifts: disregards top-edge and bottom-edge of characters with a `baseline-shift` property.
	Example	`.class {line-stacking-shift: disregard-shifts;}`
line-stacking-strategy ❸	Syntax	inline-line-height	block-line-height	max-height	grid-height
	Description	Inherited. Block elements. When all inline elements are aligned, the stack-height method is based on: ■ inline-line-height: the smallest value that contains the **extended** block progression dimension ■ block-line-height: `line-height` property value ■ max-height: the smallest value that contains the block progression dimension ■ grid-height: smallest multiple of the element `line-height` computed value that can contain the block progression
	Example	`.class1 {line-stacking-strategy: grid-height;}`

Property	Values	
text-height ❸	Syntax	auto	font-size	text-size	max-size
	Description	Inherited. Applies to: inline elements and parents of element with **display:ruby-text** property. Defines the block-progression dimension of the text content area, which is: ■ auto: based either on the em square determined by the element font-size property value or the cell-height (ascender + descender). ■ font-size: the font size based em square. ■ text-size: based on the cell-height (ascender + descender) related to the element font-size. ■ max-size: based on the maximum extent toward the before-edge and after-edge of the box obtained by considering all children elements located on the same line, ruby elements with **display:ruby-text** property and baseline shifted elements.
	Example	.class1 {text-height: text-size;}
vertical-align ❸	Syntax	auto	use-script	baseline	sub	super	top	text-top	central	middle	bottom	text-bottom	<%>	<length>
	Description	Shorthand property. Applies to: inline-level and *table-cell* elements. Defines vertical alignment of the **inline** box with the **parent** box via these values:

	inline box	parent box
■ auto	Baseline	Baseline
■ use-script	Computed baseline	Baseline
■ baseline	Alphabetic baseline	Alphabetic baseline
■ central	Central baseline	Central baseline
■ middle	Middle baseline	Middle baseline
■ sub	Lower baseline	Proper position for subscripts
■ super	Higher baseline	Proper position for superscripts
■ text-top	Top of box	Before-edge of the font
■ text-bottom	Bottom of box	After-edge of the font
■ <%> ■ <length>	Alphabetic baseline adjusted by value	Alphabetic baseline
■ top	Before edge of the extended inline box	Before-edge of the line box
■ bottom	After edge of the extended inline box	After-edge of the line box

	Example	.class1 {vertical-align: super;}

Lists and Counters Level 3

Draft → Last Call → Candidate → Recommendation
http://www.w3.org/TR/css-lists-3/

Property	Values	
list-style	Syntax	<'list-style-type'> + <'list-style-position'> + <'list-style-image'>
	Description	Shorthand property
	Example	`.class1 {list-style: lower-roman url("http://domain.com/star.gif") inside;}`
list-style-image	Syntax	<url> | <u>none</u>
	Description	Defines image as the list item marker
	Example	`.class1 {list-style-image: url("http://domain.com/dot.gif");}`
list-style-position	Syntax	inside | <u>outsides</u>
	Description	List-item marker position relative to the content box.
	Example	`.class1 {list-style-position: inside;}`
list-style-type	Syntax	[none | <u>disc</u> | circle | square] | [decimal | decimal-leading-zero | lower-roman | upper-roman | lower-greek | lower-latin | upper-latin | armenian | georgian | lower-alpha | upper-alpha]
	Description	Inherited. Styling of the list item marker, representing unordered and ordered list values: ■ armenian: e.g. A, B, G, D, etc. ■ decimal: decimal number, beginning with 1 ■ decimal-leading-zero: e.g. 01, 02, 03, etc. ■ georgian: Georgian numbering, e.g. an, ban, etc. ■ lower-alpha: e.g. a, b, c, d, e, etc. ■ lower-greek: e.g. alpha, beta, gamma, etc. ■ lower-latin: e.g. a, b, c, d, e, etc. ■ lower-roman: e.g. i, ii, iii, iv, etc. ■ upper-alpha: e.g. A, B, C, D etc. ■ upper-latin: e.g. A, B, C, D, etc. ■ upper-roman: I, II, III, IV, etc.
	Example	`.class1 {list-style-type: lower-alpha;}`
marker-side	Syntax	list-item | list-container
counter-reset	Syntax	[<custom-ident> <integer>?]+ | none
counter-set	Syntax	[<custom-ident> <integer>?]+ | none
counter-increment	Syntax	[<custom-ident> <integer>?]+ | none

Multi-column layout

Draft → Last Call → Candidate → Recommendation
w3.org/TR/2011/CR-css3-multicol-20110412

Property	Values	
column-count ❸	Syntax	<integer_number>	auto
	Description	Number of columns definition ■ auto: determined by other properties, e.g. *column-width* ■ <integer>: a numeric value
	Example	`.class1 {column-count: 3;}`
break-after ❸ break-before ❸	Syntax	auto	always	avoid	left	right	page	column	avoid-page	avoid-column
	Description	Column/page break method for the multiple column layout: ■ auto: neither force nor forbid a break ■ always	avoid: force/avoid a break ■ left	right: force 1 or 2 breaks to format the next page as a left/right page ■ page	column: force a break ■ avoid-page	avoid-column: avoid a break
	Example	`.class1 {break-after: avoid-page;}`
break-inside	Syntax	auto	avoid	avoid-page	avoid-column
columns ❸	Syntax	<'column-width'> + <'column-count'>
	Description	Shorthand property
		IE 10 FF 4ᵐ SF 3ʷ • iOS 3ʷ CH 9ʷ • An 2ʷ O 11

	Example	`.heading { column-span: 2;}`
		
		`.body {`
		`column-width:90px; column-count:3;`
		`column-rule: 3px dotted red;`
		`column-gap: 8px;    /* shown in yellow */`
		`padding: 5px; }    /* shown in blue */`

To Be or Not to Be

To be, or not to be: that is the question:

Whether 'tis nobler in the mind to suffer

The slings and arrows of outrageous fortune,

Or to take arms against a sea of troubles,

And by opposing end them? To die: to sleep;

No more; and by a sleep to say we end

The heart-ache and the thousand

Property	Values	
column-fill ❸	Syntax	auto | <u>balance</u>
	Description	■ balance: content is equally balanced between columns ■ auto: sequential fill
	Example	div {column-fill: balance;}
column-gap	Syntax	<length> | <u>normal</u>
	Description	Gap (space, gutter) between columns.
	Example	.class1 {column-gap: 1em;}
column-rule ❸	Syntax	<column-rule-width> + <border-style> + [<color> | transparent]
	Description	Shorthand property
	Example	.class1 {column-rule: 2px dotted blue;}
column-rule-color ❸	Syntax	<color>
	Description	Initial value depends on browser.
	Example	.class1 {column-rule-color: black;}
column-rule-style ❸	Syntax	<'border-style'>
	Description	The '*border-style*' property values: none | hidden | dotted | dashed | solid | double | groove | ridge | inset | outset
	Example	.class1 {column-rule-style: dotted;}
column-rule-width ❸	Syntax	<'border-width'>
	Description	Initial value: **medium**. Based on the '*border-width*' property values: <numeric> | thin | medium | thick
	Example	.class1 {column-rule-width: 3px;}
column-span ❸	Syntax	<u>1</u> | all
	Description	Defines the number of columns. ■ 1: no span across columns ■ all: span across all columns
	Example	.class1 {column-span: 1;}
column-width ❸	Syntax	<length> | <u>auto</u>
	Description	Columns width definition: ■ auto: determined by other properties, e.g. '*column-count*' ■ <length>: a numeric value
	Example	.class1 {column-width: 3.5em;}

Paged Media

Draft → Last Call → Candidate → Recommendation
http://www.w3.org/TR/2013/WD-css3-page-20130314/

| IE | FF | SF | CH | O11 |

Property	Values	
object-fit ❸	Syntax	fill	hidden	meet	slice
	Description	Applies to: replaced elements, typically images. Defines the scale method if neither 'width' nor 'height' property is 'auto': ■ fill: scale the object's height and width independently so that the content fills the containing box ■ hidden: no scale ■ meet: maximum scale while preserving the aspect ratio - width <= 'width' and height <= 'height' - fit at least one smaller side (vertical or horizontal) ■ slice: scale the object as small as possible while preserving the aspect ratio - its width >= 'width' and height >= 'height' - fit at least one larger side
	Example	`.class1 {fit: meet;}`
object-position ❸	Syntax	[[<percentage>	<length>]{1,2}	[[top	center	bottom] + [left	center	right]]]	auto
	Description	Initial value: **0% 0%**. Inherited. Applies to: replaced elements, typically images. Defines the object alignment inside the box. The values are similar to the 'background-position' values.
	Example	`.class1 {fit-position: 10% left;}`
image-orientation ❸	Syntax	auto	<angle>
	Description	Applies to: images. Defines the image angle.
	Example	`.class1 {image-orientation: 90deg;}`

Property	Values		
page	Syntax		<u>auto</u> | <identifier>
	Description		Inherited. Applies to: block-level elements.
			Specifies the page type where an element should be displayed. If a block box with inline content has a '*page*' property that is different from the preceding block box, then page break(s) would be inserted between them.
			The boxes after the page break are rendered on a page box of the named type.
	Example		```/* CSS: tables are rendered on portrait pages while the page type 'wide' is valid for the the rest of the <div> content */ @page wide {size: 20cm 10cm;} @page verticale {size: portrait;}```
			```div {page: wide;} table {page: verticale;}```
			```// the HTML document: <div>```
			```<table><tr><td></td></tr></table> <table><tr><td></td></tr></table>```
			```<p>This is rendered on a 'wide' page</p></div>```
page-break-after	Syntax		<u>auto</u> | always | avoid | left | right
page-break-before	Description		Applies to: block-level elements. Defines page break method before (after) the generated box:
			■ auto: no forced / avoided page break
			■ always: forced page break
			■ avoid: avoided page break
			■ left | right: forced page break; the next page is formatted as a left / right page
	Example		`.class1 {page-break-after: always;}`
page-break-inside	Syntax		<u>auto</u> | avoid
	Description		Applies to: block-level elements. Defines a printing page break within an element. An 'avoid ' value attempts to avoid a page break within the element.
	Example		`.class1 {page-break-inside: avoid;}`

Tip: The *page* property can specify an element, e.g. table placed on a right-hand side portrait page titled 'rotated':

```
@page vericale
{size: portrait;}
table {
page: vericale;
page-break-
before: right;}
```

Property	Values	
size	Syntax	<length> {1,2} | <u>auto</u> | [<page-size> + [portrait | landscape]]
	Description	Applies to: page context. Defines the size and orientation of the containing box for page content. The size of a page box may either be "absolute" (fixed size) or "relative" (scalable, fluid). Relative pages automatically scale the document and make optimal use of the page size: ■ auto: size and orientation of the page is set by the browser. ■ landscape | portrait: horizontal / vertical orientation The absolute values: ■ <length>: length can be set in fixed units (e.g. inches) ■ <page-size>: *Media Standardized Names* standard sizes:
	Example	`@page {size: B5 landscape;}`
orphans	Syntax	<integer>
widows	Description	Initial value: 2. Inherited. Applies to: block-level elements. A minimum number of lines of a paragraph that must be left at the bottom (orphans) or top (widows) of a page.
	Example	`.class1 {orphans: 3; widows: 3;}`

Within the Description of size, a table:

	Millimeters					Inches		
	A5	A4	A3	B5	B4	Letter	Legal	Ledger
	148x210	210x297	297x420	176x250	250x353	8.5x11	8.5x14	11x17

Ruby

Draft → Last Call → Candidate → Recommendation
http://www.w3.org/TR/css-ruby-1/

Ruby is a short caption/annotation text next to the base text, typically used in ideographic East Asian scripts. The CSS Rubi properties associated with the 'Ruby' HTML elements.

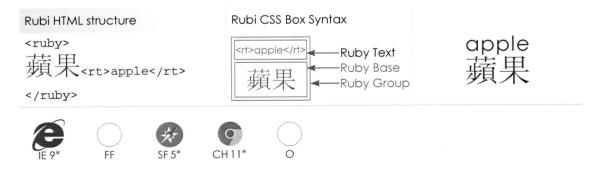

Rubi HTML structure

```
<ruby>
蘋果<rt>apple</rt>
</ruby>
```

Rubi CSS Box Syntax

<rt>apple</rt> ← Ruby Text
蘋果 ← Ruby Base
← Ruby Group

apple
蘋果

IE 9*   FF   SF 5*   CH 11*   O

Property	Values	
'ruby-align' ❸	Syntax	start | center | space-between | space-around
	Description	This property specifies how text is distributed within the ruby boxes when their contents do not exactly fill their respective boxes. ■ start: the ruby content is aligned with the start edge of its box ■ center: centered within the width of the base ■ space-between: the ruby content expands as defined for normal text justification (as defined by *text-justify*), except that if there are no justification opportunities the content is centered. ■ space-around: As for space-between except that there exists an extra justification opportunities whose space is distributed half before and half after the ruby content.
	Example	`.class1 {ruby-align: distribute-letter;}`
'ruby-merge' ❸	Syntax	separate | collapse | auto
	Description	This property controls how ruby annotation boxes should be rendered when there are more than one in a ruby container box: whether each pair should be kept separate, the annotations should be collapsed and rendered as a group, or the separation should be determined based on the space available.
	Example	`.class1 { <ruby style="ruby-merge:separate">` `<rb>`無`<rb>`む`<rt>`常`<rt>`じょう`</ruby> }`
'ruby-position' ❸	Syntax	[over | under | inter-character] && [right | left]
	Description	Applies to ruby annotation containers. Defines the position of the ruby text relative to its base. Initial value: **over right**
	Example	`.class1 {ruby-position: after;}`

Selectors

CSS Selector Types

Type	Description	Example Code
Universal	Defines property for any element	`* {font-family: Times;}`
HTML tag	Defines property for any specific HTML element	`div {height: 100%;}`

Class	Defines value for the 'class' attribute. 'Class' attribute can apply a common set of property values to a multiple elements of different types.	`.myclass {font-weight: bold;}`
		
		`<p class=myclass>1st paragraph</p>`
		`<p class=myclass>2nd paragraph</p>`

Id	Defines value for the 'id' attribute. 'Id' attribute can not have duplicate values within one HTML document.	`#heading {font-weight: bold;}`
		
		`<div id=heading>`
		`First Chapter</div>`

Group	Defines a common value for a multiple elements of different types	`h2, .myclass, #title` `{font-family: Arial;}`
Descendant	Defines value for a parent-child pair	`#heading p {color: blue;}`
Child	Defines property value that only affect elements that are children of other specific elements	`#heading > p {color: blue;}`
Universal Grandchild	Defines property value for the specified grandchild element:	
	■ *p* is at least a grandchild of the *section* element.	`section * p` `    {color: blue;}`
	■ *p* is at least a great-grandchild of the *section*	`section * * p` `    {color: blue;}`
	■ *p* is at least a grandchild of the *table* element given that the *table* is at least a great-grandchild of the *section*.	`section * * table * p` `    {color: blue;}`
Adjacent Sibling	Elements that are immediately next to each other. Not supported in IE 6.	`h1 + h2 {font-style: italic;}`
General Sibling ❸	All elements that share the same parent and elements are in the same sequence, not always immediate	`h1 ~ p {font-style: italic;}`

149

CSS3 Selectors

Draft → Last Call → Candidate → Recommendation
w3.org/TR/2011/REC-css3-selectors-20110929

Matching Attribute Selectors

Type	Description	Example Code
[att]	match when the element defines the attribute ('att').	`span[class=footer] {color:blue;}`
[att=val]	attribute value is "val".	
[att~=val]	attribute whose value is a space-separated list of keywords, one of which is "val".	
[att | =fr]	attribute has a hyphen-separated list of values beginning with "fr".	
[att^=val]	attribute value begins with the prefix "val"	`p[title^="right"] {color:blue;}`
[att$=val]	attribute whose value ends with the suffix "val"	`p[title$="wing"] {color:red;}`

[att*=val]	attribute whose value contains at least one instance of the substring "val"	`p[title*="left"]{color:gray;}`
		
		`<p title="right-wing">`
		`The right-wing conspiracy.</p>`

Pseudo-Classes

Pseudo-Class	Values	
:active	Description	Activated element by a left mouse button on multibutton mice.
	Example	`a:active {color: blue;}`
:checked ❸	Description	Element checked state (e.g., a check box)
	Example	`input:in-range`
:empty ❸	Description	Element has no children
:enabled ❸	Description	Mutually exclusive, representing enabled / disabled element
:disabled	Example	`a:enabled {color: blue;}` `a:disabled {color: black;}`
:focus	Description	Element has focus
	Example	`a:focus {color: black;}`

Pseudo-Class	Values	
:hover	Description	Element has mouse over
	Example	`a:hover {text-decoration: underline;}` `a:focus:hover {color: red;}`
:indeterminate ❸	Description	Radio and checkbox elements can be toggled, but are sometimes in an indeterminate state, neither checked nor unchecked.
:in-range	Description	Selects `<input>` elements with a value within a specified range
	Example	`input:in-range`
:invalid	Description	Selects all `<input>` elements with an invalid value
	Example	`input:invalid`
:link :visited	Description	Mutually exclusive, representing visited / unvisited link. ■ The 1st example defines the font color of all visited links. ■ The 2nd example defines the font color of all unvisited HTML links with a class 'resources'.
	Example	`a:visited {color: blue;}` `a.resources:link {color: black;}`
:lang(code)	Syntax	:lang(<language code>) { }
	Description	Element language definition
	Example	`:lang(fr) {color: blue;}`
:lang(language)	Description	Selects every `<p>` element with a *lang* attribute value "fr"
	Example	`p:lang(fr)`
:nth-child(n) ❸	Syntax	:nth-child({ <number expression> | odd | even }) { }
	Description	Matches any element that is the **n**-th child of its parent. ■ The `:nth-child(an+b)` pseudo-class notation represents an element that has **an+b-1** siblings **before** it, for any positive integer or zero value of **n**, and has a parent element. ■ For values of **a** and **b** > **0**, this divides the element's children into groups of **a** elements (the last group taking the remainder), and selecting the **b**-th element of each group. For instance, this allows to alternate the table row colors. The 1st child index is **1**.
	Example 1	Selecting a third child: `:nth-child(3) {color: blue;}`

	Example 2a	Two ways of selecting every odd row of a table :
		
		`tr:nth-child(2n+1) {color: navy;}`
		`:nth-child(odd)    {color: green;}`

Pseudo-Class	Values	

	Example 2b	Three ways of selecting every even row of a table:
		
		`tr:nth-child(2n+0)`
		`tr:nth-child(2n)`
		`tr:nth-child(even)`

	Example 3	Alternate paragraph colors in sets of 3:
		
		`p:nth-child(3n+1)`
		`p:nth-child(3n+2)`
		`p:nth-child(3n+3)`

	Example 4	When the value **b** is preceded by a "**-**", the "**+**" character is effectively replaced by the "**-**" character indicating the negative value of **b**. Example of electing the 9th, 19th, 29th, etc elements:
		
		`:nth-child(10n-1)`
		`:nth-child(10n+9)`

:nth-last-child(n) ❸	Syntax	`:nth-last-child( { <number expression> | odd | even }) { }`
	Description	The **n**-th sibling counting from the last sibling.
	Example 1	The two last rows of a table: `tr:nth-last-child(-n+2)`
	Example 2	Selecting the last 5 list items in a list: `li:nth-last-child(-n+5)`
:nth-of-type(n) ❸	Syntax	`:nth-of-type( { <number expression> | odd | even }) { }`
	Description	The **n**-th sibling of its type.
	Example	Selecting the 2nd, 5th, 8th, etc, paragraphs in a **div** element: `div > p:nth-of-type(3n-1)`
:nth-last-of-type(n) ❸	Syntax	`:nth-last-of-type( { <number expression> | odd | even }) { }`
	Description	The **n**-th sibling of its type counting from the last sibling

	Example	Two ways of selecting all h3 children except the first and last:
		
		`body > h3:nth-of-type(n+2):nth-last-of-type(n+2) { }`
		`body > h3:not(:first-of-type):not(:last-of-type) { }`

:first-child ❸ :last-child :only-child	Description	■ The 1st child element of its parent ■ The last child element of its parent ■ The only child of its parent
	Example	`li:first-child {color: blue;}`

Pseudo-Class	Values	
:first-of-type ❸ :last-of-type :only-of-type	Description	■ The 1st sibling of its type ■ The last sibling ■ The only child of that type
	Example	`li:first-of-type {color: blue;}`
:not(x) ❸	Syntax	`:not(simple selector) { }`
	Description	This negation pseudo-class would match all elements that do not match an argument in the parenthesis

	Example	`:not(div) { }`
		`:not('logo') { }`
		`input:not([type="checkbox"] { }`

:optional	Description	Selects `<input>` elements with no "required" attribute
	Example	`input:optional`
:out-of-range	Description	Selects `<input>` elements with a value outside a specified range
	Example	`input:out-of-range`
:read-only	Description	Selects `<input>` elements with a "readonly" attribute specified
	Example	`input:read-only`
:read-write	Description	Selects `<input>` elements with no "readonly" attribute
	Example	`input:read-write`
:root ❸	Description	Document root *HTML* element
:target ❸	Description	URL-defined target element. Target is specified by a number sign (#) followed by an anchor ID, called the *fragment identifier*. ■ URL with fragment identifier links to an element within the document, known as the target element. ■ By using `:target`, CSS can only style the elements on the page that match the anchor chosen, e.g. anchor 'products': `http://site.com/top.html#products`. ■ A **DIV** element can be styled by the `:target` pseudo-class.

	Example	`<style>div:target {color:blue;}</style>`
		`<a href=#products>Products/a>`
		`<div id=products>Product description</div>`

153

Pseudo-Elements

`::first-letter`	Defines style for the first letter of a paragraph (the drop cap letter)
`::first-line`	Defines style for the first line of a text
`::before`	Inserts content before an element
`::after`	Inserts content after an element
`::selection`	Part of a document that has been highlighted by the user, e.g. text

CSS At-Rules

- *At-rules* are special set of instructions to the CSS interpreter.
- *At-rules* are named because of the *@character* prefix.
- *@rules* can be defined for a specific type of elements or media.

Pseudo-Class	Values	
`@character`	Description	Character set encoding defined at the top of for the CSS document
	Example	`@charset "iso-8859-1";`
`@charset`	Description	It defines the character set used by the browser.
		It is useful if the stylesheet contains non-ASCII characters (e.g. UTF-8).
	Example	`@charset "UTF-8";`
`@font-face`	Description	Defines the Web Open Font Format (WOFF) embedding method for mostly TTF with compression and additional metadata.
		The goal is to support font distribution from a server to a client.
	Example	```@font-face {` ` font-family: VremyaCyrillic;` ` src: url(fonts/VremyaCyrillic.ttf)` ` format("opentype");` ` unicode-range: U+980-9FF;` `}```
`@import`	Description	Allows nested style sheets by importing one style sheet into another. ■ `@import` declaration must appear before any rules. ■ Used to hide certain styles from older browsers, ignoring `@import`
	Example	`@import url(mystylesheet.css);`

Pseudo-Class	Values	
@media	Description	Medi-specific CSS. Some options are: ■ all: every media ■ aural: speech synthesizers ■ braille: braille writing system ■ handheld: for handheld devices ■ print: for printers ■ screen: for computer monitors
	Example	`@media print {body {color:blue;}}`
@keyframes	Description	It defines the basis for keyframe animations on CSS properties, by allowing us to define the start and stop (and in-between) marks for what is being animated.

	Example	```@keyframes pulse {```
		``` 0% { color: #001f3f; }```
		``` 100% { color: #ff4136; }```
		```}```

@page	Description	Defines border, margin, padding and other paged media properties
	Example	`@page first {size: landscape;}`
@namespace	Description	Declares an *XML namespace* and, optionally, a prefix with which we can refer to it. **@namespace** rules must follow all **@charset** and **@import** rules, and precede all other at-rules in a style sheet.
	Example	`@namespace "http://www.w3.org/1999/xhtml";`
@supports	Description	The rule tests whether a browser supports a feature, then applies the styles for those elements if the condition is met.

	Example	```@supports (not ((text-align-last:justify)```
		
		or
		
		```(-moz-text-align-last:justify))```
		```{```
		```/* specific CSS applied to simulate text-align-last:justify */```
		```}```

Selectors API Level 1

The Level 1 API efines iterface *NodeSelector* to select DOM elements and retrieve DOM nodes that match against a group of selectors.

Two interface methods and the *NodeSelector* interface definition.

Draft → Last Call → Candidate → Recommendation
w3.org/TR/2009/CR-selectors-api-20091222

```
module dom {
   [Supplemental, NoInterfaceObject]
interface NodeSelector {
Element    querySelector(in DOMString selectors);
NodeList   querySelectorAll(in DOMString selectors); };
Document implements NodeSelector;
DocumentFragment implements NodeSelector;
Element implements NodeSelector; };
```

Method	Values	
querySelector	Description	▪ Selects the 1st matching element for a selection expression ▪ Returns a matching DOM element

	Example	```function changeClassNameToGreenToFirstLI() {```
		```var elm = document.querySelector("ul li.red");```
		```elm.className = "green"; }```

querySelectorAll	Description	▪ Selects all the matches for a selection expression ▪ Returns DOM elements array a **NodeList**

	Example	```function changeClassNameToBlueToAllLI() {```
		```var elements = document.querySelectorAll("ul li.red");```
		```for (var i = 0; i < elements.length; i++) {```
		```elements[i].className = "green"; } }```

Speech

Draft → Last Call → Candidate → Recommendation
http://www.w3.org/TR/css3-speech/

Property	Values	
cue ❸	Syntax	<'cue-before'> + <'cue-after'>?
	Description	Shorthand property
cue-before ❸ cue-after	Syntax	<URL> <decibel>? | <u>none</u>
	Description	Sounds to be played before or after the element to delimit it. ▪ URL: auditory icon resource. ▪ none: no auditory icon is used. ▪ decibel: "dB" (decibel unit), representing a change relative to the value of the *voice-volume* property within the aural "box" Syntax.
	Example	```.class1 {cue-before: url(music.mp3) +3dB;``` ``` cue-after: url(music2.mp3) 3dB;}```

Property	Values	
pause ❸	Syntax	<'pause-before'> + <'pause-after'>?
	Description	Shorthand property.
	Example	`.class1 {pause: none  200ms;}`
pause-before ❸	Syntax	<time> | <u>none</u> | x-weak | weak | medium | strong | x-strong
pause-after	Description	Pause timing and rest/prosodic boundary definitions.
rest-before ❸		■ <time>: seconds and milliseconds, e.g. '5s' or '120ms'
rest-after		■ none, x-weak, weak, medium, strong, and x-strong: prosodic strength of the break in speech output
	Example	`.class1 {pause-before: medium;}`
rest ❸	Syntax	<'rest-before'> + <'rest-after'>
	Description	Shorthand property.
	Example	`.class1 {rest: weak  strong;}`
speak ❸	Syntax	<u>auto</u> | none | normal
	Description	Inherited. Defines the method of text rendered aurally:
		■ auto: a computed value of 'none' when 'display' is 'none', otherwise resolves a value of 'normal'.
		■ none: no aural rendering
		■ normal: aural rendering regardless of its 'display' value.
	Example	`.class1 {speak: normal;}` `object.style.speak="normal"`
speak-as ❸	Syntax	<u>normal</u> | spell-out + digits + [literal-punctuation | no-punctuation]
	Description	Inherited. Defines the method of text rendered aurally:
		■ normal: language-dependent pronunciation rendering.
		■ spell-out: spells the text one letter at a time
		■ digits: speak numbers one digit at a time
		■ literal-punctuation: punctuation to be spoken literally
		■ no-punctuation: punctuation not spoken nor rendered
	Example	`.class1 { speak-as: spell-out;}`

Property	Values	
voice-duration ❸	Syntax	auto	<time>
	Example	.class1 {voice-duration: 200ms;}
voice-balance ❸	Syntax	<number>	left	center	right	leftwards	rightwards

	Description	Inherited. The balance between left/right stereo channels:
		■ <number>: '0' to '100' integer or floating point number
		  - '-100': only left channel is audible
		  - '100'
			'+100': only the right channel is audible
			  - '0': both channels have the same level
			■ left:
				center: equal to '-100'	'0'
					■ right: equal to '100'
						'+100'
						■ leftwards
							rightwards: shifts the sound to the left	right

	Example	.class1 {voice-balance: -45.5;}
voice-family ❸	Syntax	[[<name>	<generic-voice>],] + [,*]	preserve

	Description	A comma-separated list of voices in order of priority.
		■ <generic-voice> = [<age>? <gender> <integer>?]
		  - <age>: allowed values: 'child'
			'young'	'old'
				  - <gender>: allowed values: 'male'
					'female'	'neutral'
						  - <integer>: voice preference order, e.g. "2nd male voice"
						■ <name>: specific character instances, e.g. John, driver. Voice names must either be given quoted as strings, or unquoted as a sequence of one or more identifiers.
						■ <preserve>: 'voice-family' value behaves as 'inherit'

	Example	p.romeo {voice-family: romeo, young male;}
voice-rate ❸	Syntax	[normal	x-slow	slow	medium	fast	x-fast] + <percentage>
	Description	Speaking rate definition. ■ <percentage>: 50% is one half of a normal rate. ■ x-slow, slow, medium, fast, x-fast: predefined rate values
	Example	.class1 {voice-rate: fast 200ms;}

Property	Values	
voice-pitch ❸ voice-range ❸	Syntax	\<frequency> && absolute | [[x-low | low | <u>medium</u> | high | x-high] + [\<frequency> | \<semitones> | \<percentage>]]
	Description	*voice-pitch*: average voice pitch (frequency). *voice-range*: range variation of voice frequency. ■ \<frequency>: frequency value ("100Hz", "+2kHz"). ■ absolute: the frequency represents an absolute value. ■ semitones: the relative incremental change to the inherited value, expressed as a \<number> followed by "st" (semitones). ■ \<percentage>: positive/negative (incremental/ decremental) percentage values relative to the inherited value. ■ x-low, low, medium, high, x-high: a sequence of monotonically non-decreasing pitch levels (implementation and voice specific).

	Example	`.class`
		`{voice-pitch:-3.5st; voice-range: low;}`
		
		`object.style.voiceRange="100Hz"`

voice-stress ❸	Syntax	<u>normal</u> | strong | moderate | none | reduced
	Description	Strength of emphasis definition, based on a combination of pitch change, timing, and loudness.
	Example	`.class1 {voice-stress: reduced;}`
voice-volume ❸	Syntax	silent | [[x-soft | soft | <u>medium</u> | loud | x-loud] + \<decibel>]
	Description	Inherited. ■ silent: no sound is generated ■ x-soft | soft | medium | loud | x-loud: a sequence of audible volume level values: minimum to a maximum. ■ decibel: "dB" (decibel unit), representing a change relative to the given keyword value for the root element.
	Example	`.class1 {voice-volume: x-loud;}`

Table

Property	Values	
border-collapse	Syntax	collapse | <u>separate</u>
	Description	Inherited. ■ collapse: borders are collapsed into a single border, sharing a common border between table cells. ■ separate: each table cell has its own border.
	Example	`.class1 {border-collapse: collapse;}` `object.style.borderCollapse="collapse"`
border-spacing	Syntax	\<length\> \<length\>
	Description	Inherited. Distance between borders of adjacent cells if the property '*border-collapse*' is set to 'separate'.
	Example	`.class1 {border-collapse: separate;` `          border-spacing: 3px 3px;}`
caption-side	Syntax	<u>top</u> | bottom | left | right
	Description	Inherited. Defines table caption location
	Example	`.class1 {caption-side: bottom;}`
empty-cells	Syntax	<u>show</u> | hide
	Description	Inherited. Defines display mode for borders and background on empty table cells if the property '*border-collapse*' is set to 'separate'.
	Example	`.class1 {empty-cells: hide;}`
table-layout	Syntax	<u>auto</u> | fixed
	Description	Defines the table layout algorithm: ■ auto: column width is defined by the widest unbreakable content in any row ■ fixed: column widths is determined by the cells in the first row only. Faster table rendering.
	Example	`.class1 {table-layout: fixed;}`

Text Formatting Level 3

Draft → Last Call → Candidate → Recommendation
http://www.w3.org/TR/css-text-3/

Property	Values	
hanging-punctuation ❸	Syntax	none	[first + [force-end	allow-end] + last]
	Description	Inherited. For: inline elements. Punctuation mark positioning:
		■ first: an opening bracket or quote at the start of the first formatted line of an element hangs.
		■ allow-end: punctuation mark at the end of a line does not hang, because it fits without hanging.
		■ force-end: punctuation mark at the end of a line is forced to hang, even if it fits.
		■ Last: A closing bracket or quote at the end of the last formatted line of an element hangs.
		no browser support
		' f i r s t ' a l l o w - e n d ; f o r c e - e n d ;
	Example	.class1 {hanging-punctuation: force-end;}
		object.style.hangingPunctuation="force-end"
hyphens ❸	Syntax	auto	manual	none
	Description	This property controls whether hyphenation is allowed to create more soft wrap opportunities within a line of text.
		■ auto: automatic hyphenation determined by word characters, or the 'hyphenate-resource' property
		■ manual: words are only hyphenated if there are characters inside the word that suggest line breaks resources
		■ none: no hyphenation
	Example	.class1 {hyphens: manual;}
letter-spacing ❸	Syntax	normal	<length>
	Description	It specifies additional spacing between adjacent characters (commonly called tracking).
	Example	.class1 {letter-spacing: 1em;}

Property	Values	
line-break ❸	Syntax	<u>auto</u> | loose | normal | strict
	Description	Inherited. Defines line-breaking method. ■ auto: less restrictive, based on the length of the line. ■ loose: least restrictive, used for short lines, e.g. newspapers. ■ normal: most common set of line-breaking rules. ■ strict: most stringent set of line-breaking rules. IE 9 FF SF CH
	Example	`.class1 {line-break: loose;}`
overflow-wrap ❸	Syntax	<u>normal</u> | break-word
	Description	Inherited. Defines break within a word to prevent overflow. ■ normal: regular line-break behavior. ■ break-word: a word may be broken at any point. IE 9 FF 4 SF 5 CH 12 O 11
	Example	`.class1 {overflow-wrap: break-word;}`
tab-size ❸	Syntax	<integer {default:<u>8</u>}> | <length>
	Description	Inherited. Defines the width of the tab character (U+0009), measured in space characters (U+0020), when rendered.
	Example	`.class1 {tab-size: 8;}`
text-align ❸	Syntax	[<u>start</u> | end | left | right | center | justify | match-parent | start end]
	Description	Inherited. In-line content horizontal alignment to: ■ left: left edge of the line. ■ right: right edge of the line. ■ center: centered within the line. ■ justify: text is justified.

Property	Values	

	Description	New values in *CSS3*:
		
		■ start: start edge of the line.
		■ end: end edge of the line.
		■ match-parent: inherited **start** or **end** keyword is calculated from its parent's **direction** value **left** or **right**.
		■ start end: this property specifies:
		  - **start** alignment of the 1st line and a line after a line break;
		  - **end** alignment of any remaining lines.
		
		IE 9* FF 4* SF 5 • iOS 5 CH 4 • An 3 O 11*

	Example	TD {text-align: start end ;}
text-align-last ❸	Syntax	<u>auto</u> | start | end | left | right | center | justify
	Description	Inherited. Defines alignment method for the last line of text. IE9 FF SF CH
	Example	.class1 {text-align: end;}
text-indent ❸	Syntax	[[<u><length_fixed></u> | <length_%>] + [hanging + each-line]]
	Description	Initial value **0**. Inherited. Indent is a margin applied to the first line of the text block. ■ <length_fixed>: absolute margin value (e.g. px, pt). ■ <length_%>: relative margin value (e.g. %). ■ each-line: indentation affects every line in the paragraph. ■ hanging: no indentation on the 1st line. IE 9* FF 6 SF 5 • iOS 5* CH 12 • An 3* O 11 indent ←⌐→To be, or not to be, that is Whether 'tis nobler in the mi
	Example	.class1 {text-indent: 5px hanging;}

Property	Values	
text-justify ❸	Syntax	<u>auto</u> | none | inter-word | distribute
	Description	Inherited. Defines justification method used when **text-align** property is set to **justify**.
		The values *inter-ideograph*, *inter-cluster*, *cashida* removed from specification.
		■ auto: browser-defined.
		■ inter-word: defines spacing between words.
		■ distribute: defines spacing between words/characters.
		IE 9 FF SF CH
	Example	`.class1 {text-justify:  inter-word;}`
text-transform ❸	Syntax	<u>none</u> | capitalize | uppercase | lowercase | full-width
	Description	Inherited. Text styling transformation.
		■ capitalize: title-case, every word starts with capital letter.
		■ uppercase: capital letters
		■ lowercase: lower-case
		■ full-width: all characters are in full-width form
		IE 9* FF 4* SF 5* · iOS 4* CH 10* · An 3* O 11*
	Example	`.class1 {text-transform: uppercase;}`
white-space ❸	Syntax	<u>normal</u> | pre | nowrap | pre-wrap | pre-line
	Description	Inherited. Shorthand for the 'bikeshedding' and 'text-wrap' properties.
		Not all combinations are represented.
		■ normal: bikeshedding:collapse; text-wrap:normal;
		■ pre: bikeshedding:preserve; text-wrap:none;
		■ nowrap: bikeshedding:collapse; text-wrap:none;
		■ pre-wrap: bikeshedding:preserve; text-wrap:normal;
		■ pre-line: bikeshedding:preserve-breaks; text-wrap:normal;
	Example	`.class1 {white-space: pre-wrap;}`

Property	Values	
word-break	Syntax	normal | keep-all | break-all
	Description	The property specifies soft wrap opportunities between letters, i.e. where it is "normal" and permissible to break lines of text.
		■ break-all: break between 2 characters for non-CJK scripts.
		■ keep-all: CJK characters may not be broken.
		IE 9 FF 4 SF 4 • iOS 3 CH 12 • An 2 O 11
	Example	.class1 {word-break: keep-all;}
word-spacing ❸	Syntax	[normal | <length> | <percentage>]
	Description	This property specifies additional spacing between "words".
	Example	.class1 {word-spacing: 0.5em;}
word-wrap	Syntax	normal | break-word
	Description	The property specifies whether the browser may arbitrarily break within a word to prevent overflow when an otherwise-unbreakable string is too long to fit within the line box.
		It only has an effect when *white-space* allows wrapping.
		■ normal: lines may break only at allowed break points.
		■ break-word: an unbreakable "word" may be broken at an arbitrary point if there are no otherwise-acceptable break points in the line.
	Example	.class1 {word-wrap: break-word;}

Text Decoration Level 3

Draft → Last Call → Candidate → Recommendation
http://www.w3.org/TR/css-text-decor-3/

Property	Values		
text-decoration-line ❸	Syntax	<u>none</u> | [underline + overline + line-through + blink]	

	Description	Not inherited. The property defines the line decoration method. Propagated value can be specified in respect to a descendant element.		

		underline	overline	line-through
	creates propagated	underline	overline	line-through
	creates non-propagated	replace-underline	replace-overline	replace-line-through
	prevents propagated	no-underline	no-overline	no-line-through
			remove-all	
	does neither		none	

	Example	.class1 {text-decoration-line: no-overline;}
text-decoration-color ❸	Syntax	<u><color></u>
	Description	Not inherited. Defines the color of *text-decoration* property.
	Example	.class1 {text-decoration-color: #fff;}
text-decoration-style ❸	Syntax	<u>solid</u> | double | dotted | dashed | wavy
	Description	Defines the style of the text decoration line. The same values as for the *border-style* properties, plus wavy.
	Example	.class1 {text-decoration-style: solid;}
text-decoration ❸	Syntax	<text-decoration-line> + <text-decoration-color> + <text-decoration-style>
	Description	Shorthand property. The omitted *text-decoration-color* & *text-decoration-style* values are CSS2.1 backwards-compatible.
	Example	.class1 {text-decoration: none;/*CSS 2.1+*/ text-decoration: red dotted overline;}/*CSS3*/

Property	Values	
text-decoration-skip ❸	Syntax	none | [objects + spaces + ink + edges + box-decoration]
	Description	Inherited. The property defines what part of the element content should not receive any text decoration. ■ none: text-decoration is drawn for all text content. ■ objects: skip an atomic inline element, e.g. an image. ■ spaces: skip white space, including spaces: regular (U+0020), *nbsp* (U+00A0), ideographic (U+3000), tabs (U+0009), etc. ■ ink: skip glyphs preventing decoration from obscuring a glyph. ■ edges: start and end of the line inwards from the content edge. Prevents two elements side-by-side from having a single underline (a form of punctuation in Chinese).
	Example	.class1 {text-decoration-skip: spaces;}
text-underline-position ❸	Syntax	auto | alphabetic | below left | below right
	Description	Inherited. The property defines the position of an underline which is set using the *text-decoration* property/ *underline* value: ■ auto: below the text, or on the right in vertical typographic mode if the languages set to *:lang(ja)* or *:lang(ko)*. ■ alphabetic: aligned with the alphabetic baseline and likely to cross some descenders. ■ below left: aligned with the under edge of the element's content box and likely not cross the descenders. ■ below right: - Horizontal typographic mode: equal to 'below left'. - Vertical mode: similar to 'below left', except it is aligned to the right edge of the text. IE 9 FF SF CH
	Example	.under {text-underline-position: below right;}

Property	Values	
text-emphasis-style ❸	Syntax	<u>none</u> | [[filled | open] + [dot | circle | double-circle | triangle | sesame]] | <string>
	Description	Inherited. Defines emphasis marks for the element's text. ■ none: no marks. ■ filled: the shape is filled with solid color. ■ open: the shape is hollow. ■ dot: small filled dot U+2022 '•', or open dot U+25E6 '◦'. ■ circle: large filled U+25CF '●', large open U+25CB 'o'. ■ double-circle: filled U+25C9 '◉'; open U+25CE '◎'. ■ triangle: filled U+25B2 '▲', open U+25B3 '△'. ■ sesame: filled U+FE45 '﹅', open U+FE46 '﹆'. ■ <string>: defines string as marks.
	Example	`.class1 {text-emphasis-style: filled circle;}`
text-emphasis-color ❸	Syntax	<<u>color</u>>
	Description	Inherited. Defines foreground color of the emphasis marks.
	Example	`.class1 {text-emphasis-color: #fff;}`
text-emphasis ❸	Syntax	<'text-emphasis-style'> + <'text-emphasis-color'>
	Description	Shorthand property. Inherited.
	Example	`.class1 {text-emphasis: filled #000;}`
text-emphasis-position ❸	Syntax	[<u>above</u> | below] && [<u>right</u> | left]
	Description	Initial values: above right (Japanese); below left (Chinese). ■ above: over the text - horizontal typographic mode. ■ below: under the text - horizontal typographic mode. ■ right: to the right of the text - vertical typographic mode. ■ left: to the left of the text - vertical typographic mode.

<table>
<tr><td colspan="5" align="center">Preferred mark position</td></tr>
<tr><td></td><td colspan="2" align="center">Horizontal</td><td colspan="2" align="center">Vertical</td></tr>
<tr><td>Japanese</td><td>above</td><td>文</td><td rowspan="2">right</td><td rowspan="2">書
き</td></tr>
<tr><td>Chinese</td><td>below</td><td>人</td></tr>
</table>

	Example	`.class1 {text-emphasis-position: below left;}`

Property	Values	
text-shadow ❸	Syntax	none	[[<shadow>] + [,*]]
	Description	Inherited. List of multiple comma-separated shadow effects could be defined. The <shadow> value matches the 'box-shadow' property values definitions, with the exception of the 'inset' keyword.

		IE	FF 4	SF 4 • iOS 3	CH 10 • An 2	O 11

Text Shadow

	Example	.class1 {text-shadow: 3px 3px 3px gray;}

CSS Writing Modes Level 3:

Draft → Last Call → Candidate → Recommendation
http://www.w3.org/TR/css-writing-modes-3/

direction	Syntax	ltr	rtl
	Description	Text direction. ■ ltr: left-to-right. ■ rtl: right-to-left: useful for some languages, such as Hebrew.
	Example	.class1 {direction: rtl;} object.style.direction="rtl"
unicode-bidi	Syntax	normal	embed	bidi-override
	Description	Formatting definition of the *bi-directional* flow of content based on controls for language "embedding" and directional overrides. The property determines the method of mapping to the Unicode algorithm. ■ normal: no additional level of embedding. ■ embed: additional level of embedding is opened and it is given by the direction property. ■ bidi-override: override for inline-level elements.

	Example	`.class1 {unicode-bidi: embed;}`
writing-mode	Syntax	<u>horizontal-tb</u> | vertical-rl | vertical-lr
	Description	It specifies whether lines of text are laid out horizontally or vertically and the direction in which blocks progress. ■ horizontal-tb: Top-to-bottom block flow direction. The writing mode is horizontal. ■ vertical-rl: Right-to-left block flow direction. Vertical mode. ■ vertical-lr: Left-to-right block flow direction. Vertical mode.
	Example	`.class1 {writing-mode: vertical-rl;}`
text-orientation	Syntax	<u>mixed</u> | upright | sideways-right | sideways-left | sideways | use-glyph-orientation
	Description	The property specifies the orientation of text within a line. Current values only have an effect in vertical writing modes (no effect on boxes in horizontal writing modes). ■ mixed: In vertical writing modes, characters from horizontal-only scripts are set sideways, i.e. 90° clockwise from their standard orientation in horizontal text. Characters from vertical scripts are set with their intrinsic orientation. ■ upright: In vertical writing modes, characters from horizontal-only scripts are rendered upright, i.e. in their standard horizontal orientation. Characters from vertical scripts are set with their intrinsic orientation and shaped normally. ■ sideways-right: In vertical writing modes, this causes text to be set as if in a horizontal layout, but rotated 90° *clockwise*. ■ sideways-left: In vertical writing modes, this causes text to be set as if in a horizontal layout, but rotated 90° *counter-clockwise*. ■ sideways: This value is equivalent to sideways-right in *vertical-rl* writing mode and equivalent to sideways-left in *vertical-lr* writing mode. It can be useful when setting horizontal script text vertically in a primarily horizontal-only document. ■ use-glyph-orientation: defines glyph-orientation-vertical and glyph-orientation-horizontal properties that were intended to control text orientation.
	Example	`.class1 {text-orientation: sideways;}`

text-combine-upright	Syntax	none	all	[digits <integer>?]
	Description	It specifies the combination of multiple characters into the space of a single character. If the combined text is wider than 1em, the UA must fit the contents within 1em, see below. The resulting composition is treated as a single upright glyph for the purposes of layout and decoration. This property only has an effect in vertical writing modes. ■ none: No special processing. ■ all: Attempt to typeset horizontally all consecutive characters within the box such that they take up the space of a single character within the vertical line box. ■ digits <integer>?: Attempt to typeset horizontally each maximal sequence of consecutive ASCII digits (U+0030–U+0039) that has as many or fewer characters than the specified integer such that it takes up the space of a single character within the vertical line box.
	Example	.class1 {text-combine-upright: all;}

CSS Transforms:

Draft → Last Call → Candidate → Recommendation
http://www.w3.org/TR/css-transforms-1/

Property	Values	
transform ❸	Syntax	none	[[<transform-list>] + [, *]]
	Description	A list of space delimited *transform functions*. The list of transform functions available in the Appendix chapter. IE 9ᵐ FF 4ᵐ SF 3ʷ·iOS 3ʷ CH 11ʷ·An 2ʷ O 11º
	Example	.class1 {transform: rotate(40deg) scale(2.0);}

Property	Values	
transform-origin ❸	Syntax	[left | center | right | top | bottom | <percent> | <length>] | [left | center | right | <percent> | <length>] [top | center | bottom | <percent> | <length>] <length>? | [center | [left | right]] && [center | [top | bottom]] <length>?
	Description	It allows you to change the position of transformed elements. ■ 2D transformations can change the X- and Y-axis of an element. ■ 3D transformations can also change the Z-axis of an element. Initial: 50% 50%
	Example	.class1 {transform-origin: 20% 40%;}
transform-style ❸	Syntax	<u>flat</u> | preserve-3d
	Description	Initial value: 0. Defines the nesting method in space. ■ flat: rendering in 2D space ■ preserve-3d: rendering in 3D space
	Example	.class1 {transform-style: preserve-3d;}
perspective	Syntax	<u>none</u> | <number>
	Description	Applies the [perspective: number] transformation to the children of the element, not to the element itself.
	Example	.class1 {perspective: 2;}
perspective-origin ❸	Syntax	[left | center | right | top | bottom | <percent> | <length>] | [left | center | right | <percent> | <length>] [top | center | bottom | <percent> | <length>] | [center | [left | right]] && [center | [top | bottom]]
	Description	It establishes the origin for the *perspective* property. It effectively sets the X and Y position at which the viewer appears to be looking at the children of the element. Initial: 50% 50%
	Example	.class1 {transform-origin: 20% 40%;}
backface-visibility	Syntax	<u>visible</u> | hidden
	Description	Defines the back side visibility of a transformed element.
	Example	.class1 {backface-visibility: hidden;}

CSS3 'Transform' property functions

CSS Function	Description
`matrix(<number>, <number>, <number>, <number>, <number>, <number>)`	6- value matrix for 2D transformation (3x2)
`matrix3d(<number>, <number>, <number>, <number>, <number>, <number>, <number>, <number>, <number>, <number>, <number>, <number>, <number>, <number>, <number>, <number>)`	16-value matrix for 3D transformation.
`translate(<x-translation-value> + <y-translation-value>])`	2D translation by the two vectors
`translate3d(<translation-value>, <translation-value>, <translation-value>)`	3D translation by the 3 vectors
`translateX(<translation-value>)` `translateY(<translation-value>)` `translateZ(<translation-value>)`	Translation amount in the X/Y/Z direction
`scale(<x-number> + <y-number>])`	2 parameters of a 2D scaling vector
`scale3d(<number>, <number>, <number>)`	3 parameters of a 3D scaling vector
`scaleX(<number>)`	Scale operation using the X scaling vector, which is given as the parameter
`scaleY(<number>)`	Scale operation using the Y scaling vector, which is given as the parameter
`rotate(<angle>)`	Defines a 2D rotation, the angle is specified in the parameter

CSS Function	Description
rotate3d(<number>, <number>, <number>, <angle>)	Clockwise 3D rotation defined by 3 parameters
perspective(<length>)	Perspective projection matrix
rotateX(<angle>) rotateY(<angle>) rotateZ(<angle>)	Clockwise rotation angle along the X/Y/Z-axis
skewX(<angle>) skewY(<angle>)	Skew transformation angle along the X/Y-axis
skew(<x-angle>, <y-angle>])	Skew transformation angle along both X & Y-axis

Animation

Draft → Last Call → Candidate → Recommendation
http://www.w3.org/TR/css3-animations/

*See the Appendix chapter for the list of properties which can be animated.

Property	Values	
animation ❸	Syntax	[<animation-name> + <animation-duration> + <animation-timing-function> + <animation-delay> + <animation-iteration-count> + <animation-direction>] + [, *]
	Description	Shorthand property. See individual properties IE 10m FF 4m SF 5w • iOS 4w CH 11w • An 3w O 11o
	Example	.class1 {animation: "splash" 12s, "main" 20s, "splash" 12s alternate;}

Property	Values	
animation-delay ❸ animation-duration	Syntax	[<time>] + [, *]
	Description	Initial value: **0**. Animation playback-delay and playback-duration properties
	Example	`.class1 {animation-delay:2s;` `animation-duration: 50s;}`
animation-direction ❸	Syntax	[<u>normal</u> | alternate] + [, *]
	Description	Defines a reverse playback on alternate cycles. ■ normal: normal playback ■ alternate: reverse playback
	Example	`.class1 {animation-direction: alternate;}`
animation-fill-mode ❸	Syntax	[<u>none</u> | forwards | backwards | both] + [, *]
	Description	The property defines what values are applied by the animation outside the time it is executing.
	Example	`.class1 {animation-fill-mode: forwards both;}`
animation-iteration-count ❸	Syntax	[infinite | <u><number></u>] + [, *]
	Description	Initial Value: **1**. Number of animation cycles
	Example	`.class1 {animation-iteration-count: 3;}`
animation-name ❸	Syntax	[<u>none</u> | <text_string>] + [, *]
	Description	■ <text_string>: defines a list of animation sequences by name, while name is related to an animation keyframe. ■ none: no animation
	Example	`.class1 {animation-name: "splash";}`
animation-play-state ❸	Syntax	[<u>running</u> | paused] + [, *]
	Description	It defines whether the animation is running or paused.
	Example	`.class1 {animation-play-state: paused;}`

Property	Values	
animation-timing-function ❸	Syntax	[ease | linear | ease-in | ease-out | ease-in-out | cubic-bezier(<number>, <number>, <number>, <number>)] + [, *]
	Description	Defines the method how the intermediate animation frames will be calculated: ■ cubic-bezier: four values define points P1 and P2 of the curve as (x1, y1, x2, y2). Values must be in the range [0, 1] Equivalent to cubic-bezier: ■ ease: 0.25, 0.1, 0.25, 1.0 ■ linear: 0.0, 0.0, 1.0, 1.0 ■ ease-in: 0.42, 0, 1.0, 1.0 ■ ease-out: 0, 0, 0.58, 1.0 ■ ease-in-out: 0.42, 0, 0.58, 1.0

	Example	`.b1    {animation-timing-function:`
		`        linear, ease;}`
		
		`.b2    {animation-timing-function:`
		`        cubic-bezier(0.4, 0, 0.5, 1.0);}`

A figure appears in the Description cell with axes labeled "Output %" (vertical, 0.5 to 1.0) and "Input %" (horizontal, 0.5 to 1.0), showing control points P0, P1, P2, P3, captioned "Timing Function Control Points".

Transitions

Draft ➜ Last Call ➜ Candidate ➜ Recommendation
http://www.w3.org/TR/css3-transitions/

Property	Values	
animation ❸	Syntax	[none | <single-transition-property>] + <time> + <single-transition-timing-function> + <time] + [, *]
	Description	Shorthand property. See individual properties
	Example	`.class1 {animation: "splash" 12s, "main" 20s,` `"splash" 12s alternate;}`
transition-delay ❸ transition-duration	Syntax	[<time>] + [, *]
	Description	Initial value: **0**. Animation transition-delay & transition-duration

	Example	`.class { transition-delay: 2s;`
		`          transition-duration: 50s;}`
		`object.style.transitionDuration="5s"`

Property	Values	
transition-property ❸	Syntax	none | <u>all</u> | [<property_name>] + [, *]
	Description	Name of the property to which the transition is applied

	Example	`.class1 {transition-property: opacity;}`
		
		`object.style.transitionProperty="width,height"`

transition-timing-function ❸	Syntax	[<u>ease</u> | linear | ease-in | ease-out | ease-in-out | cubic-bezier(<number>, <number>, <number>, <number>)] + [, *]
	Description	Defines the method how the intermediate transition frames will be calculated: ■ cubic-bezier: four values define points P1 and P2 of the curve as (x1, y1, x2, y2). Values must be in the range [0, 1] Equivalent to cubic-bezier: ■ ease: 0.25, 0.1, 0.25, 1.0 ■ linear: 0.0, 0.0, 1.0, 1.0 ■ ease-in: 0.42, 0, 1.0, 1.0 ■ ease-out: 0, 0, 0.58, 1.0 ■ ease-in-out: 0.42, 0, 0.58, 1.0 Timing Function Control Points

	Example	`.b1 {transition-timing-function: linear, ease;}`
		
		`.b2 {transition-timing-function:`
		`     cubic-bezier(0.4, 0, 0.5, 1.0);}`

User Interface

Draft → Last Call → Candidate → Recommendation
w3.org/TR/2004/CR-css3-ui-20040511

Property	Values	
appearance ❸	Syntax	<u>normal</u> | <appearance>
	Description	Applies to: all elements. Shorthand for 'appearance', 'color', 'font', and 'cursor'. Defines an element as a standard platform (OS or browser) UI element. ■ The property sets 'appearance' to the specified value and the other properties to their appropriate system value, rendering element using platform-specific user interface control. ■ normal: resets 'appearance' to 'normal', others to 'inherit'

Property	Values	
| | Example | ```
input[type=button] {appearance: push-button;}
<!--default browser look and feel:-->
input[type=button].custom {color: blue;
                           background-color: yellow;}

<!--the related HTML5 code:-->
<input type=button value="plain button">
<input type=button value="color button"
class=custom>
``` |
| box-sizing ❸ | Syntax | <u>content-box</u> | border-box |
| | Description | Applies to: elements accepting width or height.

■ content-box: the specified width and height (and respective min/max properties) apply to the content box of the element.

■ border-box: the specified width and height on this element define the border box of the element. The content size is calculated by subtracting the border and padding values. |
| | Example | ```
div.hSplit { box-sizing: border-box;
             width: 50%; float: left;}

<!--the related HTML5 code:-->
  <div style=width:200px>
  <div class=hSplit>The left half.</div>
  <div class=hSplit>The right half.</div>

  </div>
``` |
outline	Syntax	<'outline-color'> + <'outline-style'> + <'outline-width'>
	Description	Applies to: all elements. Shorthand property. Outline is similar to borders but it does not take up space and it may be non-rectangular. The outline is always on top, drawn "over" a box, and it doesn't influence the position or size of the box. The outline has the same property values on all sides, e.g., there are no **outline-top** or **outline-right** properties.
	Example	.class1 {outline: blue thick solid;}
outline-width	Syntax	<numeric> | thin | <u>medium</u> | thick
	Description	Initial value: **medium**. Applies to: all elements. The values are the same values as the **border-width** property values.

Property	Values	
	Example	`.class1 {outline-width: thin;}`
outline-style	Syntax	auto | [none | dotted | dashed | solid | double | groove | ridge | inset | outset
	Description	Initial value: none. Applies to: all elements. The *outline-style* property accepts the same values as *border-style* property plus the value 'auto', minus 'hidden'.
	Example	`.class1 {outline-style: auto;}`
outline-color	Syntax	<color> | invert
	Description	Applies to: all elements. The color value can be 'inverted' to display an opposite value
	Example	`.class1 {outline-color: #fff;}`
outline-offset	Syntax	<length>
	Description	Applies to: all elements. Initial value: **0**. The outline offset beyond the border edge.
	Example	`.class1 {outline-offset: 5px;}`
resize ❸	Syntax	none | both | horizontal | vertical
	Description	Applies to: elements with 'overflow' value other than visible. Defines the 'user-resize' capability and axis/axes.
	Example	`.class1 {resize: horizontal;}`
text-overflow	Syntax	[clip | ellipsis | <string>]{1,2}
	Description	It specifies rendering when inline content overflows its line box edge in the inline progression direction. ■ clip: Clip inline content that overflows its block container. ■ ellipsis: Render an ellipsis character (U+2026) to represent clipped inline content, e.g. three dots "...". ■ <string>: Render the given string.
	Example	`.class1 {text-overflow: ellipsis;}`

Property	Values	
cursor ❸	Syntax	[[<URL> [<x> <y>]]* [<u>auto</u>	default	none	context-menu	help	pointer	progress	wait	cell	crosshair	text	vertical-text	alias	copy	move	no-drop	not-allowed	e-resize	n-resize	ne-resize	nw-resize	s-resize	se-resize	sw-resize	w-resize	ew-resize	ns-resize	nesw-resize	nwse-resize	col-resize	row-resize	all-scroll]]
	Description	Inherited. Applies to: all elements.

Tip: Set automatic pointer cursor to clickable elements:

```
a[href], button,
input[type=image],
label[for],
select

.hand {
cursor: pointer;}
```

General purpose cursors

- auto: context-based cursor determined by browser
- default: platform-dependent default cursor, e.g. an arrow

Links and status cursors

- context-menu: object context menu, e.g. arrow & menu
- help: reference to a help, e.g. question mark or a balloon
- pointer: a link indicator
- progress: program processing indicator, e.g. hourglass
- wait: watch or hourglass

Selection cursors

- cell: cell selection cursor, e.g. a thick plus sign
- crosshair: a "+" sign cursor: a 2D bitmap selection mode
- text: text selection indicator, e.g. a vertical I-beam
- vertical-text: vertical text selection, e.g. a horizontal I-beam

Drag and drop cursors

- alias: alias/shortcut indicator, e.g. an arrow cursor
- copy: object is being copied, e.g. arrow with a plus sign
- move: object is being moved indicator
- no-drop: the dragged item cannot be dropped, e.g. a pointer with a small circle & line through it
- not-allowed: action not allowed, e.g. circle / line through it

Resizing and scrolling cursors

- e-resize, n-resize, ne-resize, nw-resize, s-resize, se-resize, sw-resize, w-resize: an edge is to be moved indicator
- ew-resize, ns-resize, nesw-resize, nwse-resize: bidirectional resize indicator
- col-resize: column resize indicator, e.g. left / right arrows
- row-resize: column resize indicator, e.g. arrows pointing up
- all-scroll: any direction scroll indicator, e.g. cross arrows

Image cursors:

- <URL>: cursor image referenced by URL.
- <x> <y>: the position within the image / hotspot (optional)

	Example	:link,:visited { cursor: crosshair;}

Property	Values	
caret-color ❸	Syntax	<u>auto</u> | color
	Description	The caret is a visible indicator of the insertion point in an element where text is inserted by the user. This property controls the color of that visible indicator.
	Example	`.class1 {caret-color:#bb7510;}`
nav-up ❸ nav-right nav-down nav-left	Syntax	<u>auto</u> | <id> [current | root | <target-name>]
	Description	Applies to: all elements. ■ auto: browser defined. ■ <id>: consists of a '#' character followed by a unique ID. ■ <target-name>: text string, a target frame for the navigation. The keyword 'root' indicates the full window.
	Example	`.class1 {nav-up: #a1 root;}`

CSS4 Preview

Just to be clear, CSS4 does not exist per se. After CSS3, everything to do with CSS is separated into modules. This topic covers modules that come after CSS3, such as Text Formatting Level 4 and Selectors Level 4. CSS Working Group, however, calles it CSS4 term: *https://wiki.csswg.org/spec/css4-ui*

Text Formatting Level 4

Draft ➜ Last Call ➜ Candidate ➜ Recommendation
http://drafts.csswg.org/css-text-4/

Property	Values	
text-space-collapse ❸	Syntax	<u>collapse</u> | discard | [[preserve | preserve-breaks] + [trim-inner + consume-before + consume-after]
	Description	White space collapse method within the element. ■ collapse: collapses sequences of white space into a single character (or in some cases, no character). ■ preserve: prevents collapsing sequences of *whitespace*. Line feeds are preserved as forced line breaks. ■ preserve-breaks: collapses white space, while preserving line feeds as forced line breaks. ■ discard: "discards" all white space in the element. ■ trim-inner: discards *whitespace* at the beginning and at the end of the element. ■ consume-before / consume-after: collapses all collapsible *whitespace* before the start/end of the element.
	Example	`.class1 {text-space-collapse: collapse;}`

Property	Values	
text-space-trim	Syntax	none | trim-inner + discard-before + discard-after
		The property defines trimming behavior at the beginning/ end of a box.
text-wrap ❸	Syntax	<u>normal</u> | nowrap | balance
	Description	Inherited. Text wrapping method definition: ■ normal: regular text wrapping. ■ none: no wrapping, which is normally a cause of overflow. ■ balance: same as *normal* for inline-level elements. For block-level elements that contain line boxes as direct children, line breaks are chosen to balance the inline-size those line boxes consume, if better balance than *normal* is possible.
	Example	`.class1 {text-wrap: balance;}`
wrap-before ❸ wrap-after ❸	Syntax	<u>auto</u> | avoid | avoid-line | avoid-flex | line | flex
	Description	These properties specify modifications to break opportunities in line and flex line breaking. ■ auto: Lines may break at allowed break points before and after the element, as determined by the line-breaking rules in effect. ■ avoid: Flex and line breaking is suppressed before/after the element: the UA may only break before/after the element if there are no other valid break points in the line. If the text breaks, line-breaking restrictions are honored as for `auto`. ■ avoid-line: Same as `avoid`, but only for line breaks. ■ avoid-flex: Same as `avoid`, but only for flex line breaks. ■ line: Force a line break before/after the element if this is a valid line break point. ■ flex: Force a flex line break before/after the element if this is a valid flex line break point and the element is a flex item in a multi-line flex container.
	Example	`.class1 {wrap-before: avoid;}`
wrap-inside ❸	Syntax	<u>auto</u> | avoid
	Description	auto: Lines may break at allowed break points within the element, as determined by the line-breaking rules in effect. avoid: Line breaking is suppressed within the element: the UA may only break within the element if there are no other valid break points in the line.
	Example	`.class1 {wrap-inside: avoid;}`

Property	Values	
hyphenate-character ❸	Syntax	<u>auto</u> | <text_string>
	Description	Defines a shown character when a hyphenation occurs
	Example	`.class1 {hyphenate-character: "\2010";}`
hyphenate-limit-zone ❸	Syntax	<u>0</u> | <length_%> | <length_Fixed>
	Description	Inherited. Defines the maximum of unfilled space before justification that is left in the line before hyphenation is triggered to pull part of a word from the next line.
	Example	`.class1 {hyphenate-limit-zone: 50%;}`
hyphenate-limit-chars ❸	Syntax	<u>auto</u> | <integer>{1,3}
	Description	Defines a minimum before/after number of characters in a hyphenated word. A single 'auto' value means 2 for before/after, and 5 for the word total.
	Example	`.class1 {hyphenate-limit-chars: auto 3;}`
hyphenate-limit-lines ❸	Syntax	<u>no-limit</u> | <integer>
	Description	Inherited. Defines maximum number of successive hyphenated lines in a block-level element.
	Example	`.class1 {hyphenate-limit-lines: 2;}`
hyphenate-limit-last ❸	Syntax	<u>none</u> | always | column | page | spread
	Description	It defines hyphenation method at the end of element, column, page and spread (a set of two left/right pages) ■ none: no hyphenation restrictions ■ always: the last full line of the element, or the last line before any column, page, or spread break inside the element should not be hyphenated. ■ column: he last line before any column, page, or spread break inside the element should not be hyphenated. ■ page: the last line before page or spread break inside the element should not be hyphenated. ■ spread: the last line before any spread break inside the element should not be hyphenated.
	Example	`.class1 {hyphenate-limit-last: always;}`

Property	Values	
text-spacing ❸	Syntax	<u>normal</u> | none | [trim-start | space-start] + [trim-end | space-end | allow-end] + [trim-adjacent | space-adjacent] + no-compress + ideograph-alpha + ideograph-numeric + punctuation
	Description	Spacing method between adjacent characters on the same line using trimming (kerning) method for the blank half of a *full-width character width* punctuation character.

This method is additive with the word/letter-spacing properties.

- normal: trim the blank half of full-width closing punctuation if it does not fit prior to justification - end of each line, equivalent to 'space-start allow-end trim-adjacent'.
- none: no extra space is created.
- ideograph-numeric: creates 1/4em extra spacing between ideographic letters and non-ideographic numerals.
- ideograph-alpha: creates 1/4em extra spacing between ideographic and non-ideographic text, e.g. Latin-based.
- punctuation: creates extra non-breaking spacing around punctuation as required by language-specific typography.
- space-start: don't trim
- trim-start: trim the opening punctuation - beginning of line.
- space-end: don't trim
- trim-end: trim
- allow-end: don't trim if it does not fit prior to justification for the closing punctuation - end of each line.
- space-adjacent \| trim-adjacent: don't trim \| trim punctuation when not at the start or at the end of the line.
- no-compress: the blank portions of full-width punctuation must not be trimmed during the justification process.

IE 9   FF   SF   CH

| | Example | p {text-spacing: trim-start space-end;} |

25 New Selectors. Syntax Summary

This summary includes both Level 1-3 selectors and new Level 4 selectors

http://www.w3.org/TR/selectors4/

Pattern	Represents	Section	Level
*	any element	Universal selector	2
E	an element of type *E*	Type (tag name) selector	1
E:not(s1, s2)	an *E* element that does not match either compound selector *s1* or compound selector *s2*	Negation pseudo-class	4-Mar
E:matches(s1, s2)	an *E* element that matches compound selector *s1* and/or compound selector *s2*	Matches-any pseudo-class	4
E.warning	an *E* element belonging to the class warning (the document language specifies how class is determined).	Class selectors	1
E#myid	an *E* element with ID equal to *myid*.	ID selectors	1
E[foo]	an *E* element with a foo attribute	Attribute selectors	2
E[foo="bar"]	an *E* element whose foo attribute value is exactly equal to bar	Attribute selectors	2
E[foo="bar" i]	an E element whose foo attribute value is exactly equal to any (ASCII-range) case-permutation ofbar	Attribute selectors: Case-sensitivity	4
E[foo~="bar"]	an *E* element whose foo attribute value is a list of whitespace-separated values, one of which is exactly equal to bar	Attribute selectors	2
E[foo^="bar"]	an *E* element whose foo attribute value begins exactly with the string "bar"	Attribute selectors	3
E[foo$="bar"]	an *E* element whose foo attribute value ends exactly with the string bar	Attribute selectors	3
E[foo*="bar"]	an *E* element whose foo attribute value contains the substring bar	Attribute selectors	3
E[foo|="en"]	an *E* element whose foo attribute value is a hyphen-separated list of values beginning with en	Attribute selectors	2
E:dir(ltr)	an element of type *E* in with left-to-right directionality (the document language specifies how directionality is determined)	The :dir() pseudo-class	4
E:lang(zh, *-hant)	an element of type *E* tagged as being either in Chinese (any dialect or writing system) or otherwise written with traditional Chinese characters	The :lang() pseudo-class	4-Feb

Pattern	Represents	Section	Level
E:any-link	an *E* element being the source anchor of a hyperlink	The hyperlink pseudo-class	4
E:link	an *E* element being the source anchor of a hyperlink of which the target is not yet visited	The link history pseudo-classes	1
E:visited	an *E* element being the source anchor of a hyperlink of which the target is already visited	The link history pseudo-classes	1
E:local-link	an *E* element being the source anchor of a hyperlink of which the target is the current document	The local link pseudo-class	4
E:local-link(0)	an *E* element being the source anchor of a hyperlink of which the target is within the current domain	The local link pseudo-class	4
E:target	an *E* element being the target of the referring URL	The target pseudo-class	3
E:scope	an *E* element being a designated contextual reference element	The scope pseudo-class	4
E:current	an *E* element that is currently presented in a time-dimensional canvas	Time-dimensional Pseudo-classes	4
E:current(s)	an *E* element that is the deepest :current element that matches selector *s*	Time-dimensional Pseudo-classes	4
E:past	an *E* element that is in the past in a time-dimensional canvas	Time-dimensional Pseudo-classes	4
E:future	an *E* element that is in the future in a time-dimensional canvas	Time-dimensional Pseudo-classes	4
E:active	an *E* element that is in an activated state	The user action pseudo-classes	1
E:hover	an E element that is under the cursor, or that has a descendant under the cursor	The user action pseudo-classes	2
E:focus	an E element that has user input focus	The user action pseudo-classes	2
E:enabled	a user interface element *E* that is enabled or disabled, respectively	The :enabled and :disabled pseudo-classes	3
E:disabled			
E:checked	a user interface element *E* that is checked/selected (for instance a radio-button)	The selected-option pseudo-class	3
E:indeterminate	a user interface element *E* that is in an indeterminate state (neither checked nor unchecked)	The indeterminate-value pseudo-class	4

Pattern	Represents	Section	Level
E:default	a user interface element E that	The default option pseudo-class :default	3-UI/4
E:in-range	a user interface element E that	The validity pseudo-classes	3-UI/4
E:out-of-range			
E:required	a user interface element E that is required	The optionality pseudo-classes	3-UI/4
E:optional			
E:read-only	a user interface element E that	The mutability pseudo-classes	3-UI/4
E:read-write			
E:root	an E element, root of the document	Structural pseudo-classes	3
E:empty	an E element that has no children (not even text nodes)	Structural pseudo-classes	3
E:first-child	an E element, first child of its parent	Structural pseudo-classes	2
E:nth-child(n)	an E element, the $n\text{-}th$ child of its parent	Structural pseudo-classes	3
E:last-child	an E element, last child of its parent	Structural pseudo-classes	3
E:nth-last-child(n)	an E element, the $n\text{-}th$ child of its parent, counting from the last one	Structural pseudo-classes	3
E:only-child	an E element, only child of its parent	Structural pseudo-classes	3
E:first-of-type	an E element, first sibling of its type	Structural pseudo-classes	3
E:nth-of-type(n)	an E element, the $n\text{-}th$ sibling of its type	Structural pseudo-classes	3
E:last-of-type	an E element, last sibling of its type	Structural pseudo-classes	3
E:nth-last-of-type(n)	an E element, the $n\text{-}th$ sibling of its type, counting from the last one	Structural pseudo-classes	3
E:only-of-type	an E element, only sibling of its type	Structural pseudo-classes	3
E:nth-match(n ofselector)	an E element, the $n\text{-}th$ sibling matching selector	Structural pseudo-classes	4
E:nth-last-match(n ofselector)	an E element, the $n\text{-}th$ sibling matching selector, counting from the last one	Structural pseudo-classes	4
E:column(selector)	an E element that represents a cell in a grid/table belonging to a column represented by an element that matches selector	Grid-Structural pseudo-classes	4
E:nth-column(n)	an E element that represents a cell belonging to the nth column in a grid/table	Grid-Structural pseudo-classes	4
E:nth-last-column(n)	an E element that represents a cell belonging to the nth column in a grid/table, counting from the last one	Grid-Structural pseudo-classes	4
E F	an F element descendant of an E element	Descendant combinator	1
E > F	an F element child of an E element	Child combinator	2

Pattern	Represents	Section	Level
E + F	an *F* element immediately preceded by an *E* element	Next-sibling combinator	2
E ~ F	an *F* element preceded by an *E* element	Following-sibling combinator	3
E /foo/ F	an *F* element ID-referenced by an *E* element's foo attribute	Reference combinator	4
E! > F	an *E* element parent of an *F* element	Determining the subject of a selector +Child combinator	4

Removed from W3C Editor's Draft

Features that were dropped from CSS3-UI (e.g. the 2004 CR) are eligible to be considered for CSS4-UI, but they will need a strong justification as having been ignored by implementations for 6+ years means there was likely something wrong with them and they need major revising. In addition, features dropped from other CSS3 specs or trimmed when bringing over to CSS3-UI are also considered here.

- appearance
- nav properties (nav-index)
- text-overflow string plus
- text-overflow block hint
- text-overflow start end values
- user-select

CSS3 Browser Compatibility Summary

	Desktop					Mobile		
	IE	FireFox	Safari	Chrome	Opera	iOS	Opera	Android
Advanced bg-image	9	4	5	6	10.5	3.2	10	2.1*
Advanced Selectors	9	3.5	3.2	6	10.5	3.2	10	2.1
Border Images	?	3.5	3.2	6	10.5	3.2	✕	2.1
Border Radius	9	4	5	6	10.5	3.2 x	11	2.1 x
Box Sizing	8	3	3.2	6	10.5	3.2	10	2.1
Box-Shadow	9	3.5	3.2	6	10.5	3.2	11	2.1
CSS3 Animation	?	5 x	4 x	6 x	?	3.2 x	✕	2.1 x
CSS3 Transitions	?	4	3.2	6	10.5	3.2	10	2.1
Flexible Box Layout	10 x	3.5 x	3.2 x	6 x	?	3.2 x	✕	2.1 x
Generated Content	8	3	3.2	6	10.5	3.2	10	2.1
HSL-Alpha Colors	9	3	3.2	6	10.5	3.2	10	2.1
Media Queries	9	3.5	4	6	10.5	3.2	10	2.1
Multi-Backgrounds	9	3.6	3.2	6	10.5	3.2	10	2.1
Multi-column Layout	10	3.5 x	3.2 x	6 x	11.1	3.2 x	✕	2.1 x
Opacity	9	3	3.2	6	10.5	3.2	10	2.1
Position: fixed	7	3	3.2	6	10.5	✕	10	2.2*
SVG/CSS backgrounds	9	4	5	6	10.5	3.2*	10	3
Table Display	8	3	3.2	6	10.5	3.2	10	2.1
Text Overflow	7	?	3.2	8	11	3.2	11 x	2.1
Transformations	9 x	3.5 x	3.2 x	6 x	10.5 x	3.2 x	11	2.1 x
Text Shadow	?	3.5	4	6	10.5	3.2	10	2.1
Transforms	10 x	?	5 x	?	?	3.2	✕	✕
Web Fonts	9	3.5	3.2	6	10.5	4.2	10	2.1*
Word Wrap	7 +	3.5 +	3.2 +	6 +	10.5 +	3.2 +	10 +	2.1 +

* Indicates partial support

x Indicates required proprietary extension, e.g. *-moz-*, *-webkit-*, *-o-*, *-ms-*.

? Indicates unknown support

✕ Indicates no support

In the Chapter 6

6. HTML5 APIs

What is API

In addition to a new markup specifications, HTML5 offers scripting application programming interfaces (APIs). API is a collection of programming methods and standards for accessing a software application to be powered by the API service. The HTML5 APIs provide various native Rich Internet Application functionality without the use of plugins, simplifying development and improving user experience. This chapter provides basic fundamental information about most common HTML5 APIs.

HTML5 and Related Technologies

Not all of the mentioned HTML5 related technologies are included in the W3C HTML5 specification, but they are part of the WHATWG HTML specification. Other HTML5 related technologies, which are not part of either the W3C HTML5 or the WHATWG HTML specification, are published by W3C separately.

HTML5

Taxonomy & Status (October 2014)

- Recommendation/Proposed
- Candidate Recommendation
- Last Call
- Working Draft
- Non-W3C Specifications
- Deprecated or inactive
- Not covered in this book

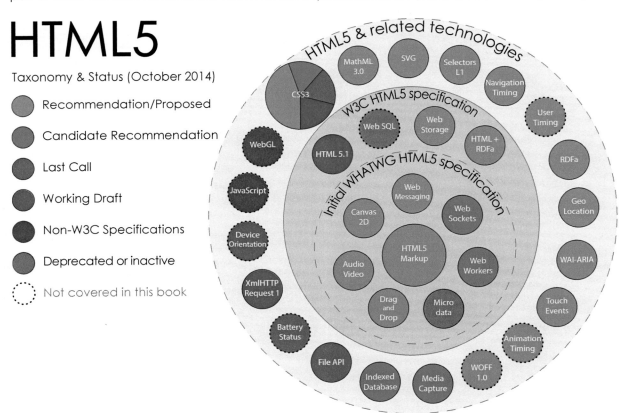

Semantics

Semantic Web

The next generation of the World Wide Web will be the Semantic Web, which will significantly improve the level of efficiency with which we use the web. The web will evolve into one ocean of standardized machine-readable semantic *metadata*, one global database of uniformly formatted semantic entities. I will call these entities "semantic objects". Every entity will become a semantic object and every entity will have assigned standardized semantic properties: any product, person, concept, entity, even a single word. For instance, a personal computer will have the properties: type, manufacturer, color, weight, etc. Semantic data will be fetched, analyzed and processed by various web applications, portlets and widgets, helping us search, shop, sell, market, travel, research, invent, create, communicate, socialize, etc. While the current web is very fragmented, inefficient and redundant, the future semantic web will be unified, efficient, and significantly less redundant. There are a few types of technologies available to assign semantic structured information:

- *RDF* - the standardized machine-readable language *RDF* describes object semantic properties / relationships, using a concept of *triple*: entity-property-value (subject-predicate-object). RDF/XML implementation is relatively difficult to publish requiring to maintain huge parallel databases.

- *Microformats* - method of embedding semantics within the attributes of HTML markup tags.

- *Microdata* - method to create pieces of custom metadata and embed it into HTML web pages.

- *RDFa* - combines simplicity of embedding metadata into web pages with the use of a wide range of existing specialized RDF vocabularies, e.g. taxonomies, contacts, copyrights, geolocation.

- *Schema.org* - launched in 2011 by Bing, Google and Yahoo, proposing to mark up website content as metadata, using *microdata*, according to their schemas.

 **Microdata** Working Group Note
http://www.w3.org/TR/microdata/

Microdata API extends HTML by adding custom semantic vocabularies offering a standardized way to embed machine-readable custom semantic properties in HTML document. At a high level, *microdata* is expressed by of a group of name-value pairs which can be nested. The groups are called *items*, and each name-value pair is a *property*. Example:

- The **itemscope** attribute creates an item
- The **itemprop** attribute adds a property to an item
- Two of these items have the same property 'price'
- An element can introduce multiple properties at once, e.g. type, color, operating system:
  ```
  <span itemprop="type-desktop
  color-beige os-winows7">Dell PC</span>
  ```

```
<div itemscope>

<p>Bread $<span itemprop=price>
2.50</span>.</p>

</div>

<div itemscope>

<p>Milk $<span itemprop=price>
3.20</span>.</p>

</div>
```

- The global document object will have **getItems()** function for supported browsers: **function microdataSupport() {return !!document.getItems;}**.
- Search engines utilize HTML-based microdata. Browsers, on the other hand, will take advantage of *microdata* DOM API functions.

Global Microdata attributes

Global attributes can be used to specify *items*.

Attribute	Description
itemscope	A boolean attribute that creates a group of name-value pairs called an *item*
itemtype	URL which defines an *item* vocabulary name
itemid	Global unique identifier for an *item*
itemprop	Property definition of an *item*
itemref	Non-descendent properties of element with the *itemscope* attribute can be associated with the item via reference to an element ID

Property types

Description	Code

<ul><li>To make *microdata* reusable, it is necessary to define item *type*, which can be identified as namespace URL.</li><li>An item can only have one type which gives the context for the properties, consequently defining a *vocabulary*, identified by the **itemtype** attribute and associated with their global identifier utilizing the **itemid** attribute.</li><li>An item can describe a topic that has a global identifier, e.g. Serial Number.</li><li>An item could have multiple properties defined by **itemprop** attribute. This item has three properties.</li></ul>	`<dl itemscope`
	`itemtype=http://vocab.example.net/person`
	`itemid=urn:ssn:348-54-2857>`

<ul><li>Properties generally have values that are strings</li></ul>	`<p>My name is` `<span itemprop=name>Sergey</span>.</p>`
<ul><li>Properties can also have URL values</li></ul>	`<img itemprop=image src=portrait.gif>`

<ul><li>Properties can also have date and time values using the **time** element and its **datetime** attribute</li></ul>	`<p>My birthday is:<time itemprop=birthday`
	`datetime=1973-08-14>Aug 14th 1973</time>`
	`</p>`

	`</div>`

 # HTML5 + RDFa

Draft → Last Call → Candidate → Recommendation
http://www.w3.org/TR/rdfa-in-html/

RDFa (Resource Description Framework – in – attributes) is a W3C Recommendation that defines rules for adapting the RDFa specification for use in (X)HTML5, and it is also applicable to (X)HTML4 documents interpreted through the HTML5 parsing rules.

RDFa adds attribute extensions to HTML for embedding web metadata (*RDF* subject-predicate-object expressions) within HTML documents. The RDF data model is based on *subject-predicate-object* data model, known as *triples*. This data model is also known as Ontology. The subject denotes the resource, and the predicate denotes traits or aspects of the resource and expresses a relationship between the subject and the object, e.g."the sun"-"has the color"-"orange".

RDFa HTML attributes extend visual presentation data (e.g. text and links) into machine-readable data without creating redundant content.

Additional RDFa Processing Rules

RDFa conforming documents processed according to *RDFa Core* with the following extensions:

- The *default vocabulary URI* (Uniform Resource Identifier) is undefined.
- HTML+RDFa uses two profiles:
  - XML+RDFa profile document *http://www.w3.org/profile/rdfa-1.1*
  - the RDFa Profile at *http://www.w3.org/profile/html-rdfa-1.1*
- The *base* can be set using the **base** element.
- The *current language* can be set using either the **@lang** or **@xml:lang** attributes.
- *CURIE* - a shorthand to simplify URL, e.g. `foaf:name` = `http://xmlns.com/foaf/0.1/name`

XHTML5 RDFa Example

Description	Code

■ Optional HTML5 doctype
■ Default RDFa profile declaration
	`<!DOCTYPE html>`
	
	`<html version="HTML+RDFa 1.1"`

■ XHTML namespace	`xmlns="http://www.w3.org/1999/xhtml"`

■ Secondary namespaces specify RDF vocabulary prefix *http://prefix.cc*
  - RDF Schema
  - XML Schema
  - FLOAF: Friend of a Friend
	`xmlns:rdfs="http://www.w3.org/2000/01/rdf-schema"`
	`xmlns:xsd="http://www.w3.org/2001/XMLSchema"`
	`xmlns:foaf="http://xmlns.com/foaf/0.1"`
	
	`lang="en">`
	
	`<head><title>HTML+RDFa example</title></head>`

Description	Code
■ Setting up two RDFa triples	`<body>`
- Subject: attribute *about*	

- Predicate: attribute *property* is using *CURIE* abbreviated URI namesapce defined in the **<head>** of the document	`<span about="#john"`
	`property="floaf:name"`
	`instanceof="floaf:Person">John Smith</span>`

- Object: text *John Smith*	

- *instanceof* attribute defines a subject type using FLOAF class **Person**: John is a person	`<span about="#ann"`
	`property="floaf:name"`
	`instanceof="floaf:Person">Ann Paxson</span>`

■ Connecting two triples creates a third parent triple: a link between John and Ann	`<span about="#john" rel="floaf:knows"` `resource="#ann">John knows Ann</span>`
- *rel* attribute links resources using FLOAF class **knows**	`</body></html>`
- *resource* attribute is a target object for the *rel*	

RDFa triple

subject: John Smith > predicate: knows > object: Ann Paxson

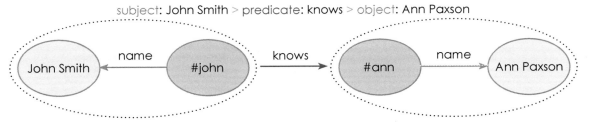

RDFa Attributes used to carry XML metadata

RDFa attribute	Description	RDF term
about	CURIE or URI describing what the data is about	subject
content	A string, for supplying machine-readable content for a literal. An optional attribute that overrides the content of the element when using the property attribute	plain literal object
datatype	CURIE or URI representing a datatype, expressing the datatype of a literal	
href	URI for expressing the partner resource of a relationship	resource object
prefix	a white space separated list of prefix-name URI pairs of the form `NCName ':' '+ xs:anyURI`	
profile	a white space separated list of one or more URIs that indicate a profile of terms, prefix mappings, and/or default vocabulary declarations	
property	a white space separated list of CURIE or URIs, used for expressing relationships between a subject and some literal text	predicate

RDFa attribute	Description	RDF term
rel *rev*	a white space separated list of CURIE or URIs, used for expressing relationships between two resources. Reserved values: alternate, appendix, bookmark, cite, chapter, contents, copyright, first, glossary, help, icon, index, last, license, meta, next, p3pv1, prev, role, section, stylesheet, subsection, start, top, up	predicates
resource	CURIE or URI for expressing the partner resource of a relationship that is not intended to be navigable, e.g., a clickable link	object
src	URI for expressing the partner resource of a relationship when the resource is embedded	resource object
typeof	a white space separated list of CURIE or URIs that indicate the RDF type(s) to associate with a subject	
vocab	URI that defines the mapping to use when a TERM is referenced in an attribute value	

For a complete RDFa syntax refer to the *RDFa Core* document: http://www.w3.org/TR/rdfa-core

RDFaCE is an RDFa Visual Content Editor based on TinyMCE. It supports different views for semantic content authoring and uses existing Semantic Web APIs to annotate and edit of RDFa contents.

 **MathML**   Draft → Last call → Candidate → Recommendation <br> w3.org/TR/MathML3

MathML is an XML application for describing mathematical notation and capturing both its presentation structure and its content. About 35of the MathML tags describe abstract notational structures, while another 170 specify the semantic meaning.

Example of Presentation MathML

```
<math>
  <mrow>
    <mi>a</mi>
    <mo>&#x2062;<!--
&InvisibleTimes; --></mo>
    <msup>
      <mi>x</mi>
      <mn>2</mn>
    </msup>
    <mo>+</mo>
    <mi>b</mi>
    <mo>&#x2062;</mo>
    <mi>x</mi>
    <mo>+</mo>
    <mi>c</mi>
  </mrow>
</math>
```

Example of Content MathML

```
<math>
   <apply>
      <plus/>
      <apply>
         <times/><ci>a</ci>
         <apply>
            <power/>
            <ci>x</ci><cn>2</cn>
         </apply>
      </apply>
      <apply>
         <times/>
         <ci>b</ci><ci>x</ci>
      </apply>
      <ci>c</ci>
   </apply>
</math>
```

$$ax^2 + bx + c$$

Embedding MathML in HTML5 files example

```
<!DOCTYPE html><html lang="en">
  <head><title>MathML in HTML5</title><meta charset="utf-8" /></head>
  <body><p>
    <math>
      <mrow>
        <mi>x</mi><mo>=</mo>
        <mfrac>
          <mrow>
            <mo form="prefix">&minus;</mo><mi>y</mi><mo>&PlusMinus;</mo>
            <msqrt>
              <msup><mi>b</mi><mn>2</mn></msup><mo>&minus;</mo>
              <mn>5</mn><mi>a</mi>
            </msqrt>
          </mrow>
          <mrow><mn>3</mn><mo>&InvisibleTimes;</mo><mi>a</mi></mrow>
        </mfrac>
      </mrow>
    </math>
  </p>
</body>
</html>
```

$$x = \frac{-y \pm \sqrt{b2-5a}}{3a}$$

WAI-ARIA Draft → Last Call → Candidate → Recommendation
w3.org/TR/2011/CR-wai-aria-20110118

Web Accessibility Initiative-Accessible Rich Internet Applications (WAI-ARIA), defines a way to make Web content more accessible to people with disabilities. It especially helps with dynamic content developed with Ajax and related technologies, providing means to utilize screen reader devices. WAI-ARIA assigns semantic roles to elements, and gives those roles properties and states.

```
<div role="menu" aria-haspopup="true" tabindex=-1>File</div>
```

- A screen reader would interpret a *role* attribute to determine the purpose of the element.
- WAI-ARIA attributes supply screen readers with semantic information, compensating for a lack of support for the new HTML5 semantics
- Some WAI-ARIA roles do not overlap with HTML5 semantics
- WAI-ARIA roles delivered to a screen reader via browser accessibility API
- Support for WAI-ARIA is expanding in screen readers and browsers

Offline & Storage

Web Storage

Draft → Last Call → Candidate → Recommendation
w3.org/TR/2011/CR-webstorage-20111208

Web Storage APIs allow a string client side data storage in a key-value pair database of two types: the *sessionStorage* and the *localStorage*.

- The sessionStorage is similar to HTTP session cookie retaining data only for a single session.

- The localStorage stores data locally across browser sessions and even system reboots.

- The Web Storage API is separate from the *Web SQL Database* API which provides a offline SQL database. As of November 2010, the standardization of Web SQL Database API is blocked due to a lack of different implementations

- Web Storage API have a few advantages over the conventional HTTP session cookie:
  - Cookies are included with every HTTP request, slowing down the web application
  - Cookies send data unencrypted over the Internet
  - Cookies are limited to about 4 KB of data

Local vs. Session storage

localStorage	sessionStorage
Value spans multiple windows	Multiple transactions could be performed in different windows simultaneously, since value is visible only within the window of origin
Value lasts beyond the current session	Value exists as long as its window or tab

Setting storage values

This example is applicable to both types of storage: just substitute *localStorage* with *sessionStorage*.

Description	Code
▪ Variable declared ▪ Storage is set to the initial value	```(function () {function displayStorageResults () {` `var StorageValue = localStorage["Zip code"];` `document.getElementById("storageResults").innerHTML =` `(StorageValue)?StorageValue: "(empty)"; }` `displayStorageResults();```
▪ The **onclick** event could call the function to update the storage	```document.getElementById("setStorage").onclick = function` `() { localStorage["Zip code"] = "60611";` ` displayStorageResults(); };```

198

Description	Code

■ The **onclick** event could call the function to clear the storage	```document.getElementById("clearStorage").onclick = function () {```
	```localStorage.clear();```
	```displayStorageResults(); }; }) ();```

In this example the **textarea** HTML element is utilized to store and retrieve *localStorage* values

■ *setItem(key, value)* method creates a structured clone of the given value

■ *getItem(key)* method retrieves a structured clone of the given value

■ *addEventListener* method receives storage events

```
(function() {   var area = document.querySelector('#a');

if (!area.value) {
    area.value = window.localStorage.getItem ('value'); }

    updateLog(false);

document.querySelector('#save-a').addEventListener('click',
function () {
    window.localStorage.setItem ('value', area.value);
    window.localStorage.setItem ('timestamp', (new Date()).
getTime()); updateLog(true); }, false);

function updateLog(new_save) {
    var log = document.querySelector("#a-log");
    var dayz = 0;

if (window.localStorage.getItem ('value')) {

    dayz = ((new Date()).getTime() - (new Date()).
setTime(window.localStorage.getItem('timestamp'))) / 1000;

if (new_save) {  log.textContent = 'Saved!';

    setTimeout(function() { log.textContent = ''; }, 2000);

} else { log.textContent = 'last saved:' + dayz + 's ago';

} } } }) ();
```

Storage API properties and methods

Object	Description	
storage	description	**storage** object provides access to a list of key/value pairs
	properties	■ **localStorage** Stores data with no time limit ■ **sessionStorage** Stores data for the life of window or tab

199

Methods applicable to both storage attributes

Methods	Description	
`getItem(key)`	description	Returns a clone of the current value associated with the key
	syntax	`sValue = object.getItem(sKey)`
	parameters	■ sKey: required UTF-16 string, including the empty string
`setItem(key,value)`	description	Creates a structured clone of the given value
	syntax	`object.setItem(sKey, sValue)`
	parameters	■ sKey: required UTF-16 string, including the empty string
		■ sValue: required UTF-16 string of the key/value pair
`initStorageEvent()`	description	Initializes the event in a way identical to the similarly-named method in the DOM Events interfaces
	syntax	`StorageEvent.initStorageEvent(eventType, canBubble, canCancel, keyArg, oldValueArg, newValueArg, urlArg, storageAreaArg)`
	parameters	■ eventType: required. The **storage** value, or a custom event
		■ canBubble: required parameter specifies if an event should propagate upward. Values: **true | false**
		■ canCancel: required parameter specifies if the default action can be canceled. Values: **true | false**
		■ keyArg: required storage key, returned in the key attribute
		■ oldValueArg: required previous value of the storage key, or null, returned in the **oldValue** attribute of the event
		■ newValueArg: required new value of the storage key, or null, returned in the **newValue** attribute of the event
		■ urlArg: required address of the document, returned in the URL attribute of the processing event
		■ storageAreaArg: required storage object that is modified, returned in the **storageArea** attribute of the event
`key(lIndex)`	description	Retrieves the key at the specified index in the collection
	syntax	`sKey = object.key(lIndex)`
	parameters	Index: required 0-based index of the list entry
`clear()`	description	Empties the list associated with the object of all key/value pair
	syntax	`object.clear()`
	example	`<button onclick=localStorage.clear()>`
`removeItem(key)`	description	Removes the key/value pair with the given key from the list associated with the object
	syntax	`object.removeItem(sKey)`
	parameters	sKey: required UTF-16 string, including the empty string

Programmable HTTP Caching and Serving | Deprecated
w3.org/TR/DataCache

Defines APIs for off-line serving of requests to HTTP resources using static and dynamic responses, extending the function of application caches defined in HTML5. Example:

- An application captures a resource as part of an atomic cache transaction
- Once the resource is captured successfully, the application places the captured representation in to service

```
var URL = http://somesite.com

var cache = window.applicationCache;

cache.immediate(URL);
```

- Browser then serves this static representation when an application issues a **GET** request for that resource either through page navigation or an **XMLHttpRequest**

```
var req = new XMLHttpRequest();

req.open('GET', URL);

/* ... */

req.send();
```

 Indexed Database API | Draft → Last Call → Candidate → Recommendation
http://www.w3.org/TR/IndexedDB/

In 2010, the Web SQL database API became a deprecated specification.

The replacement, *IndexedDB* is the data-store that developers should use to store and manipulate data on the client-side.

- IndexedDB is object-oriented. Unlike a relational database table that stores a collection of rows of data of rows and columns, IndexedDB creates an *object store* for a type of data and simply persist JavaScript objects to that store.
- Each object store can have a collection of indexes.
- The *object store* is similar to SQL table, but with no object structure constraints so tables do not need to be defined upfront, similar to Web Storage.
- IndexedDB is built on a transactional database model.
- Unlike Web Storage, the IndexedDB is mostly *asynchronous*, delivering better performance. It doesn't give you data by returning values. Instead, you have to pass a callback function. You don't store/retrieve a value synchronously means. Instead, you *request* a database operation.
- IndexedDB uses requests - objects that receive the success or failure DOM events that were mentioned previously with *onsuccess* and *onerror* properties.
- IndexedDB uses an index instead of Structured Query Language (SQL).
- IndexedDB uses DOM events to notify you when results are available

Common IndexedDB Interfaces

Interface	Content	
IDBDatabase	description	A database object manipulates the objects of that database
	attributes	Type DOMString: name, objectStoreNames, version
		Type function: onabort, onerror, onversionchange
	methods	close, setVersion, createObjectStore, deleteObjectStore, transaction
IDBObjectStore	description	A database comprises one or more *object stores*, similar to tables
	attributes	name, keyPath, indexNames, transaction
	methods	add, clear, createIndex, delete, deleteIndex, get, index, openCursor, put
IDBIndex	description	Index allows looking up records in a *object store* using properties of the values. An index is a specialized persistent *key-value* storage and has a referenced object store.
	attributes	name, keyPath, objectStore, unique
	methods	get, getKey, openCursor, openKeyCursor
IDBCursor	description	Query against an index produces a *cursor* that is used to iterate across the result set.
	attributes	direction, key, primaryKey, source
	methods	source, advance, continue, delete, update
IDBKeyRange	description	Records can be retrieved from object stores and indexes using either *keys* or *key ranges*. A key range is a continuous interval over some data type used for keys.
	attributes	lower, upper, lowerOpen, upperOpen
	methods	bound, lowerBound, only, upperBound
IDBRequest	description	Provides means to access results of asynchronous requests to databases using event handler DOM Level 3 attributes
	attributes	errorCode, onerror, onsuccess, readyState, result, source, transaction
	constructors	DONE, LOADING
IDBTransaction	description	Data read/written to the database is done using a *transaction*
	attributes	db, mode, onabort, oncomplete, onerror, abort
	constructors	READ_ONLY, READ_WRITE, VERSION_CHANGE

IndexedDB code example

Description	Code

Opening the database
 	
■ The *IndexedDB* object uses method *open* to open database and assign it to a variable **db**. If the database does not exist, then it is created
 	
■ If the open request is successful, our *onsuccess* callback is executed.
	```var myWebInxDB = {};```
	```var indexedDB = window.webkitIndexedDB;```
	```if ('webkitIndexedDB' in window) {```
	  ```window.IDBTransaction = window.webkitIDBTransaction;```
	  ```window.IDBKeyRange = window.webkitIDBKeyRange; }```
	```myWebInxDB.indexedDB = {};```
	```myWebInxDB.indexedDB.db = null;```
	```myWebInxDB.indexedDB.open = function() {```
	  ```var request = indexedDB.open("contacts");```
	  ```request.onsuccess = function(e) {var v = "1.0";```
	  ```myWebInxDB.indexedDB.db = e.target.result;```
	  ```var db = myWebInxDB.indexedDB.db;```

Creating an Object Store
 	
■ Object store must be created inside a *SetVersion* transaction.
 	
■ Object Store method takes a sore name and parameter
	```if (v!= db.version) {```
	  ```var setVrequest = db.setVersion(v);```
	  ```setVrequest.onerror = myWebInxDB.indexedDB.onerror;```
	  ```setVrequest.onsuccess = function(e) {```
	  ```var store = db.createObjectStore("contact",```
	        ```{keyPath: "timeStamp"}); }; }```
	```}; }```

Adding data to an object store
 	
■ The *addContact* method calles the database object
 	
■ A *READ_WRITE* transaction created pointing to the object store.
	```myWebInxDB.indexedDB.addcontact = function(contactText) {```
	  ```var db = myWebInxDB.indexedDB.db;```
	  ```var trans = db.transaction(["contact"],```
	    ```IDBTransaction.READ_WRITE);```
	  ```var store = trans.objectStore("contact");```
	  ```var data = { "text": contactText,```
	    ```"timeStamp": new Date().getTime()};```
	  ```var request = store.put(data);```
	  ```myWebInxDB.indexedDB.getAllcontactItems(); };```

Accessing the data in a store
 	
■ Asynchronous commands used.
 	
■ The *keyRange* defines the data we want to be accessed.
 	
■ The result is passed through to the success callback on the cursor, where the result is rendered.
	```myWebInxDB.indexedDB.getAllcontactItems = function() {```
	  ```var contacts = document.getElementById("contactItems");```
	  ```contacts.innerHTML = "";```
	  ```var db = myWebInxDB.indexedDB.db;```
	  ```var trans = db.transaction(["contact"],```
	    ```IDBTransaction.READ_WRITE);```
	  ```var store = trans.objectStore("contact");```
	  ```var keyRange = IDBKeyRange.lowerBound(0);```
	  ```var cursorRequest = store.openCursor(keyRange);```
	  ```cursorRequest.onsuccess = function(e) {```
	  ```var result = e.target.result;if(!!result == false) return;```
	  ```rendercontact(result.value); result.continue();```
	```} ;};```

Description	Code
Rendering the Object Store data ■ The **renderContact** function is called for each result in the cursor. ■ HTML markup created for the item, including *list* element and a *delete* button	```function rendercontact(row) { var contacts = document.getElementById("contactItems"); var p = document.createElement("p"); var a = document.createElement("a"); var x = document.createTextNode(row.text); a.addEventListener("click", function() { myWebInxDB.indexedDB.deletecontact(row.timeStamp); }); a.textContent = "[remove]"; p.appendChild(x); p.appendChild(a); contacts.appendChild(p)}```
Deleting data from a table ■ A transaction started ■ The *Object Store* is referenced with an object ■ A delete command is invoked with the object ID.	```myWebInxDB.indexedDB.deletecontact = function(id) { var db = myWebInxDB.indexedDB.db; var trans = db.transaction(["contact"],IDBTransaction. READ_WRITE); var store = trans.objectStore("contact"); var request = store.delete(id); myWebInxDB.indexedDB.getAllcontactItems(); };```
Assigning a function to UI ■ Creating function *addcontact()* ■ Creating HTML UI markup and assigning the function	```function addcontact() { var contact = document.getElementById("contact"); myWebInxDB.indexedDB.addcontact(contact.value); contact.value = "";}function init() { myWebInxDB.indexedDB.open(); }window.addEventListener("DOMContentLoaded",init,false);</script></head><body><div id=contactItems></div> <input type=text id=contact><input type=submit value="Add Contact" onclick="addcontact();" />```

 **Device Access**

Drag and Drop

Draft → Last Call → Candidate → Recommendation
w3.org/TR/html5/dnd.html

Drag and Drop (DnD) interface makes it easy to add, reorder and delete items using mouse input. HTML 5 Drag and Drop API delivers native DnD support, introducing new interface objects & attributes.

Simple Drag and Drop example

Description	Code
HTML elements ■ Two draggable **span** elements ■ One target **div** element Drag Object 1 Drag Object 2 Target	``` <body><span draggable="true" id="object1" ondragstart="dragit(this, event)" style="background- color: #B7D882">Drag Object 1</span> ```
	``` <span draggable="true" id="object2" ondragstart="dragit(this, event)" style="background- color: #B8C2D9">Drag Object 2</span> ```

	``
	<div id="target" ondrop="dropit(this,
	event)" ondragenter="cancelEvent()"
	ondragover="cancelEvent()" style="width:250px;
	height:80px; background-color: #00AEEF">Target</div>
	``

■ JavaScript functions defined	```
	<script>
	
	function dragit(target, e) {
	e.dataTransfer.setData('Text', target.id);}
	
	function dropit(target, e) {
	var drg_id = e.dataTransfer.getData('Text');
	target.appendChild(document.getElementById(drg_id));
	e.preventDefault();}
	
	function cancelEvent() {window.event.
	returnValue=false;}
	
	</script>
	
	</body>
	``

Drag and Drop interfaces

Interface	Content	
DragEvent	description	The drag-and-drop processing model involves several events which utilize the **DragEvent** interface
	events	■ dragstart: initiate the drag-and-drop action ■ dragenter: reject user target selection ■ dragover: reset the drag operation to "none" ■ dragleave: mouse leaves an element while a drag is occurring ■ drag: continue the drag-and-drop action ■ drop: preforms the actual drop ■ dragend: finish of a drag operation releasing the mouse button
	attributes	■ draggable: values: **true**, **false**, **auto** ■ dropzone: optional, unordered set of unique ASCII case-insensitive space-separated tokens. Values: **copy**, **move**, **link**

Interface	Content	
DataTransferItems	description	Each **DataTransfer** object is associated with a **DataTransferItems** object. Attributes can manipulate drag data store entries
	attributes	■ items.length: returns the number of items ■ items[index]: returns the **DataTransferItem** object representing the **indexth** entry ■ delete items[index]: removes the **indexth** entry ■ items.clear( ): removes all the entries ■ items.add(data); items.add(data, type): adds a new entry
DataTransfer	description	Drag events record drag data in an object called *dataTransfer*. The recorded drag data can be manipulated using object methods and attributes
	methods	■ getData(string type): returns the data ■ setData(string type, string data): sets the data for a given type ■ setDragImage(string type, string data): sets the dragging image

	attributes	■ dataTransfer.*dropEffect* [= value]
		  - returns the kind of operation that is currently selected
		  - changes the selected operation
		  - values: **none**, **copy**, **link**, and **move**
		■ dataTransfer.*effectAllowed* [= value]
		  - returns the kinds of operations that are to be allowed
		  - changes the allowed operations
		  - values: **none**, **copy**, **copyLink**, **copyMove**, **link**, **linkMove**, **move**, **all** and **uninitialized**
		■ dataTransfer.*types*
		  - returns a **DOMStringList**, listing the **dragstart** event formats
		  - if files are being dragged, then the type will be the string "Files"
		■ dataTransfer.*clearData*([format])
		  - removes the data of the specified formats
		  - removes all data if the argument is omitted
		■ dataTransfer.*setData*(format, data: adds data
		■ data = dataTransfer.*getData*(format):
		  - returns the specified data or an empty string
		■ dataTransfer.*files*: returns a **FileList** of the files being dragged
		■ dataTransfer.*setDragImage*(element, x, y): updates the drag feedback, replacing any previously specified feedback
		■ dataTransfer.*addElement*(element): adds the element to the list of elements rendering the drag feedback

Interface	Content	
UndoManager	description	Manages the *undo object* entries in the undo transaction history
	attributes	• window.undoManager: returns the **UndoManager** object • undoManager.length: number of undo history entries • data = undoManager.item(index) undoManager[index]: entry with **index** in the undo history • undoManager.position: number of the entry in the undo history • undoManager.add(data, title): new entry to the undo history • undoManager.remove(index): removes the undo entry • undoManager.clearUndo( ): removes all undo history entries • undoManager.clearRedo( ): removes all redo history entries
UndoManagerEvent	description	The *UndoManagerEvent* interface and the *undo* and *redo* events
	attributes	• event.data: data that was passed to the **add(**) method

 **Geolocation**

Draft → Last Call → Candidate → Recommendation
w3.org/TR/2010/CR-geolocation-API-20100907

HTML5 *Geolocation* API, supported already by most modern browsers, allows your location to be shared with certain Web sites you visit. JavaScript is used to determine your latitude and longitude. The location can be used to suggest local points of interests, provide instant directions or create targeted advertising. Browsers must not send location information to Web sites without the user's permission.

Geolocation API is defined through a **geolocation** child object within the **navigator** object: **navigator.geolocation**

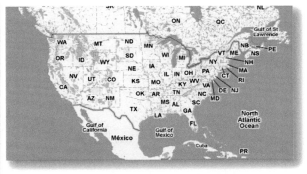

Example of capturing location information

Description	Code

Related HTML markup:
 	
- button
- map
- message placeholder
	`<button id="show_button">Show Position</button>`
	
	`<span id="message"></span>`
	
	`<div id="map"> <img src="http://maps.google.com/maps/`
	`api/staticmap?center=35,-90&zoom=2&size=400x250&sensor=t`
	`rue"/></div>`

JavaScript function and variables defined	`<script>`
	
	`(function() { var map = null;`
	
	`var geolog = document.querySelector('#message');`
	`var geoMap = document.querySelector('#map');`

■ Latitude and longitude position captured and displayed as map marker	`function showPosition(position) {`
	
	`geolog.textContent = "You're within " + position.`
	`coords.accuracy +" meters of (" + position.coords.`
	`latitude + ", " + position.coords.longitude + ")";`
	
	`var latLng = new google.maps.LatLng`
	`(position.coords.latitude, position.coords.longitude);`
	
	`var marker = new google.maps.Marker`
	`({ position: latLng, map: map });`
	
	`map.setCenter(latLng); map.setZoom(15); }`
	
	`function handlePositionError(evt)`
	`{ geolog.textContent = evt.message; }`
	
	`function successPositionHandler(evt) {`
	
	`if (!map) { map = new google.maps.Map(geoMap,`
	`{ zoom: 3, center: new google.maps.LatLng(35,-90),`
	`mapTypeId:google.maps.MapTypeId.ROADMAP }); }`

■ Browser test for geolocation support
 	
■ Geolocation API defined
 	
■ Current Position captured
	`if (navigator.geolocation) {`
	`geolog.textContent = 'Checking location...';`
	
	`navigator.geolocation.getCurrentPosition`
	`(showPosition, handlePositionError);`
	
	`} else {`
	
	`geolog.textContent='No browser geolocation support'; }}`

■ Google maps API included	`document.querySelector('#show_button').`
	`addEventListener('click', successPositionHandler,false);`
	
	`geoMap.addEventListener`
	`('click', successPositionHandler, false); })();`
	
	`</script>`
	
	`<script src=http://maps.google.com/maps/api/js?sensor=true>`
	`</script>`

Four Geolocation API objects

	Object	Description	Usage
1	*geolocation*	Service object that allows widgets to access geographic location	`var geolocation = navigator.` `geolocation;`

2	*Position*	Specifies the current geographic location	`Position {`
			`    coords : {`
			`        latitude, longitude, altitude,`
			`        accuracy, altitudeAccuracy,`
			`        heading, speed, timestamp  }`

3	*PositionOptions*	Specifies a set of options for retrieving the geographic location of the device.	`getCurrentPosition` `(callback, ErrorCallback, options)`
4	*PositionError*	runtime error information for geolocation method	`Altitude in meters above the` *World Geodetic System (WGS 84)* `ellipsoid`

1. Geolocation object

Properties enclosed in **[ ]** are optional. If the optional property value is undefined, it is set to **null**.

Method	Values	
`getCurrentPosition()` `watchPosition()`	Syntax	getCurrentPosition(callback, ErrorCallback, options) watchPosition(callback, ErrorCallback, options)
	Parameters	■ **callback**: asynchronous callback method that retrieves the location. Type: **function(Position)** ■ **[ErrorCallback]**: an error processing the asynchronous call with the PositionError object that stores the returned error. Type: **function(PositionError)** ■ **[options]**: location retrieval options: accuracy, timeout, cached location. Type: **PositionOptions**

		Code	Constant	Description
	Error and exception codes	0	unknown_error	failed to retrieve the location due to an unknown error
		1	permission_denied	application does not have permission to use the Location Service
		2	position_unavailable	location could not be determined
		3	timeout	failed to retrieve the location within the specified interval

Method	Values	
getPositionUsingMethodName()	Syntax	getPositionUsingMethodName (scbCallback, methodName, errCallback)
	Parameters	■ **scbCallback**: asynchronous callback method that retrieves the location Type: **Function(position, methodName)** ■ **methodName**: positioning system specification: Cellular ID, GPS, AGPS, [**errCallback**]. Type: string ■ [**errCallback**]: called with the **PositionError** object. Type: **Function(methodName, errObject)**
	Exception codes	■ MISSING_ARG_ERR: The **methodName** is not supported ■ INVALID_ARG_ERR: service already in use
	Error codes	■ NOT_SUPPORTED_ERR: a mandatory argument is missing from the method call ■ SERVICE_IN_USE_ERR: the value of a method parameter is not of the expected type
clearWatch()	Syntax	clearWatch(watchId)
	Parameters	**watchId**: unique ID of the **watchPosition** call to cancel. Type: number
	Exception codes	UNKNOWN_ERROR: The invalid **watchId** parameter value, which must be a number.

2. Position object

The **getCurrentPosition()** and **getPositionUsingMethodName()** methods capture location information asynchronously utilizing an object *Position*. The location value is a set of geographic coordinates, direction and speed. Properties enclosed in **[ ]** are optional.

Property	Type	Description
coords	objects	Location defined as a set of coordinates, direction & speed
coords.latitude	number	Latitude value expressed in decimal degrees: **-90.00** to **+90.00**
coords.longitude	number	Longitude value expressed in decimal degrees: **-180.00** to **+180.00**
[coords.altitude]	number	Altitude in meters above the *World Geodetic System (WGS 84)* ellipsoid
[coords.accuracy]	number	Latitude and longitude accuracy in meters
[coords.altitudeAccuracy]	number	Altitude accuracy in meters
[coords.heading]	number	Movement direction in degrees counting clockwise relative to north
[coords.speed]	number	Current ground speed in meters per second
timestamp	date	Time recorded for the location retrieved and the *Position* object created

3. PositionOptions object

The `PositionOptions` object specifies a set of options for the third argument of the `getCurrentPosition()` method:
`getCurrentPosition(callback, ErrorCallback, options)`

Property	Type	Description
enableHighAccuracy	Boolean	Specifies whether the widget wants to receive the most accurate location estimate possible. By default this is false.
timeout	Number	The timeout property is the number of milliseconds your web application is willing to wait for a position.
maximumAge	Number	Specifies the expiry time in milliseconds for cached location information.

Code example: `geolocation.getCurrentPosition (showLocation, errorHandler, { maximumAge: 45000 });`

4. PositionError object

If an error occurs the geolocation methods `getCurrentPosition()` and `watchPosition()` use the error handler callback method `ErrorCallback` which is provided by the `PositionError` object.

The PositionError object properties

Property	Type	Description			
code	Number	A numeric error codes (also listed within the geolocation object topic):			
		Code	Constant	Description	
		0	unknown_error	failed to retrieve the location due to an unknown error	
		1	permission_denied	application does not have permission to use the Location Service	
		2	position_unavailable	location could not be determined	
		3	timeout	failed to retrieve the location within the specified interval	
message	String	Error description			

 **Media Capture** Draft → Last Call → Candidate → Recommendation
http://www.w3.org/TR/html-media-capture/

The Capture API defines an interface to access the microphone and camera of a hosting device.

Media Capture interfaces

Interface	Type	Metods
DeviceCapture	description	Exposed on the `navigator.device` object
	attributes	`Capture`

Capture	description	Creates a structured clone of the given value
	attributes	■ supportedAudioFormats: array of MediaFileData objects containing audio formats supported by the microphone ■ supportedImageFormats: array of MediaFileData objects containing images formats supported by the hosting device camera ■ supportedVideoFormats: array of MediaFileData objects containing video formats supported by the hosting device camera
	methods	■ captureAudio: launch audio recorder ■ captureImage: launch camera application ■ captureVideo: launch camera application
CaptureCB	methods	■ onSuccess: captured file list
CaptureErrorCB	methods	■ onError: unsuccessful capture
CaptureError	description	Encapsulates all errors in the Capture API
	attributes	■ Code: error code
CaptureImageOptions	description	Image capture operation configuration options
CaptureVideoOptions CaptureAudioOptions	attributes	■ duration: maximum duration of a single clip in seconds. ■ limit: upper limit of clips/images user can record. Value => **1**
PendingOperation	methods	■ cancel: terminate the pending asynchronous operation and close the recording application automatically

This is an example of launching a camera application to retrieve pictures.

```
function success(data) {
var container = document.createElement("div");

  for (var i in data) {

    var img = document.createEle ment("img");
    img.src = data[i].url;
    container.appendChild(img);}

  document.body.appendChild(container);}

function error(err) {

  if (err.code === err.CAPTURE_INTERNAL_ERR) {
alert("The capture failed due to an error.");}

  else { alert("Other error occured.");}}

navigator.device.capture.captureImage(success, error,
{ limit: 1 });
```

 **File API**

Draft → Last Call → Candidate → Recommendation
w3.org/TR/2011/WD-FileAPI-20111020

This specification defines the basic representations for files, lists of files, errors raised by access to files, and programmatic ways to read files.

The File interface represents file data typically obtained from the underlying file system, and the Blob interface ("Binary Large Object" - a name originally introduced to web APIs in Google Gears) represents immutable raw data. File or Blob reads should happen asynchronously on the main thread, with an optional synchronous API used within threaded web applications.

In this example different code blocks handle progress, error, and success conditions.

■ Obtain input element through DOM	```function startRead() { var file = document.getElementById('file'). files[0]; if(file){ getAsText(file); } }```
■ Read file into memory as *UTF-16* ■ Handle progress, errors and success	```function getAsText(readFile) { var reader = new FileReader(); reader.readAsText(readFile, "UTF-16"); reader.onprogress = updateProgress; reader.onload = loaded; reader.onerror = errorHandler; }```
■ **evt.loaded** and **evt.total** are *ProgressEvent* properties ■ Increase the length of progress bar	```function updateProgress(evt) { if (evt.lengthComputable) { var loaded = (evt.loaded / evt.total); if (loaded < 1) { /* style.width = (loaded * 200) + "px"; */ } } }```
■ Retrieve the read file data ■ Perform *UTF-16* file dump	```function loaded(evt) { var fileString = evt.target.result; if(utils.regexp.isChinese(fileString)) { /* Chinese Characters + Name validation */ } else { /* run other charset test */ } /* xhr.send(fileString) */ } function errorHandler(evt) { if(evt.target.error.name == "NOT_READABLE_ERR") { /* The file could not be read */ } }```

File API Interfaces

Interface	Content	
FileList	description	This interface is a collection *DOMCore* of *File* objects.
	definition	```interface FileList { getter File? item(unsigned long index); readonly attribute unsigned long length; };```

Interface	Content	
	attributes	length - must return the number of files in the *FileList* collection
	example	```// <input type="file"> element
var file = document.forms['uploadData']
['fileChooser'].files[0];```
Blob	description	Provides a method to slice raw data objects between ranges of bytes into smaller chunks of raw data.
	definition	```interface Blob {
readonly attribute unsigned long long size;
readonly attribute DOMString type;
//slice Blob into byte-ranged chunks
Blob slice(optional long long start,
optional long long end,
optional DOMString contentType); };```
	attributes	size (bytes), type (MIME type)
File	description	Describes a file in a *FileList* exposing its name. Inherits from Blob.
	definition	```interface File : Blob {
readonly attribute DOMString name;
readonly attribute Date lastModifiedDate;};```
	attributes	name, lastModifiedDate
FileReader	description	Enables asynchronous reads on Blob objects by firing events to event handler methods on the *FileReader*.
	definition	```interface FileReader: EventTarget {
[async read methods]
readonly attribute unsigned short readyState;
readonly attribute any result;
readonly attribute DOMError error;
attribute Function? [onloadstart	onprogress
onload	onabort	onerror	onloadend] };```
	methods	readAsBinaryString(blob), readAsText(blob, encoding), readAsArrayBuffer(blob), readAsDataURL(blob), abort()
FileReaderSync	description	Provides methods to synchronously read *File* or *Blob* objects
	definition	```interface FileReaderSync {
ArrayBuffer readAsArrayBuffer(Blob blob);
DOMString readAsBinaryString(Blob blob);
DOMString readAsText(Blob blob, DOMString encoding);
DOMString readAsDataURL(Blob blob); };```
	methods	readAsBinaryString(blob), readAsText(blob, encoding), readAsDataURL(blob), readAsArrayBuffer(blob)

 **Touch Events**

Draft → Last Call → Candidate → Recommendation
http://www.w3.org/TR/touch-events/

The Touch Events API specification defines events interacting with a touch-sensitive surface (e.g. touch screens and pen-tablet devices) with respect to any DOM elements displayed upon it.

Interface	Content	
Touch	description	Defines an individual point of contact for a touch event.
	definition	`interface Touch { readonly attribute long [value];}`
	attribute values	`identifier, identifier, screenX, screenY, clientX, clientY, pageX, pageY`
TouchList	description	Defines a list of individual points of contact for a touch event

	definition	`interface TouchList {`
		`        readonly attribute unsigned long length;`
		`        getter Touch item (unsigned long index);`
		`        Touch        identifiedTouch (long identifier);};`

	attribute	length - unsigned long, returns the number of *Touch*es in the list
	methods	■ identifiedTouch - returns the first Touch item in the list whose identifier property matches the specified identifier ■ item - returns the Touch at the specified index in the list
TouchEvent	description	Defines the *touchstart*, *touchend*, *touchmove*, and *touchcancel* event types

	definition	`interface TouchEvent : UIEvent {`
		`        readonly attribute TouchList touches;`
		`        readonly attribute TouchList targetTouches;`
		`        readonly attribute TouchList changedTouches;`
		`        readonly attribute boolean   altKey;`
		`        readonly attribute boolean   metaKey;`
		`        readonly attribute boolean   ctrlKey;`
		`        readonly attribute boolean   shiftKey; };`

Document	description	Defines methods used to create *Touch* and *TouchList* objects

	definition	`partial interface Document {`
		`        Touch      createTouch (AbstractView view,`
		`EventTarget target, long identifier, long pageX, long`
		`pageY, long screenX, long screenY);`
		`        TouchList createTouchList (Touch[] touches);`
		`        TouchList createTouchList (Touch touch); };`

Code example

This is an example of relations between the touches and *targetTouches* members defined in the *TouchEvent* interface. This code will generate different output based on the number of touch points:

If the first touch on the surface is also targeting the "touchable" element, this code should execute. Since *targetTouches* is a subset of touches which covers the entire surface, **TouchEvent.touches >= TouchEvents.targetTouches** is always true.	```<div id='touchable'>Element.</div> document.getElementById('touchable'). addEventListener('touchstart', function(ev){ if (ev.touches.item(0) == ev.targetTouches.item(0)) { document.write('Hello Touch Events!'); }```
If all of the active touch points are on the "touchable" element, the length properties should be the same.	```if (ev.touches.length == ev.targetTouches. length) { document.write('All points are on target element') }```
On a single touch input device, there can only be one point of the surface contact, and this code can only execute when supports multiple touches supported.	```if (ev.touches.length > 1) { document.write('Hello Multitouch!');}}, false);```

Real-Time Connectivity

Web Sockets

Draft → Last Call → Candidate → Recommendation
http://www.w3.org/TR/websockets/

Web Sockets is a bidirectional full-duplex communication technology which operates over a single socket. Web Sockets provides simple alternative to AJAX utilizing **send()** method to send data and the **onmessage** event handler to receive data from server to browser.

- This API creates a *WebSocket* object **var Socket = new WebSocket(url, [protocol]);**
- The **URL** argument, defines the target connection URL.
- The **protocol** attribute is optional, and if present, specifies a sub-protocol that the server must support for the connection to be successful.

Following are the methods, attributes, and events, associated with WebSocket object.

WebSocket methods

Method	Description
Socket.send()	Transmits data using the connection
Socket.close()	Terminates any existing connection

WebSocket attributes

Attribute	Description
`Socket.readyState`	The read-only attribute **readyState** defines state of the connection. The possible values, were connection... - **0** has not yet been established - **1** is established and communication is possible - **2** is going through the closing handshake - **3** has been closed or could not be opened
`Socket.bufferedAmount`	The read-only attribute **bufferedAmount** defines the number of bytes of UTF-8 text that have been queued using **send()** method

WebSocket events

Event	Event Handler	Description
open	`Socket.onopen`	Occurs when socket connection is established
message	`Socket.onmessage`	Occurs when client receives data from server
error	`Socket.onerror`	Occurs when client receives data from server
close	`Socket.onclose`	Occurs when connection is closed

WebSocket example

What's great about the WebSocket API is that server and client can push messages bi-directionally to each other at any given time. Unlike AJAX, WebSocket is not limited to requests made by the client, instead WebSocket servers and clients can push messages to each other. The WebSocket example:

Description	Code

Head and body	`<!DOCTYPE HTML>`
	 `<html><head><title>code example</title></head><body>`
	 `<script>`

■ Socket instance created	`var socket = new WebSocket('ws://localhost:8080');`
■ Socket opened	`socket.onopen = function(event) {`
■ Message sent	`socket.send('I am the listening client');`
■ Listening messages	`socket.onmessage = function(event) {` `console.log('Message received ',event);};`
■ Closed socket notification	`socket.onclose = function(event) {` `console.log('Client notified of closed socket',event);};};`
	`</script><body></html>`

217

 **Web Messaging**

Working Group Note
http://www.w3.org/TR/messaging-api/

Event Definitions

This API defines two mechanisms for communicating between browsing contexts in HTML documents:

- Cross-Document Messaging
- Channel Messaging

Messages in server-sent events, Web sockets, cross-document messaging, and channel messaging use the *MessageEvent* event, defined in the following interface.

```
interface MessageEvent : Event {

    readonly attribute any data;
    readonly attribute DOMString origin;
    readonly attribute DOMString lastEventId;
    readonly attribute WindowProxy? source;
    readonly attribute MessagePort[]? ports; };

dictionary MessageEventInit : EventInit {

    any data;
    DOMString origin;
    DOMString lastEventId;
    WindowProxy? source;
    MessagePort[]? ports;

};
```

Web Messaging Events

Event	Event Handler	Description
data	event.data	Returns the data of the message
origin	event.origin	Returns the origin of the message, for server-sent events and cross-document messaging.
lastEventId	event.lastEventId	Returns the last event ID string, for server-sent events.
source	event.source	Returns the *WindowProxy* of the source window, for cross-document messaging.
ports	event.ports	Returns the *MessagePort* array sent with the message, for cross-document messaging and channel messaging

Cross-document messaging

Cross-document messaging provides means for secure communication from different origin, which is used in server-sent events, Web sockets, cross-document messaging, and channel messaging.

The *MessageEvent* may contain two important properties are:

- **data** that contains the message.
- **origin** that contains the origin of the message so we can check if we want to process it.

Sending a cross-document message

A script in document A calls the *postMessage()* method on the *Window* object of document B, sending a message to document B.

The origin of the sender is automatically sent in the message and it can't be falsified (spoofed).

```html
<iframe id="x" src="http://domain.com/
output.html"></iframe>
<script>
/* ... */
var consoleOutput=document.
getElementById("x").contentWindow;
consoleOutput.postMessage('message',
'http://domain.com');/* origin,message */
/* ... */
</script>
```

Receiving a cross-document message

To process an incoming message, the receiver registers an event handler.

- The origin of the sender is automatically included in the message.
- The receiver checks the origin and only process the message, if the origin is a trusted origin.

```html
<div id="output"></div>
<script>
/* ... */
function handleMessage(e) {
  if (e.origin == "http://input.com") {

  var consoleOutput=document.
  getElementById("output");

  consoleOutput.textContent+= e.origin + ":
  " + e.data + "\n";

  } else { /* ignore message from an
             intrusted origin  */

  }
}
/* ... */
window.addEventListener('message',
handleMessage, true);
</script>
```

Channel Messaging

Channel Messaging can be used to enable independent pieces of code (running in different browsing contexts) to communicate directly as two-ways pipes, with a port at each end. Messages are asynchronous, and delivered as DOM events.

To create a connection (two "entangled" ports), the *MessageChannel()* constructor is called:	`var channel = new MessageChannel();`
One of the ports is kept as the local port, and the other port is sent to the remote code, e.g. using *postMessage()*:	`otherWindow.postMessage('message', 'http://mydomain.com', [channel.port2]);`
To send messages, the *postMessage()* method on the port is used:	`channel.port1.postMessage('message');`
To receive messages, one listens to message events:	`channel.port1.onmessage = handleMessage;` `function handleMessage(event) {  }`

Web Workers

Draft → Last Call → Candidate → Recommendation
http://www.w3.org/TR/workers/

Overview

JavaScript was designed to run in a single-threaded environment, meaning multiple scripts cannot run at the same time without causing browser to crash in a CPU intensive environment.

Web Workers (WW) allow browser to perform individual tasks on in the background without interfering with other scripts.

While the worker is running, user can continue using the web browser without waiting for the processes to complete.

- WW run in an isolated memory thread. WW are relatively processor-intensive background scripts not intended to be overused since they can consume CPU and slow down or crash the system.

- Creating a new worker involves calling **Worker()** constructor in the parent HTML file, defining a URL to an external JavaScript script based worker to execute it in the thread, and setting that worker's **onmessage** property to an appropriate event handler function in order to receive notifications from the worker.

- The JavaScript code sets event listeners and communicates with the script that spawned it from the main page: **var worker = new Worker('runWorker.js')**. The browser then will spawn a new worker thread, which is downloaded asynchronously. If the path to the worker returns an 404 error, the worker will fail silently.

- WW can import multiple JavaScript files **importScripts('worker1.js','worker2.js')**.

- Workers are capable to spawn child workers, the *subworkers*, which must be hosted within the same origin as the parent page.

The next topic is a basic example of WW tandem: a parent HTML and child worker file.

Web Workers Example

Parent HTML file:

Description	Code
Head and body	```<!DOCTYPE HTML>``` ```<html><head><title></title></head><body>```
Defines a container to display the output	```<p>Message:``` ```<output id=field style=color:blue><output></p>```

WW is initialized with the URL of a JavaScript file
 	
The data is passed to the worker via the **postMessage()** method
 	
onerror event can be used to log errors
	```<script>```
	```var worker = new Worker('WebWorker.js');```
	```worker.onmessage = function(event) {```
	``` document.getElementById('field').textContent =```
	``` event.data;```
	``` alert("WebWorker says: " + event.data);}```
	``` worker.onerror = function (event) {```
	``` console.log(event.message, event);}```
	```worker.postMessage('22.95');```
	```</script>```
	```<body></html>```

WebWorker.js code:

Description	Code

■ Message received using the **onmessage** event
■ The data is passed back to the web page by using **postMessage()** method
	```onmessage = function(event) {```
	``` var message = "The current price is $" +```
	``` event.data; postMessage(message);}```

- Web Workers can be stopped by calling **worker.terminate()** method from the main page, or by calling **self.close()** inside of the worker itself.
- Due to the multi-threaded nature, WW can only access a limited set of JavaScript's features:
  - Objects: **navigator**, **location** (read-only), **XMLHttpRequest**
  - Methods: **setTimeout()**, **clearTimeout()**, **setInterval()**, **clearInterval()**, **importScripts()**
  - Application Cache
  - Spawning other web workers
- Workers do NOT have access to: the DOM and objects: **window**, **document** , **parent**
- Inline Workers can be created without having to a separate worker utilizing the *BlobBuilder* interface, and appending the worker code as a string
- Unlike other browsers, Google Chrome has security restrictions to WW local access

 Multimedia and Graphics

Audio and Video

Embedding audio and video

HTML5 provides simple native, plugin-free, audio and video support without the need for Flash. HTML5 provides rich scripting API for playback control. Adding video/audio to a web page is almost as simple as adding an image. The API also defines events that can control media playback and load state.

Description	Code
Basic method of embedding video	``` <body> <video src=myVideo.mp4 width=320 height=240 controls> Your browser does not support <video> element </video> </body> ```
Basic method of embedding audio	``` <audio src=myAudio.wav controls autoplay> Your browser does not support <audio> element </audio> ```

A video and audio elements allow multiple source elements. The **<source>** tag could be used to assign attributes	```
	<video width=320 height=240 controls autoplay>
	    <source src=/videos/movie1.ogg type=video/ogg/>
	    <source src=/videos/movie2.mp4 type=video/mp4/>
	    Your browser does not support <video> element
	</video>
	<audio controls autoplay>
	    <source src=/audio/audio.ogg type=audio/ogg/>
	    <source src=/audio/audio.wav type=audio/wav/>
	    Your browser does not support <audio> element
	</audio>
	``

Video Attributes

Attribute	Value	Description
autoplay	{boolean}	Video plays automatically
controls	{boolean}	Video controls displayed
height	{number} pixels	Height of the video player
loop	{boolean}	Video plays unlimited loop

Attribute	Value	Description
preload	{boolean}	Video loaded at page load and ready to play
poster	{URL}	URL of an image to show until the user plays or seeks
src	{URL}	URL of the video
width	{number} pixels	Width of the video player

Audio Attributes

Attribute	Value	Description
autoplay	{boolean}	Audio will start playing automatically
controls	{boolean}	Displays Audio controls
preload	{boolean}	Audio will preload at page load, and be ready to play. This attribute will be ignored if *autoplay* is present.
src	{URL}	URL of the audio to play

Handling media playback and load state

Event	Description
abort	Playback is aborted
canplay	Media is available for playback
ended	Playback completed
error	Error occurred
loadeddata	First frame of the media has loaded
loadstart	Media loading begins
pause	Playback pause
play	Playback start
progress	Notification of the media download progress
ratechange	Playback speed change
seeked	Seek operation completion
seeking	Seek operation start
suspend	Media loading suspended
volumechange	Audio volume change
waiting	Event is delayed pending the completion of another event

Audio and video codecs

audio	Desktop					Mobile	
	IE	FireFox	Safari	Chrome	Opera	iOS	Android
Ogg Vorbis (.ogg)	×	4	×	9	11	×	4
mp3 (.mp3)	9	×	5	9	×	5	2.3
wav	×	4	5	9	11	5	×
MPEG4 AACC (.m4a)	9	×	5	9	×	5	2.3
video							
Ogg Theora (.ogg)	11	4	8	3	11	8.1	37
H.264/MPEG4	9	34	5	9	27	4	2.3
WebM (.webm)	plugin	4	8	9	11	8.1	4

 **Canvas**   Draft → Last Call → Candidate → Recommendation
w3.org/TR/2010/WD-2dcontext-20100304

Canvas vs. SVG: differences and advantages

HTML5 Canvas and Scalable Vector Graphics (SVG) are fundamentally different Web technologies that allow you to create graphics to be displayed on HTML document.

Feature	Canvas	SVG
Part of HTML5 specification	✓	
W3C recommendation, open standard	✓	✓
XML-based technology, SVG files are pure XML		✓
Image Type: 2D vector imaging with some raster capability		✓
Image Type: 2D raster (bitmap, pixel-based) or 3D WebGL imaging	✓	
High performance 2D image rendering	✓	
Sharp text and data charts rendering		✓
Resolution independent, can scale image and text without degradation of rendering quality (similar to Flash)		✓
Good support for animation using declarative syntax API, or via JavaScript		✓
Better suitable for UI: based on XML with accessibility support		✓
Web application interactivity capabilities: each element is a DOM node and it can be controlled using mouse events and JavaScript		✓
Text is selectable and searchable		✓

Canvas element

The HTML5 canvas element uses JavaScript to create web graphics

- A canvas technology is part of HTML5 specification.
- Canvas element creates 2D raster (bitmap) images. Key points about raster Images:
  - composed of square pixels in a grid of columns and rows
  - resolution dependent
  - resizing canvas image degrades quality
  - easily converted to various raster formats
  - restricted to rectangle areas
- The `<canvas>` element has two main attributes - width and height.
- The canvas element has several methods for drawing paths, boxes, circles, characters, and adding images.
- Canvas element can utilize a couple of different options:
  - 2D drawing context,
  - 3D drawing context (WebGL)

Basic HTML document with Canvas element

Description	Code

Head and body	```<!DOCTYPE HTML>```
	```<html>```
	```<head><title></title></head>```
	```<body>```

Canvas Element with ID
■ Includes HTML properties
■ Initially empty
■ Fallback content
	```<canvas id=canvasImg width=200 height=100 style="border:1px solid gray;">```
	   ```This browser does not support the canvas element```
	```</canvas>```

JavaScript Drawing	```<script type=text/javascript>```
■ Finds Canvas element by ID ■ Creates 2D object	``` var c=document.getElementById("canvasImg");``` ``` var cxt=c.getContext("2d");```
■ Creates rectangular object: position 10, 10; size 180 x 60	``` cxt.fillRect(10,10,180,60);``` ```</script>```
	```<body>```

Moving canvas script into a function

Description	Code

Head	```<!DOCTYPE HTML>```
	```<html><head><title></title>```
	
	```<script type=text/javascript>```

■ JavaScript function
■ Creates drawing
 - basic circle
 - position and size attributes
	```function drawCircle() {```
	
	   ```var c=document.getElementById("canvasImg");```
	   ```var cxt=c.getContext("2d");```
	
	   ```cxt.beginPath();```
	   ```cxt.arc(100,100,50,0,Math.PI*2,true);```
	   ```cxt.closePath();```
	   ```cxt.stroke();}```
	
	```</script> </head>```

Body
 	
■ onLoad event calls function
■ Canvas Element renders the function-defined drawing
	```<body onload="drawCircle()">```
	
	```<canvas id=canvasImg width=200 height=100 style="border:1px solid gray;">```
	
	```This browser does not support <canvas> element```
	
	```</canvas> <body>```

Basic Canvas methods and properties

Method or Property	Description
```beginPath()```	Resetting the current path
```moveTo(x, y)```	Creating a new subpath with the point defined
```closePath()```	The current subpath is closed, and a new subpath is started

```fill()```
 	
```stroke()```
	The subpaths fill and stroke applied using current fill style

```fillStyle```
 	
```strokeStyle```
	Shape's fill and stroke style

```bezierCurveTo(cp1x, cp1y, cp2x, cp2y, x, y)```	The point is added to the path, connecting to the previous point by a Bezier curve using control points. The **x** & **y**: the end point coordinates. The **cp1x** & **cp1y** / **cp2x** & **cp2y**: the 1st / 2nd control point coordinates
```quadraticCurveTo(cpx,cpy,x,y)```	The point is added to the current path, connected to the previous point by a quadratic Bezier curve
```addColorStop(offset, color)```	Color stop with a color to the gradient with offset value range of **0.0-1.0**

Method or Property	Description
drawImage(image, dx, dy)	An image or canvas object with **x** and **y** coordinates
createRadialGradient(x0, y0, r0, x1, y1, r1)	Two gradient circles: 1. Coordinates **(x1,y1)** and radius **r1** ; 2. Coordinates **(x2,y2)** and radius **r2**
createLinearGradient(x0, y0, x1, y1)	Linear gradient represented by the start **(x1,y1)** & end points **(x2,y2)**
font [= value]	Font settings property
textAlign [= value]	Text alignment property. Values: start, end, left, right, center.
textBaseline [= value]	Baseline alignment property. Values: top, hanging, middle , alphabetic, ideographic and bottom
fillText(text,x,y[, maxWidth])	Text fill property at the coordinates **x** and **y**
strokeText(text, x, y [, maxWidth])	Text stroke property at the coordinates **x** and **y**
createPattern(image, repetition)	Image defined as pattern. The second argument values are: repeat, repeat-x, repeat-y, and no-repeat.
shadowColor [= value]	Shadow color property
shadowOffsetX [= value] shadowOffsetY [= value]	Shadow offset **X** and offset **Y** properties
shadowBlur [= value]	Shadow blur property
save() restore()	Canvas - save and restore states methods
rotate(angle)	Rotate method
scale(x, y)	Scale method: horizontal and vertical scale factor parameters
transform(m11, m12, m21, m22, dx, dy)	Transformation matrix arguments
setTransform(m11, m12, m21, m22, dx, dy)	Transformation matrix redefined to the matrix given by the arguments
setInterval(callback, time);	Repeatedly executable code. Time parameter: milliseconds
setTimeout(callback, time);	Once executable code. Time parameter: milliseconds

Canvas methods in action: drawing

Object	Code
| Lines | ```
cxt.moveTo(100,160); cxt.lineTo(460,40);
cxt.strokeStyle="blue";  //line color
cxt.lineWidth=4;         //line width
cxt.stroke();
``` |
```

Object	Code

Rectangle	```cxt.fillRect(15,15,120,60);```
	
	```cxt.clearRect(20,20,110,50);```
	
	```cxt.strokeRect(15,15,120,60);```

Path: circle	```cxt.fillStyle="#FF0000";```
	
	```cxt.beginPath();```
	```cxt.arc(100,100,50,0,Math.PI*2,true);```
	```cxt.closePath();```
	```cxt.stroke();```
	
	```cxt.fill();```

Path: triangle	```cxt.beginPath();```
	
	```cxt.moveTo(160,160);```
	```cxt.lineTo(120,50);```
	```cxt.lineTo(50,120);```
	
	```cxt.closePath();```
	```cxt.stroke();```

Gradient	```var grd=cxt.createLinearGradient(0,0,180,60); //gradient```
	
	```grd.addColorStop(0, "red"); //gradient color definition```
	
	```grd.addColorStop(0.5,"blue");```
	
	```cxt.fillStyle=grd; //object fill style defined```
	
	```cxt.fillRect(10,10,100,60); //Creates rectangle```

Oval	```var centerX = 200; var centerY = 50; //location and size```
	```var height = 80; var width = 250;```
	```cxt.beginPath(); cxt.moveTo(centerX,centerY - height/2);```
	
	```//right half of oval```
	```cxt.bezierCurveTo(centerX+width/2,centerY+height/2,centerX```
	```+width/2,centerY-height/2,centerX,centerY-height/2);```
	
	```cxt.bezierCurveTo(centerX-width/2, //left half of oval```
	```centerY-height/2,centerX-width/2,```
	```centerY+height/2,centerX, centerY+height/2);```
	
	```cxt.lineWidth=4; //fill & stroke styling```
	```cxt.strokeStyle="black"; cxt.stroke();```
	```cxt.fillStyle="#C9A761"; cxt.fill(); cxt.closePath();```

228

Object	Code
| Raster Image  | ```javascript
var img = new Image();
img.src = '/images/portrait.jpg';
``` |

 Scalable Vector Graphic

Draft → Last Call → Candidate → Recommendation
w3.org/TR/SVG

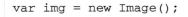

Scalable Vector Graphic (SVG) is an XML-based language for 2-D vector graphics.

- SVG is not part of HTML5 specification, however it is an W3C open standard
- Images created using geometrical element such as points, lines, Bézier curves, and shapes, which are based on mathematical equations
- SVG images can be scaled without degradation, behaving similarly to Flash graphics
- SVG files are pure XML files which could be created in any text editor
- Currently Adobe Illustrator and some other tools are capable of exporting and importing SVG graphics. Eventually we should expect more visual SVG authoring tools
- SVG can be created
    - inline: within the HTML document
    - by embedding a stand alone .SVG file

Basic HTML document with inline SVG

Description	Code
| Head and body | ```html
<!DOCTYPE HTML>
<html><head><title></title></head><body>
``` |
| Defines an SVG document fragment | ```html
<svg xmlns=http://www.w3.org/2000/svg>
``` |
| ■ Defines a rectangle with fill, stroke, position and size attributes<br>■ Fallback content | ```html
<rect stroke=black fill=blue stroke-width=2
x=15px y=15px width=200px height=100px>

This browser does not support the canvas element

</svg>
<body>
``` |

6 ways of creating SVG in HTML Document

Technique	Commentary	
<embed> tag	Description	The **<embed>** tag is not a standard HTML tag. It utilizes Adobe SVG Viewer. The **<embed>** tag is not compatible with a valid XHTML document
	Example	`<embed src=image.svg width=200 height=200 type=image/svg+xml pluginspage=http://www.adobe.com/svg/viewer/install/>`
<object> tag	Description	The **<object>** tag is a standard HTML tag and is supported by all modern browsers. This method does not allow scripting.
	Example	`<object data=image.svg width=200 height=200 type=image/svg+xml codebase=http://www.adobe.com/svg/viewer/install/>`
<iframe> tag	Description	The **<iframe>** tag can be used to render SVG graphics.
	Example	`<iframe src="image.svg" width="90" height="90"></iframe`
Inline	Description	Inline SVG only with XHTML5 document, using MIME Type **application/xhtml+xml** or **text/xml**, or in modern browsers
	Example	`<svg width="200" height="200" version="1.1" xmlns="http://www.w3.org/2000/svg">`
		`<circle cx="100" cy="80" r="60" stroke="#ffffff" stroke-width="1" fill="blue">`
		`</svg>`
JavaScript	Description	JavaScript can be used to create canvas, graphic object (circle) and object attributes
	Example	`<div id="svgimage"></div>`
		`<script type="text/javascript">`
		`var svg = document.createElementNS ("http://www.w3.org/2000/svg", "svg"), circle = document.createElementNS ("http://www.w3.org/2000/svg", "circle");`
		`svg.setAttribute("version", "1.1"); circle.setAttribute("r", "60"); circle.setAttribute("cx", "100"); circle.setAttribute("cy", "80"); circle.setAttribute("fill", "blue"); circle.setAttribute("stroke", "black"); svg.appendChild(circle); document.getElementById("svgimage").appendChild(svg);`
		`</script>`

Technique	Commentary	
Raphaël JavaScript Library raphaeljs.com	Description	Raphaël is a small JavaScript library that could be used to build vector graphics. The **raphael.js** file can be downloaded and included into the **<head>** of HTML document. Various predefined shapes and transformations then can be accessed from the library.

	Example	```var paper = Raphael(10, 50, 320, 200);```
		
		```// Circle at x = 50, y = 40, with radius 10```
		```var circle = paper.circle(50, 40, 10);```
		
		```// Fill and stroke attributes```
		```circle.attr("fill", "blue");```
		```circle.attr("stroke", "black");```

SVG Shapes

Object	Code	Description

	```<?xml version="1.0" standalone="no"?>```
	```<!DOCTYPE svg PUBLIC "-//W3C//DTD SVG 1.1//```
	```EN" "http://www.w3.org/Graphics/SVG/1.1/DTD/```
	```svg11.dtd">```
	
	```<svg width="100%" height="100%" version="1.1"```
	```xmlns="http://www.w3.org/2000/svg">```
	
	```<rect width="300" height="100"/>```
	
	```</svg>```
		Sample stand-alone, self-contained SVG document. The code can be created in text editor and saved, e.g. image.svg

Circle	```<circle cx="100" cy="80" r="60"``` ```stroke="black" stroke-width="1" fill="blue"/>```	Common properties ■ r: radius

Ellipse	```<ellipse cx="300" cy="150" rx="200" ry="80"```
	```style="fill:green;"```
	```stroke:rgb(0,0,100); stroke-width:2"/>```
		■ x & y: left and right position
		■ cx: x of the center coordinate
		■ cy: y of the center coordinate

Line	```<line x1="0" y1="0" x2="300" y2="300"``` ```style="stroke:black; stroke-width:2"/>```	■ rx: horizontal radius ■ ry: vertical radius

Polygon	```<polygon points="200,100 350,220 150,260"```
	```style="fill:blue; stroke:#000;```
	```stroke-width:1"/>```
		Path data commands
		
		■ A: elliptical Arc
		■ C: 'curveto'

Polyline	```<polyline points="0,0 0,20 20,20 20,30 30,```
	```40 40,60" style="fill:white; stroke:red;```
	```stroke-width:2"/>```
		■ H: horizontal 'lineto'
		■ L: 'lineto'
		■ M: 'moveto'

Rectangle	```<rect x="30" y="30" rx="30" ry="30"```
	```width="240" height="120"```
	```style="fill:red; stroke:black;```
	```stroke-width:3; opacity:0.7"/>```
		■ S: smooth 'curveto'
		■ Q: quadratic Belzier curve
		■ T: smooth quadratic Belzier curve
		■ V: vertical 'lineto'

Path	```<path d="M250 150 L150 350 L350 350 Z"/>```	■ Z: closepath

Performance & Integration

XMLHttpRequest

Draft → Last Call → Candidate → Recommendation
http://www.w3.org/TR/XMLHttpRequest/

The *XMLHttpRequest* specification defines scripted functionality in web browser for transferring data between a client and a server. XMLHttpRequest is essential in the *Ajax* web development technique, that allows updating of a small region within the browser window without refreshing the page.

Method	Commentary	
open	Description	The *XMLHttpRequest* object must be initialized through the *open* method, that can accept up to five parameters, but requires only two, to initialize a request. The **Method** parameter values: GET, POST, HEAD, PUT, DELETE, OPTIONS.
	Example	`open(Method, URL, Asynchronous, UserName, Password)`
setRequestHeader	Description	After the initialization, the *setRequestHeader* method can send HTTP headers with the request.
	Example	`setRequestHeader(Name, Value)`
send	Description	The *send* method is utilized to send an HTTP request, containing a single parameter (the content).
	Example	`send(Data)`

The onreadystatechange event listener

When the *open* method is activated with the *Asynchronous* parameter set to true, the *onreadystatechange* event listener will be instantly activated for each of the following actions that change the *readyState* property of the XMLHttpRequest object.

```
xmlhttp.onreadystatechange = function() {
    alert(xmlhttp.readyState); };
xmlhttp.open("GET","somepage.xml",true);
xmlhttp.send(null);
```

The HTTP response

After a successful call to the *send* method, the *responseXML* property of the XMLHttpRequest object will contain a DOM document object, and the *responseText* property will contain the response of the server in plain text by a web browser.

Navigation Timing

This specification defines an interface that provides Web applications with timing information. This specification does not define how to use these interfaces to collect, store, and report this data.

An example of how to use the interfaces:

Draft → Last Call → Candidate → Recommendation
w3.org/TR/navigation-timing

```
var t = performance.timing;
var n = performance.navigation;

if (t.loadEventEnd > 0) {
  var page_load_time = t.loadEventEnd -
t.navigationStart;
  if (n.type == n.TYPE_NAVIGATE) {
    alert (page_load_time);
  }
}
```

Interface	Commentary	

PerformanceTiming	Definition	`interface PerformanceTiming {`
		`readonly attribute unsigned long long`
		`[attribute value]; };`

	Attribute Values	`unloadEventStart;`
		`unloadEventEnd;redirectStart; redirectEnd;`
		`fetchStart; domainLookupStart;`
		`domainLookupEnd; connectStart; connectEnd;`
		`secureConnectionStart; requestStart;`
		`responseStart; responseEnd; domLoading;`
		`domInteractive; domContentLoadedEventStart;`
		`domContentLoadedEventEnd; domComplete;`
		`loadEventStart; loadEventEnd;`

PerformanceNavigation	Definition	`interface PerformanceNavigation {`
		`const unsigned short TYPE_NAVIGATE = 0;`
		`const unsigned short TYPE_RELOAD = 1;`
		`const unsigned short TYPE_BACK_FORWARD = 2;`
		`const unsigned short TYPE_RESERVED = 255;`
		`readonly attribute unsigned short type;`
		`readonly attribute unsigned short`
		`redirectCount; };`

window.performance	Definition	`interface Performance {`
		`readonly attribute PerformanceTiming timing;`
		`readonly attribute PerformanceNavigation`
		`navigation; };`
		
		`[Supplemental]`
		`interface Window {`
		`[Replaceable] readonly attribute Performance`
		`performance;  };`

Browser Compatibility

	Desktop					Mobile		
	IE	FireFox	Safari	Chrome	Opera	iOS	Opera	Android
Audio & Video	9	4	4	6	11	4	11	2
Canvas (basic)	9	2	3	4	9	3	10	2
Device Orientation	11	*10	8	7	8	7.1	8.1	4.4
Drag and Drop	6	4	4	6	24	8.1	8	37
File API	11	31	6.1	13	24	8.1	8	4.4
FileReaer API	11	31	6.1	13	24	8.1	8	4.4
Geolocation	9	4	5	5	11	3	11	2
Indexed Database	*10	4	8	11	24	*8.1	8	4.4
Inline SVG	9	4	6	7	9	5	8	4
MathML	11	5	6	41	*12	5	8	37
Media Capture	11	10	8	3	24	8.1	8	3
Navigation Timing	9	7	8.1	13	24	3	8	2
Offline HTTP Caching	10	4	4	6	11	3	11	2
Touch Events	*10	*36	8	31	24	3	11	2
WAI-ARIA	8	5	*4	*12	*11	*5	*5	*38
Web Storage	8	4	4	6	11	3	8	2
WebSockets	*10	*10	4	14	*11	4	*11	4.4
Web Messaging	*10	3	4	13	4	3	10	2
Web Workers	10	4	4	4	11	5	8	38
XMLHttpRequest 1, 2	10	4	5	4	*12	5	8	3

* indicates partial support

? indicates unknown support

8 indicates no support and the browser version

In the Chapter 7

7. Appendix

Online Resources

Web companion for this book	http://html5.belisso.com
All W3C standards and Drafts	http://www.w3.org/TR
HTML5 Reference	http://dev.w3.org/html5/html-author
Index of Elements	http://www.w3.org/TR/html401/index/elements.html
HTML, CSS, SVG cheat sheet	http://www.w3.org/2009/cheatsheet
HTML5 Arena	http://www.html5arena.com
CSS selector test	http://tools.css3.info/selectors-test/test.html
Your browser HTML5/CSS3 support test	http://www.findmebyip.com
Your browser HTML5 support test	http://html5test.com
HTML5 cross-browser Polyfills	https://github.com/Modernizr/Modernizr/wiki
CSS3 property tests	http://www.westciv.com/iphonetests
Check cross-browser compatibility	http://browsershots.org
W3C HTML validator	http://validator.w3.org
W3C CSS3 validator	http://jigsaw.w3.org/css-validator
HTML5 validator	http://html5.validator.nu

HTML5 and CSS3 desktop tools

Name	Description	Platform	Licence
Adobe Dreamweaver CS5.5	HTML5 and CSS3 WYSIWYG editing	Windows, Mac	Commercial
Adobe Flash CS5+	Exports to HTML5 Canvas	Windows, Mac	Commercial
Adobe Illustrator CS5+	Exports to SVG and CSS3	Windows, Mac	Commercial
Adobe Edge	HTML5 animation authoring tool	Windows, Mac	Beta
Apple iAd Producer	HTML5 authoring tool	Mac	Free
Tumult Hype	HTML5 animation authoring tool	Mac	Commercial
Total Validator	(X)HTML5 and accessibility validation	Windows, Mac, Linux	Free (basic)
ActiveState Komodo 6	HTML5 and CSS3 markup editing	Windows, Mac, Linux	Free (basic)

Name	Description	Platform	Licence
Panic Coda	HTML5 and CSS3 markup editing	Mac	Commercial
TextMate with HTML5 bundle	HTML5 and CSS3 markup editing	Mac	Commercial
The Free HTML Editor 9.4	HTML5 and CSS3 markup editing	Windows	Free
CoffeeCup HTML Editor	HTML5 and CSS3 WYSIWYG editing	Windows	Commercial
CSE HTML Validator 10.0	(X)HTML5 and CSS3 validation	Windows	Commercial
Open Validator 2.7	(X)HTML5 validation	Windows, Mac	Free
Sencha Animator	CSS3 animation	Windows, Mac, Linux	
Sketsa SVG Editor 6.4	SVG editing	Windows	Commercial
Google Swiffy Flash extension	Exports Flash to HTML5	Windows, Mac	Beta
Apatana Studio 3	HTML5 and CSS3 markup editing	Windows, Mac, Linux	Free

X11 color keywords

Color Name	Hex RGB	Decimal	Color Name	Hex RGB	Decimal
AliceBlue	#F0F8FF	240,248,255	Chartreuse	#7FFF00	127,255,0
AntiqueWhite	#FAEBD7	250,235,215	Chocolate	#D2691E	210,105,30
Aqua	#00FFFF	0,255,255	Coral	#FF7F50	255,127,80
Aquamarine	#7FFFD4	127,255,212	CornflowerBlue	#6495ED	100,149,237
Azure	#F0FFFF	240,255,255	Cornsilk	#FFF8DC	255,248,220
Beige	#F5F5DC	245,245,220	Crimson	#DC143C	220,20,60
Bisque	#FFE4C4	255,228,196	Cyan	#00FFFF	0,255,255
Black	#000000	0,0,0	DarkBlue	#00008B	0,0,139
BlanchedAlmond	#FFEBCD	255,235,205	DarkCyan	#008B8B	0,139,139
Blue	#0000FF	0,0,255	DarkGoldenrod	#B8860B	184,134,11
BlueViolet	#8A2BE2	138,43,226	DarkGray	#A9A9A9	169,169,169
Brown	#A52A2A	165,42,42	DarkGreen	#006400	0,100,0
BurlyWood	#DEB887	222,184,135	DarkKhaki	#BDB76B	189,183,107
CadetBlue	#5F9EA0	95,158,160	DarkMagenta	#8B008B	139,0,139

Color Name	Hex RGB	Decimal	Color Name	Hex RGB	Decimal
DarkOliveGreen	#556B2F	85,107,47	Ivory	#FFFFF0	255,255,240
DarkOrange	#FF8C00	255,140,0	Khaki	#F0E68C	240,230,140
DarkOrchid	#9932CC	153,50,204	Lavender	#E6E6FA	230,230,250
DarkRed	#8B0000	139,0,0	LavenderBlush	#FFF0F5	255,240,245
DarkSalmon	#E9967A	233,150,122	LawnGreen	#7CFC00	124,252,0
DarkSeaGreen	#8FBC8F	143,188,143	LemonChiffon	#FFFACD	255,250,205
DarkSlateBlue	#483D8B	72,61,139	LightBlue	#ADD8E6	173,216,230
DarkSlateGray	#2F4F4F	47,79,79	LightCoral	#F08080	240,128,128
DarkTurquoise	#00CED1	0,206,209	LightCyan	#E0FFFF	224,255,255
DarkViolet	#9400D3	148,0,211	LightGoldenrodYellow	#FAFAD2	250,250,210
DeepPink	#FF1493	255,20,147	LightGreen	#90EE90	144,238,144
DeepSkyBlue	#00BFFF	0,191,255	LightGrey	#D3D3D3	211,211,211
DimGray	#696969	105,105,105	LightPink	#FFB6C1	255,182,193
DodgerBlue	#1E90FF	30,144,255	LightSalmon	#FFA07A	255,160,122
FireBrick	#B22222	178,34,34	LightSeaGreen	#20B2AA	32,178,170
FloralWhite	#FFFAF0	255,250,240	LightSkyBlue	#87CEFA	135,206,250
ForestGreen	#228B22	34,139,34	LightSlateGray	#778899	119,136,153
Fuchsia	#FF00FF	255,0,255	LightSteelBlue	#B0C4DE	176,196,222
Gainsboro	#DCDCDC	220,220,220	LightYellow	#FFFFE0	255,255,224
GhostWhite	#F8F8FF	248,248,255	Lime	#00FF00	0,255,0
Gold	#FFD700	255,215,0	LimeGreen	#32CD32	50,205,50
Goldenrod	#DAA520	218,165,32	Linen	#FAF0E6	250,240,230
Gray	#808080	128,128,128	Magenta	#FF00FF	255,0,255
Green	#008000	0,128,0	Maroon	#800000	128,0,0
GreenYellow	#ADFF2F	173,255,47	MediumAquamarine	#66CDAA	102,205,170
Honeydew	#F0FFF0	240,255,240	MediumBlue	#0000CD	0,0,205
HotPink	#FF69B4	255,105,180	MediumOrchid	#BA55D3	186,85,211
IndianRed	#CD5C5C	205,92,92	MediumPurple	#9370DB	147,112,219
Indigo	#4B0082	75,0,130	MediumSeaGreen	#3CB371	60,179,113

Color Name	Hex RGB	Decimal	Color Name	Hex RGB	Decimal
MediumSlateBlue	#7B68EE	123,104,238	RoyalBlue	#4169E1	65,105,225
MediumSpringGreen	#00FA9A	0,250,154	SaddleBrown	#8B4513	139,69,19
MediumTurquoise	#48D1CC	72,209,204	Salmon	#FA8072	250,128,114
MediumVioletRed	#C71585	199,21,133	SandyBrown	#F4A460	244,164,96
MidnightBlue	#191970	25,25,112	SeaGreen	#2E8B57	46,139,87
MintCream	#F5FFFA	245,255,250	Seashell	#FFF5EE	255,245,238
MistyRose	#FFE4E1	255,228,225	Sienna	#A0522D	160,82,45
Moccasin	#FFE4B5	255,228,181	Silver	#C0C0C0	192,192,192
NavajoWhite	#FFDEAD	255,222,173	SkyBlue	#87CEEB	135,206,235
Navy	#000080	0,0,128	SlateBlue	#6A5ACD	106,90,205
OldLace	#FDF5E6	253,245,230	SlateGray	#708090	112,128,144
Olive	#808000	128,128,0	Snow	#FFFAFA	255,250,250
OliveDrab	#6B8E23	107,142,35	SpringGreen	#00FF7F	0,255,127
Orange	#FFA500	255,165,0	SteelBlue	#4682B4	70,130,180
OrangeRed	#FF4500	255,69,0	Tan	#D2B48C	210,180,140
Orchid	#DA70D6	218,112,214	Teal	#008080	0,128,128
PaleGoldenrod	#EEE8AA	238,232,170	Thistle	#D8BFD8	216,191,216
PaleGreen	#98FB98	152,251,152	Tomato	#FF6347	255,99,71
PaleTurquoise	#AFEEEE	175,238,238	Turquoise	#40E0D0	64,224,208
PaleVioletRed	#DB7093	219,112,147	Violet	#EE82EE	238,130,238
PapayaWhip	#FFEFD5	255,239,213	Wheat	#F5DEB3	245,222,179
PeachPuff	#FFDAB9	255,218,185	White	#FFFFFF	255,255,255
Peru	#CD853F	205,133,63	WhiteSmoke	#F5F5F5	245,245,245
Pink	#FFC0CB	255,192,203	Yellow	#FFFF00	255,255,0
Plum	#DDA0DD	221,160,221	YellowGreen	#9ACD32	154,205,50
PowderBlue	#B0E0E6	176,224,230			
Purple	#800080	128,0,128			
Red	#FF0000	255,0,0			
RosyBrown	#BC8F8F	188,143,143			

Web color keywords

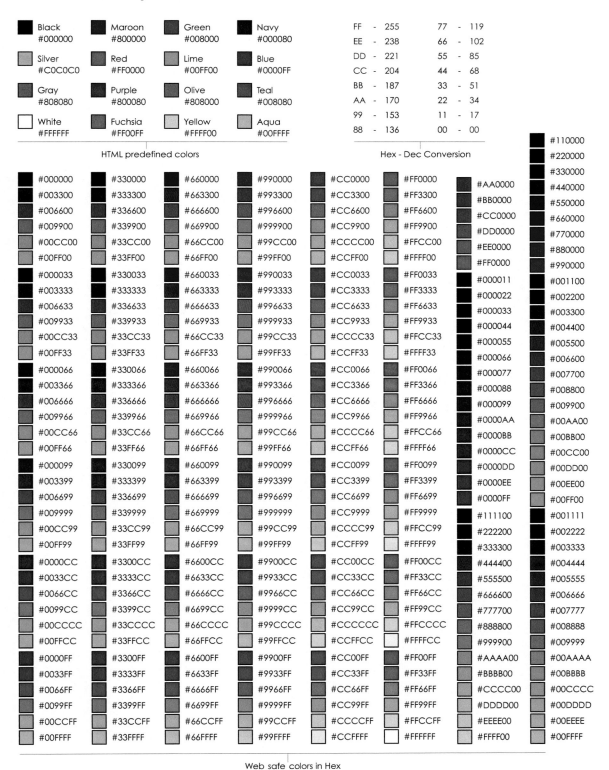

■ Black #000000	■ Maroon #800000
■ Silver #C0C0C0	■ Red #FF0000
■ Gray #808080	■ Purple #800080
□ White #FFFFFF	■ Fuchsia #FF00FF
■ Green #008000	■ Navy #000080
■ Lime #00FF00	■ Blue #0000FF
■ Olive #808000	■ Teal #008080
■ Yellow #FFFF00	■ Aqua #00FFFF

HTML predefined colors

Hex - Dec Conversion

FF	-	255	77 - 119	
EE	-	238	66 - 102	
DD	-	221	55 - 85	
CC	-	204	44 - 68	
BB	-	187	33 - 51	
AA	-	170	22 - 34	
99	-	153	11 - 17	
88	-	136	00 - 00	

Web safe colors in Hex

HTML special characters

Character	HTML Entity	ISO Latin-1 code	Name or meaning
–	&ndash;	&#8211;	en dash
—	&mdash;	&#8212;	em dash
¡	&iexcl;	&#161;	inverted exclamation
¿	&iquest;	&#191;	inverted question mark
"	&quot;	&#34;	quotation mark
"	&ldquo;	&#8220;	left double curly quote
"	&rdquo;	&#8221;	right double curly quote
'	&lsquo;	&#8216;	left single curly quote
'	&rsquo;	&#8217;	right single curly quote
«	&laquo;	&#171;	guillemets, european-style quotation marks
»	&raquo;	&#187;	
(blank space)			non-breaking space
&	&amp;	&#38;	ampersand
¢	&cent;	&#162;	cent
©	&copy;	&#169;	copyright
÷	&divide;	&#247;	divide
>	&gt;	&#62;	greater than
<	&lt;	&#60;	less than
µ	&micro;	&#181;	micron
·	&middot;	&#183;	middle dot
¶	&para;	&#182;	pilcrow (paragraph sign)
±	&plusmn;	&#177;	plus/minus
€	&euro;	&#8364;	Euro currency
£	&pound;	&#163;	British Pound Sterling
®	&reg;	&#174;	registered
§	&sect;	&#167;	section
™	&trade;	&#153;	trademark
¥	&yen;	&#165;	Japanese Yen

Properties that can be animated

Property Name	Type
background-color	color
background-image	only gradients
background-position	percentage, length
border-bottom-color	color
border-bottom-width	length
border-color	color
border-left-color	color
border-left-width	length
border-right-color	color
border-right-width	length
border-spacing	length
border-top-color	color
border-top-width	length
border-width	length
bottom	length, percentage
color	color
crop	rectangle
font-size	length, percentage
font-weight	number
grid-*	various
height	length, percentage
left	length, percentage
letter-spacing	length
line-height	number, length, %
margin-bottom	length

Property Name	Type
margin-left	length
margin-right	length
margin-top	length
max-height	length, percentage
max-width	length, percentage
min-height	length, percentage
min-width	length, percentage
opacity	number
outline-color	color
outline-offset	integer
outline-width	length
padding-bottom	length
padding-left	length
padding-right	length
padding-top	length
right	length, percentage
text-indent	length, percentage
text-shadow	shadow
top	length, percentage
vertical-align	keywords, length, %
visibility	visibility
width	length, percentage
word-spacing	length, percentage
z-index	integer
zoom	number

Dedication

For Natasha and Nika. I love you!

For people who read books.

Acknowledgements

Special thanks to the W3C, WHATWG and other contributors:

Ian 'Hixie' Hickson, Tim Berners-Lee, Aankhen, Aaron Boodman, Aaron Leventhal, Adam Barth, Adam de Boor, Adam Hepton, Adam Roben, Addison Phillips, Adele Peterson, Adrian Bateman, Adrian Sutton, Agustín Fernández, Ajai Tirumali, Akatsuki Kitamura, Alan Plum, Alastair Campbell, Alejandro G. Castro, Alex Bishop, Alex Nicolaou, Alex Rousskov, Alexander J. Vincent, Alexey Feldgendler, Алексей Проскуряков (Alexey Proskuryakov), Alexis Deveria, Allan Clements, Amos Jeffries, Anders Carlsson, Andreas, Andreas Kling, Andrei Popescu, André E. Veltstra, Andrew Clover, Andrew Gove, Andrew Grieve, Andrew Oakley, Andrew Sidwell, Andrew Smith, Andrew W. Hagen, Andrey V. Lukyanov, Andy Heydon, Andy Palay, Anne van Kesteren, Anthony Boyd, Anthony Bryan, Anthony Hickson, Anthony Ricaud, Antti Koivisto, Arne Thomassen, Aron Spohr, Arphen Lin, Aryeh Gregor, Asbjørn Ulsberg, Ashley Sheridan, Atsushi Takayama, Aurelien Levy, Ave Wrigley, Ben Boyle, Ben Godfrey, Ben Lerner, Ben Leslie, Ben Meadowcroft, Ben Millard, Benjamin Carl Wiley Sittler, Benjamin Hawkes-Lewis, Bert Bos, Bijan Parsia, Bil Corry, Bill Mason, Bill McCoy, Billy Wong, Bjartur Thorlacius, Björn Höhrmann, Blake Frantz, Boris Zbarsky, Brad Fults, Brad Neuberg, Brad Spencer, Brady Eidson, Brendan Eich, Brenton Simpson, Brett Wilson, Brett Zamir, Brian Campbell, Brian Korver, Brian Kuhn, Brian Ryner, Brian Smith, Brian Wilson, Bryan Sullivan, Bruce D'Arcus, Bruce Lawson, Bruce Miller, C. Williams, Cameron McCormack, Cao Yipeng, Carlos Gabriel Cardona, Carlos Perelló Marín, Chao Cai, Channy Yun, Charl van Niekerk, Charles Iliya Krempeaux, Charles McCathieNevile, Chris Apers, Chris Cressman, Chris Evans, Chris Morris, Chris Pearce, Christian Biesinger, Christian Johansen, Christian Schmidt, Christoph Plenio, Christopher Aillon, Chriswa, Clark Buehler, Cole Robison, Colin Fine, Collin Jackson, Corprew Reed, Craig Cockburn, Csaba Gabor, Csaba Marton, Cynthia Shelly, Daniel Barclay, Daniel Bratell, Daniel Brooks, Daniel Brumbaugh Keeney, Daniel Cheng, Daniel Davis, Daniel Glazman, Daniel Peng, Daniel Schattenkirchner, Daniel Spång, Daniel Steinberg, Danny Sullivan, Darin Adler, Darin Fisher, Darxus, Dave Camp, Dave Hodder, Dave Lampton, Dave Singer, Dave Townsend, David Baron, David Bloom, David Bruant, David Carlisle, David E. Cleary, David Egan Evans, David Flanagan, David Gerard, David Håsäther, David Hyatt, David I. Lehn, David John Burrowes, David Matja, David Remahl, David Smith, David Woolley, DeWitt Clinton, Dean Edridge, Dean Edwards, Debi Orton, Derek Featherstone, Devdatta, Dimitri Glazkov, Dimitry Golubovsky, Dirk Pranke, Divya Manian, Dmitry Titov, dolphinling, Dominique Hazaël-Massieux, Don Brutzman, Doron Rosenberg, Doug Kramer, Doug Simpkinson, Drew Wilson, Edmund Lai, Eduard Pascual, Eduardo Vela, Edward O'Connor, Edward Welbourne, Edward Z. Yang, Eira Monstad, Eitan Adler, Eliot Graff, Elizabeth Castro, Elliott Sprehn, Elliotte Harold, Eric Carlson, Eric Law, Eric Rescorla, Eric Semling, Erik Arvidsson, Erik Rose, Evan Martin, Evan Prodromou, Evert, fantasai, Felix Sasaki, Francesco Schwarz, Francis Brosnan Blazquez, Franck 'Shift' Quélain, Frank Barchard, Fumitoshi Ukai, Futomi Hatano, Gavin Carothers, Gareth Rees, Garrett Smith, Geoffrey Garen, Geoffrey Sneddon, George Lund, Gianmarco Armellin, Giovanni Campagna, Graham Klyne, Greg Botten, Greg Houston, Greg Wilkins, Gregg Tavares, Gregory J. Rosmaita, Grey, Gytis Jakutonis, Håkon Wium Lie, Hallvord Reiar Michaelsen Steen, Hans S. Tømmerhalt, Hans Stimer, Henri Sivonen, Henrik Lied, Henry Mason, Hugh Winkler, Ian Bicking, Ian Davis, Ignacio Javier, Ivan Enderlin, Ivo Emanuel Gonçalves, J. King, Jacques Distler, James Craig, James Graham, James Justin Harrell, James M Snell, James Perrett, James

Robinson, Jamie Lokier, Jan-Klaas Kollhof, Jason Kersey, Jason Lustig, Jason White, Jasper Bryant-Greene, Jatinder Mann, Jed Hartman, Jeff Balogh, Jeff Cutsinger, Jeff Schiller, Jeff Walden, Jeffrey Zeldman, Jennifer Braithwaite, Jens Bannmann, Jens Fendler, Jens Lindström, Jens Meiert, Jeremy Keith, Jeremy Orlow, Jeroen van der Meer, Jian Li, Jim Jewett, Jim Ley, Jim Meehan, Jjgod Jiang, João Eiras, Joe Clark, Joe Gregorio, Joel Spolsky, Johan Herland, John Boyer, John Bussjaeger, John Carpenter, John Fallows, John Foliot, John Harding, John Keiser, John Snyders, John-Mark Bell, Johnny Stenback, Jon Ferraiolo, Jon Gibbins, Jon Perlow, Jonas Sicking, Jonathan Cook, Jonathan Rees, Jonathan Worent, Jonny Axelsson, Jorgen Horstink, Jorunn Danielsen Newth, Joseph Kesselman, Joseph Pecoraro, Josh Aas, Josh Levenberg, Joshua Randall, Jukka K. Korpela, Jules Clément-Ripoche, Julian Reschke, Jürgen Jeka, Justin Lebar, Justin Sinclair, Kai Hendry, Kartikaya Gupta, Kathy Walton, Kelly Norton, Kevin Benson, Kornél Pál, Kornel Lesinski, Kristof Zelechovski, Krzysztof Maczyński, Kurosawa Takeshi, Kyle Hofmann, Léonard Bouchet, Lachlan Hunt, Larry Masinter, Larry Page, Lars Gunther, Lars Solberg, Laura Carlson, Laura Granka, Laura L. Carlson, Laura Wisewell, Laurens Holst, Lee Kowalkowski, Leif Halvard Silli, Lenny Domnitser, Leons Petrazickis, Lobotom Dysmon, Logan, Loune, Luke Kenneth Casson Leighton, Maciej Stachowiak, Magnus Kristiansen, Maik Merten, Malcolm Rowe, Mark Birbeck, Mark Miller, Mark Nottingham, Mark Pilgrim, Mark Rowe, Mark Schenk, Mark Wilton-Jones, Martijn Wargers, Martin Atkins, Martin Dürst, Martin Honnen, Martin Kutschker, Martin Nilsson, Martin Thomson, Masataka Yakura, Mathieu Henri, Matias Larsson, Matt Schmidt, Matt Wright, Matthew Gregan, Matthew Mastracci, Matthew Raymond, Matthew Thomas, Mattias Waldau, Max Romantschuk, Menno van Slooten, Micah Dubinko, Michael Engelhardt, Michael 'Ratt' Iannarelli, Michael A. Nachbaur, Michael A. Puls II, Michael Carter, Michael Daskalov, Michael Enright, Michael Gratton, Michael Nordman, Michael Powers, Michael Rakowski, Michael(tm) Smith, Michal Zalewski, Michel Fortin, Michelangelo De Simone, Michiel van der Blonk, Mihai Şucan, Mihai Parparita, Mike Brown, Mike Dierken, Mike Dixon, Mike Schinkel, Mike Shaver, Mikko Rantalainen, Mohamed Zergaoui, Mounir Lamouri, Ms2ger, NARUSE Yui, Neil Deakin, Neil Rashbrook, Neil Soiffer, Nicholas Shanks, Nicholas Stimpson, Nicholas Zakas, Nickolay Ponomarev, Nicolas Gallagher, Noah Mendelsohn, Noah Slater, NoozNooz42, Ojan Vafai, Olaf Hoffmann, Olav Junker Kjær, Oldřich Vetešník, Oli Studholme, Oliver Hunt, Oliver Rigby, Olivier Gendrin, Olli Pettay, Patrick H. Lauke, Paul Norman, Per-Erik Brodin, Perry Smith, Peter Karlsson, Peter Kasting, Peter Stark, Peter-Paul Koch, Phil Pickering, Philip Jägenstedt, Philip Taylor, Philip TAYLOR, Prateek Rungta, Pravir Gupta, Rachid Finge, Rajas Moonka, Ralf Stoltze, Ralph Giles, Raphael Champeimont, Remco, Remy Sharp, Rene Saarsoo, Rene Stach, Ric Hardacre, Rich Doughty, Richard Ishida, Richard Williamson, Rigo Wenning, Rikkert Koppes, Rimantas Liubertas, Riona Macnamara, Rob Ennals, Rob Jellinghaus, Robert Blaut, Robert Collins, Robert Nyman, Robert O'Callahan, Robert Sayre, Robin Berjon, Rodger Combs, Roland Steiner, Roman Ivanov, Roy Fielding, Ryan King, S. Mike Dierken, Salvatore Loreto, Sam Dutton, Sam Kuper, Sam Ruby, Sam Weinig, Sander van Lambalgen, Sarven Capadisli, Scott González, Scott Hess, Sean Fraser, Sean Hayes, Sean Hogan, Sean Knapp, Sebastian Markbåge, Sebastian Schnitzenbaumer, Seth Call, Shanti Rao, Shaun Inman, Shiki Okasaka, Sierk Bornemann, Sigbjørn Vik, Silvia Pfeiffer, Simon Montagu, Simon Pieters, Simon Spiegel, skeww, Stanton McCandlish, Stefan Haustein, Stefan Santesson, Steffen Meschkat, Stephen Ma, Steve Faulkner, Steve Runyon, Steven Bennett, Steven Garrity, Steven Tate, Stewart Brodie, Stuart Ballard, Stuart Parmenter, Subramanian Peruvemba, Sunava Dutta, Susan Borgrink, Susan Lesch, Sylvain Pasche, T. J. Crowder, Tab Atkins, Tantek Çelik, TAMURA Kent, Ted Mielczarek, Terrence Wood, Thomas Broyer, Thomas Koetter, Thomas O'Connor, Tim Altman, Tim Johansson, Toby Inkster, Todd Moody, Tom Pike, Tommy Thorsen, Travis Leithead, Tyler Close, Vladimir Katardjiev, Vladimir Vukićević, voracity, Wakaba, Wayne Carr, Wayne Pollock, Wellington Fernando de Macedo, Weston Ruter, Will Levine, William Swanson, Wladimir Palant, Wojciech Mach, Wolfram Kriesing, Yang Chen, Ye-Kui Wang, Yehuda Katz, Yi-An Huang, Yngve Nysaeter Pettersen, Yuzo Fujishima, Zhenbin Xu, Zoltan Herczeg, and Øistein E. Andersen.

8. Index

Symbols

X

44201038R00146

Made in the USA
Middletown, DE
31 May 2017